SCIENCE FAIR PROJECTS

Invent, Devise, Create and Win

Edited by Byron G. Wels

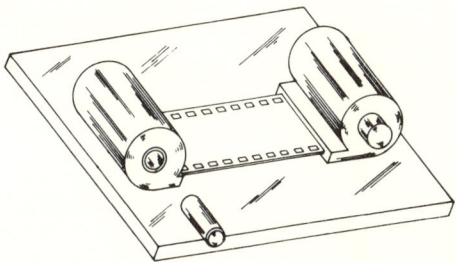

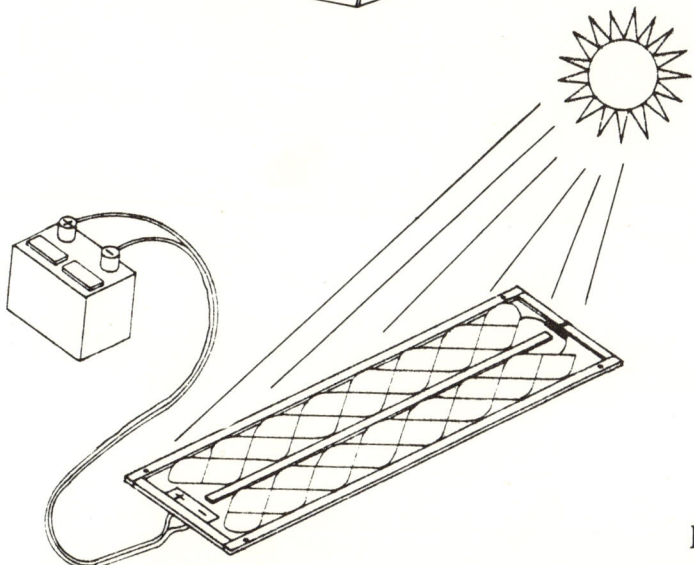

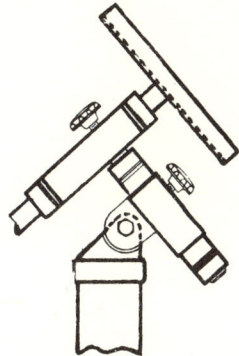

DRAKE PUBLISHERS INC.

NEW YORK • LONDON

DEDICATION

If I had to name one man in this country who has done more to start
youngsters on the way to scientific success, it would have to be an old
and dear friend, whose very name has come to mean science today.
With great affection and respect, I dedicate this work to

Norman W. Edmund

Published in 1976 by
Drake Publishers Inc.
801 Second Avenue
New York, N. Y. 10017

Library of Congress Cataloging in Publication Data

Wels, Bryon G
    Science fair projects.

    1. Science -- Experiments -- Juvenile literature.
I. Title.
Q164.W44   502'.8   76-16359
ISBN 0-8473-1301-8

Printed in the United States of America

Contents

Introduction

Each year, in schools all over the country, Science Fair competitions are held. The winners at each school continue to district competitions, then to city-wide run-offs. The winners in each city attend county and then state championships, and finally, a national competition is held for the outstanding science project in the country.

Each year, youngsters are told when the competitions will take place. And each year, many otherwise sharp students wait until the very last minute to prepare their entries. What happens? A slap-dash effort is made, there is no time to do the proper research and work, and the result is disappointment.

There are certain things that may not seem to have a thing to do with science but that can help students get closer to the winner's circle. The author, a former judge at competitions, has some basic advice: although the judges at the nationals may be top scientists who will understand what you're into -- to get to them, you will have to be selected by the judges at your own local school, and one of the judges might be your English teacher. Will she pass you up because you don't look neat, your spelling is bad, or your hair is too long? To be fair, competition must be systematic, and to win in the system, you can't fight it. No matter how GOOD your project is, give it some back-up by knowing all about the subject, make a nice appearance and a good presentation. Be alert, be prepared to answer questions on the subject, and don't forget to thank the judges for looking.

This is an "idea book." While I've made every effort to give you good, solid information, remember that thousands of other students are reading the very same words you are. Select a project from the book as an idea only; then do something new with it yourself, to make it a real winner.

Judges are only human too. When I served as a judge at a Science Fair at a large, midwestern city, we took a break for lunch. One of the lady judges, looking pretty frazzled, said to me "If I see one more unfertilized egg, I'll scream!"

So do something different. And by all means, do it by yourself. Judges can be pretty sharp, and they can quickly and easily recognize Dad's helping hand. Maybe Dad CAN do a better, neater job than you can, but if the work is obviously your own, you'll do lots better in the judge's eyes.

Before giving you the last word, I'd like to thank the Edmund Scientific Co., of Barrington, N. J. They've done a fantastic job of cooperating with me to produce this work. They're also the best people to see for the materials you're going to need.

So get into the book, absorb as much as you can, then select your project and get to work. And by the way, GOOD LUCK!

Byron G. Wels

Chapter 1

LIGHT

Ever since the sun first shone on man's earliest endeavors, he has been fascinated with light. Now that science has made new apparatus available to him, man's interest in light has increased, for he can study it, learn about it, and make light perform at his command. In this section, we will have the opportunity to shed "new light on light."

WHIRLING WONDERS DISCS

Whirling Wonders is a scientific toy which permits the study of various principles involved in motion. Most of our study is made of still objects but when motion is introduced many changes take place. Among the phenomena involved, are laws of inertia, centrifugal force, psychological and physiological effects to name a few. Principle among the effects is optical illusion. The full importance, understanding, and use of the subject has not yet been approached. Greater knowledge of the subject will enhance our living just as motion pictures have.

One of the early approaches to our modern motion picture industry, was an instrument known as the zoetrope. Your kit contains a zoetrope and is a fine stepping off point for the investigation of Whirling Wonders.

Figure 1

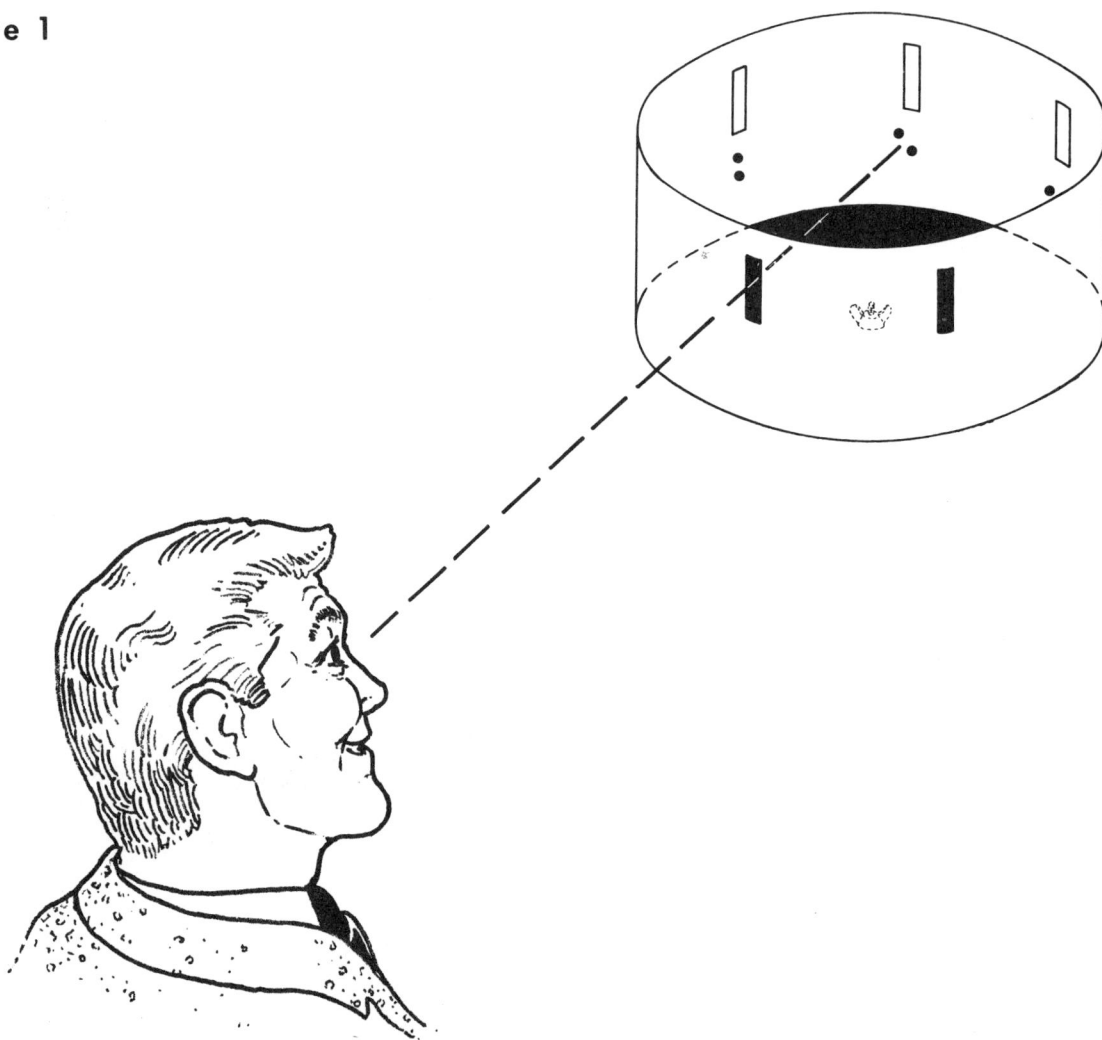

Cut out the long strip, bend it around and glue it to a plain disc as is shown in the illustration, Fig. 1. Mount this on a stick, such as a lollipop stick, so it can be rotated. As the zoetrope rotates, view the light and dark spots from outside through the slits as they pass in front of your eye. As you slowly change speeds, you will note one of the dots appears to go around the other dot. What actually happens here is that the eye is permitted to take a fleeting glance through the slit at the two dots. The brain remembers this picture until the next slit and the corresponding set of dots is brought into view. When this is done fast enough, an illusion is created of motion. You may if you care to, draw upon a strip of paper, another series of events and place them over the dots. It can be a boy jumping over a log, a dog running, or even a bouncing ball. In the case of the bouncing ball, draw a little straight line representing the surface on which the ball is bounced; one straight line for instance, for each set of dots on the zoetrope, and in the same position. Above each line draw one position of the ball. Have the ball come down to the line, strike the line, and go back up. With a little practice you will be able to make many strips of your own ideas. If you reverse the direction of rotation, driving the zoetrope backwards, it will reverse the illusion. Too great a speed will destroy the effect of the zoetrope.

Contained in your Whirling Wonders, are six black and white printed discs. Take any one of the first five as shown in the illustration, and attach it to the lollipop stick. Start it rotating gradually and with a relaxed stare, gaze at the center of the disc. As the speed is slowly increased, the black and white will be blended into hues of green and red and brown. At first, this may not be seen because you may not know exactly what you are looking for. However, going through the first five discs, there will be at least one of them which will function very nicely for your set of eyes. Everyone's eyes do not respond in exactly the same manner. Once you find the disc that works most easily, stay with it and examine it in motion at various speeds. You will learn how to see the colors with relaxed vision and they will become more brilliant. Try the same thing by reversing the disc's motion. Again too much speed is not desirable. You will often notice that the optimum of speed will vary depending on the amount of lighting that you have upon the disc. If you hold the disc very close to a bright light, the speed will be different to see colors than when the disc is held in more general lighting. What happens here is that the eye sees alternate black and white but it sees it so fast that the brain cannot record it as distinct black and white, but alternates between black and white so fast that you think you are seeing colors.

The sixth disc is mounted and rotated in much the same manner, but behind the slot place the little red Christmas tree lamp and (this lamp is lighted) as the disc is rotated in front of this light, your eye sees black, red, and white as the speed is increased. The brain tries to keep with it and confuses you into thinking that you see the red bulb turn to green. Motion also effects real color as can be demomstrated by the three discs in your set which are represented in the figure.

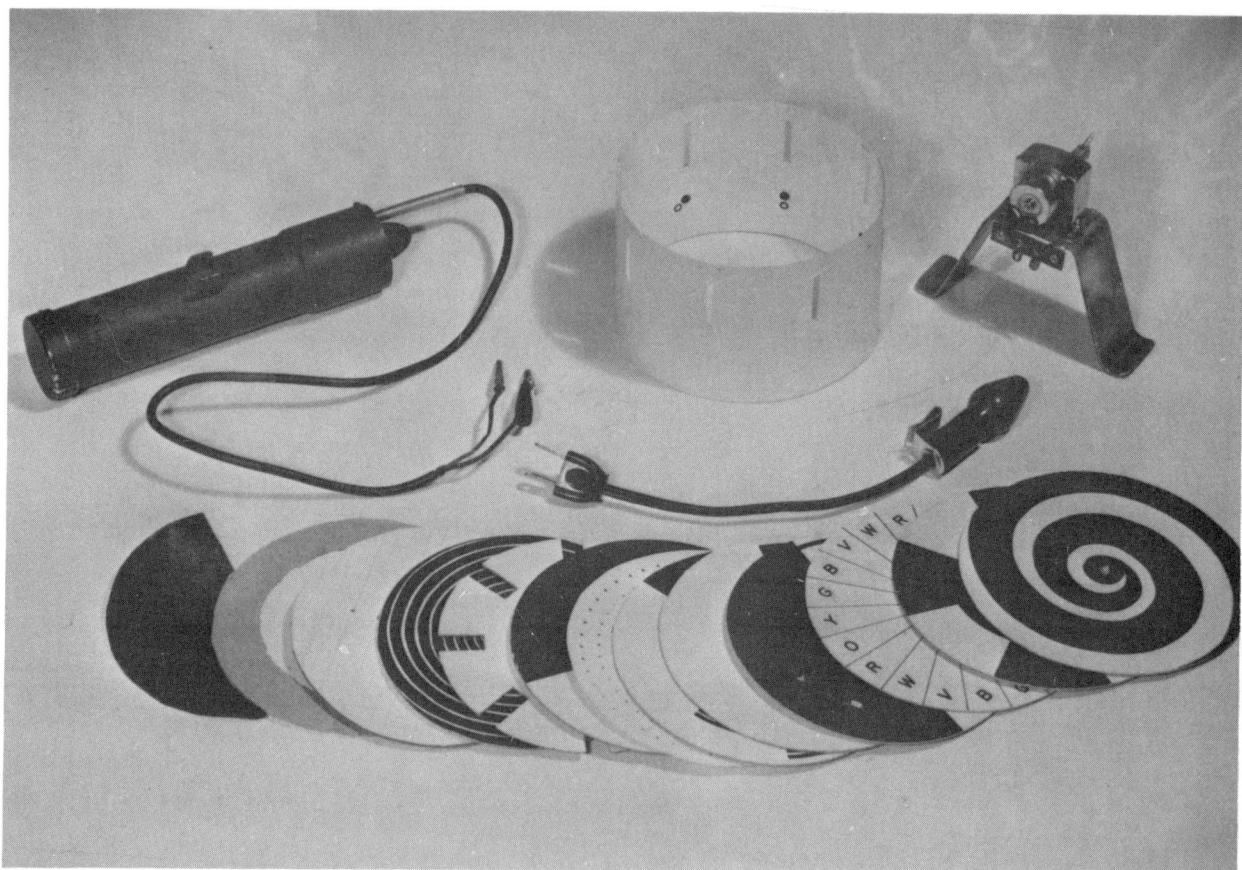

The first disc has on it a series of letters each representing a color such as red, which is "R", orange which is "O", and "Y" which is yellow. By coloring with water colors or crayons and rotating it, various speeds will give different effects. It is also an interesting experiment to rotate it under different color lights.

The second disc is a disc of stripes. It is not necessary to color the stripes, but every other stripe may be colored (such as red). At a certain speed it will be noted that the striped lines appear to be concentric circles. At low speed the disc appears to be in four sections. Two of the sections have straight lines and the other two sections are blurred.

The third disc may also be alternately colored such as blue, yellow, blue yellow; or red, blue, red, blue, and rotated in the same manner as the others. As part of the experiment concerning this particular disc, it is interesting to rotate it under a single fluorescent light at various speeds noting how the converging lines seem to multiply and they also appear to move backwards. This is a stroboscopic effect caused by the blinking in the fluorescent light in relation to the speed of rotation of the disc.

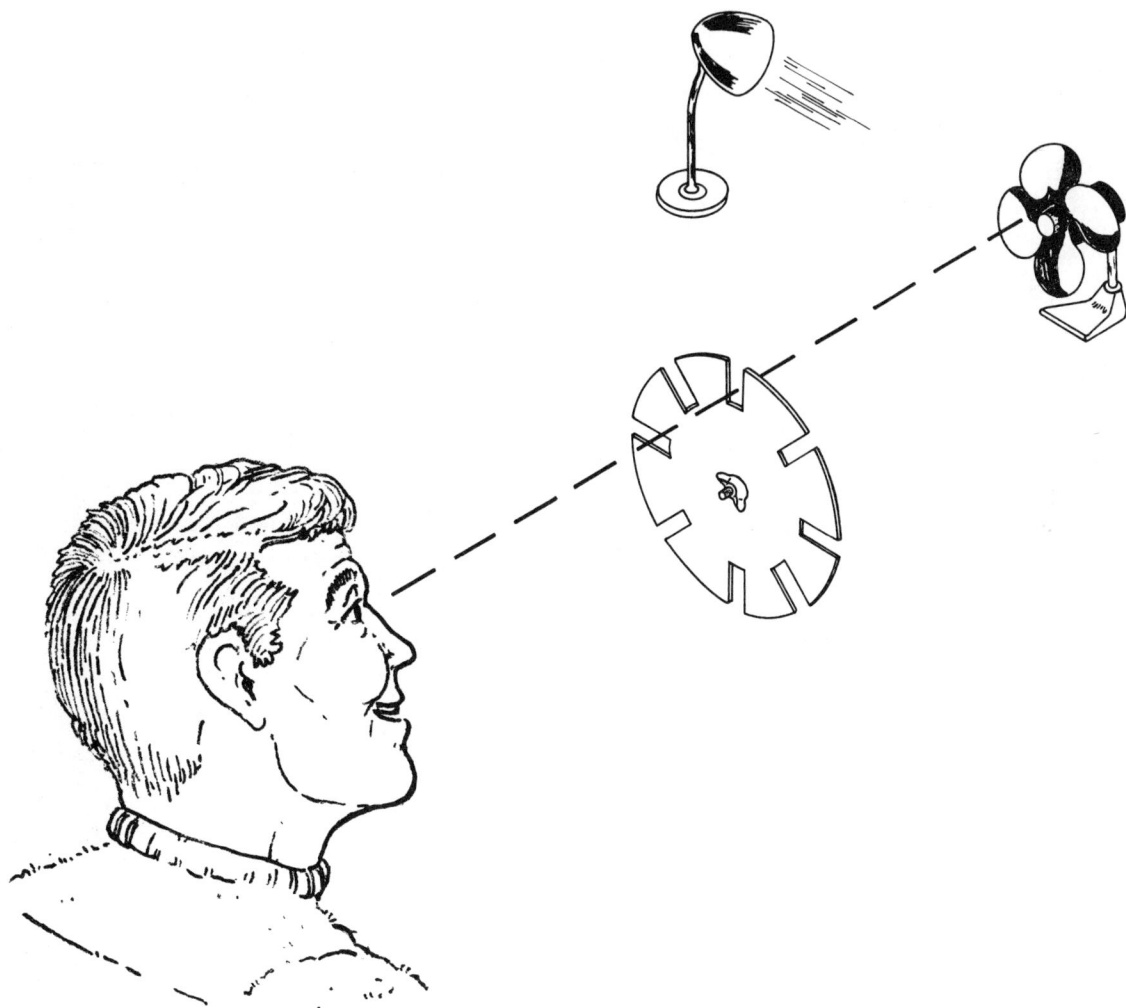

There is contained in your kit a stroboscopic disc. This is the disc that has eight slots cut in its periphery. Mount this disc in a similar manner as the others and start it rotating. View an electric fan or other rotating device through these slits by holding the disc relatively close to your eye as in the illustration. When the proper speed is reached, the fan or rotating device will appear to stand still. As the speed is changed further, the device will appear to move backwards. This effect has often been seen in the theatre where a wagon wheel or airplane propeller appears to stop moving forward and rotates in the opposite direction. With this simple device, it is actually possible to determine the speed of rotation or the speed of a moving object in a straight line. This is done by estimating as close as possible the speed the stroboscope disc is moving and multiplying this by eight to give you the number of slits that are passing before your eye in a given unit of time. For instance, if the disc is rotating at a hundred revolutions per minute, there are eight slits. That would mean 800 slits are passing your eye per minute. At this speed a fan blade appears to stand still when viewed. The fan blade will be making 800 revolutions per minute. A camera placed in front of the disc photographing through a time exposure an object moving on the other side of the disc, the object will appear on the developed film as a series of individual pictures. The known speed of the rotating disc with the number of gaps on the picture will give the speed of the object.

Several interesting effects can be observed by rotating the spiral configuration. Rotation clockwise gives the impression of moving into a tube, counter-clockwise of moving out of a tube. It is interesting to stare at the center of rotation of this disc for a minute then look away and stare at a fixed object and note how there is created an illusion of motion about this fixed object. This is the same effect that is found by driving an automobile over a straight road for a long period of time.

Next take the disc in this series whose periphery has a ring cemented on it. Mount this with the ring on the top side. Spin the disc at full speed. Notice how the ring (when the mount is moved slightly) tends to remain in the position in which it was, but when advanced to the new position it wobbles back and forth, slowly quieting down to a stable position of rotation. This is the way a gyroscope tends to operate by attempting to stay in the same place in which it rotates. With the disc spinning at full speed, notice how long it takes for the disc to come to a coasting stop as compared to any of the other discs in the set. This is the flywheel principle. It is interesting to observe centrifugal force in operation with this disc. In the center of the disc place a small piece of cardboard or a small button and start the disc rotating slowly as possible then introduce more speed. Quickly the button will move from the center of rotation to the periphery of the wheel, or be flung completely off. If it weren't for gravity this is exactly what would happen to the things on the surface of the earth.

There is a disc with four holes, one in the center and three moving out progressively from it. When the disc is mounted on the center hole, it rotates evenly and generally without vibration. If it is mounted on the second hole out from the center and held in the hand as rotation is increased, you will see and feel your hand vibrating under the eccentric motion of this wheel. Note how fast the wheel seems to be turning and then without altering its speed, place it firmly on a table top and hold it securely there and notice how the speed increases and the vibration decreases. This demonstrates the importance of always having flywheels and similar devices in proper balance.

Take the thin paper disc and pierce it with a large needle at each black dot. Always pierce it from the same side and try to get all the holes the same basic meter. Once a hole has been pierced, do not crush the excess paper on the far side back into the hole, but carefully go on to pierce the other holes. Mount this disc and start it rotating at top speed. Place the large end of the little glass tube in your mouth and place the small end very close to the rotating disc. Blow a constant stream of air through the tube and move the tube from the center of the disc to the outside. You will hear a musical scale. The air moving through the little rotating holes is chopped off, and this sets up a vibration which produces sound. It is possible to make a disc of this nature and actually play a song. Rotate this disc in front of a single fluorescent tube. At the right speed a set of dots will appear to move backward and another set forward. Several blank discs are contained in the kit so that you can try some experiments of your own. Any one of the subjects is full of potential discovery and application.

You will find that some of the foregoing experiments can best be demonstrated by using a motor to rotate the discs. For this purpose we suggest a flashlight battery operated motor;

FIBER OPTICS ILLUMINATOR

This unit provides high intensity illumination for use with fiber optic bundles, or light pipes. Bushings are provided to adapt the 1/2" output orifice to match the diameter of the desired fiber optic bundle.

Bushings for 3/8, 5/16, 1/4, 3/16, and 1/8" are included, and aluminum foil can be used to space out other sizes. For maximum light, the light pipe should be inserted with the tip well into the light chamber. Secure it there with the large screw for large sizes and with the small set screws on small sizes.

This unit was designed for use with glass bundles. If plastic light fibers are used, the heat may soften the ends inserted into the light chamber. However, normally this will not affect operation.

The Illuminator is protected by a thermo-stat which turns off the lamp in case of overheating (it automatically resets as it cools down). The lamp supplied (Edmund replacement No. 41,154) has a rated life of 25 hours at full brightness—longer at reduced brilliance. A long life (200 hours rating) alternative replacement (No. 41,544) is also available, but has reduced light output. For maximum lamp life, turn the three position switch to fan for a few minutes before turning off Illuminator.

A happy adaptation of the standard Edmund special effects projector, the regular lens is packed with the unit, and merely substituting this lens allows other uses. Slides and color wheels placed in the "gate" of the projector will project, and can also be used to color the fiber optics. See the Edmund catalog for other attachments and color effects.

DISC SETS

The recent upsurge of interest in unique lighting has brought with it a demand for all sorts of light coloring and light polarizing tools. You can use the Edmund plastic and glass discs to make a wide variety of these tools for yourself. The discs can be used to make color disc-slides that rotate inside of the gate of an Edmund projector. Or they can be used to make color wheels and polarizing spinners that rotate in front of the projector. Either will fill your screen or falls with splashes of changing color, or vary the color tones of your favorite slides.

MAKING DISC SLIDES

The disc slide is made to be rotated inside of the Edmund visual effects projector. The projector is adapted by adding a bracket and motor as shown in Figure 1. (It is provided with mounting studs for this purpose.) A disc-slide is placed on the motor shaft and rotates inside of the projector gate. The colored shapes on the disc will continually move across the screen, entering at one side, exiting at the other.

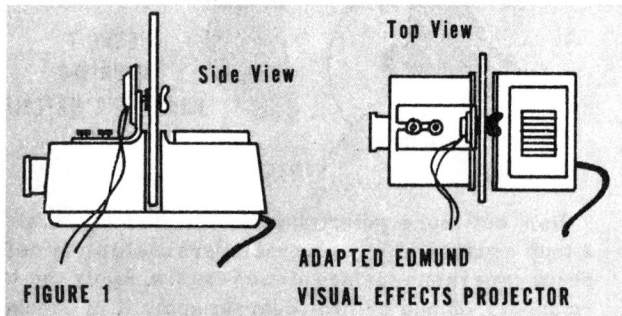

FIGURE 1   ADAPTED EDMUND VISUAL EFFECTS PROJECTOR

The shapes can be realistic, surrealistic, or totally abstract. The choice is yours. You can paint them on with transparent paints, or you can cut sheets of colored filter material into interesting shapes and sandwich them between two discs.

FLOW PAINTING

You don't have to be handy with a paint brush to make beautiful hand painted slides. Flow painting calls for almost no brush work. Just apply a drop of transparent paint to the surface of one of your discs, as shown. Then squirt thinner onto the dot with a dropper or a syringe. Hold the disc vertically then horizontally and watch the flow patterns develop. Repeat the process with another color. Apply a drop of paint. Then squirt on the thinner. Do not mix complimentary colors on the same disc. For instance, don't mix red and green

Drop of blue paint   FIGURE 2   Eyedropper with thinner

Blue and yellow flow together via thinner to make green   Drop of yellow paint

as this will give you a mud brown.

For interesting effects, flow-paint both of your discs and let them dry, then sandwich them together, rotating both inside the projector gate.

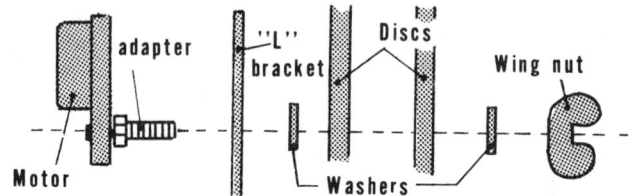

FIGURE 3 DETAIL FOR MOUNTING 2 DISCS IN GATE OF VISUAL EFFECTS PROJECTOR

Here you can use complimentary colors. The dominant colors in one disc can compliment the dominant colors in the other. For instance, paint one disc with red and pink, the other with blue and green. Although the discs can be placed with painted sides facing each other, facing them away from each other gives illusion of depth.

Texture the painted surfaces of your slides for a 3-dimensional effect. This is done by applying transparent paint to the disc in the pattern of your choice, or no pattern at all, and dabbing the paint with some porous object. A cigarette filter provides good texturing effects. A piece of tissue paper, sand paper, or even a dry brush will also work well. Or you may want to texture the surface with a piece of hair, or thread. Lay the hair on the wet painted disc, and peel it off when the paint dries. You can even scrape the dried paint with a razor blade or ball point pen. You can probably think of a dozen other texturing techniques. Try them all, since each will give you a slightly different texture and a vastly different effect when projected.

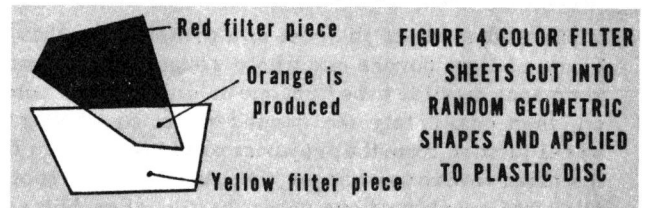

Red filter piece   Orange is produced   Yellow filter piece   FIGURE 4 COLOR FILTER SHEETS CUT INTO RANDOM GEOMETRIC SHAPES AND APPLIED TO PLASTIC DISC

For the artist who prefers scissors, razor blade, or Exacto knife to a paint brush, there are sheets of colored filter material available. These can be cut into squares, triangles, or just jagged shapes. Sandwich the sections of the colored filter material between two discs. You can let some of the colors overlap. A yellow sheet overlapping a blue one will give you a section of green. (Figure 4.) Red overlapping yellow will provide an orange image, but overlapping dark colors will give you black shadows.

MOVING MONTAGE

For a totally different effect, cut some old slides or movie film into sections and sandwich them between two Edmund discs. The fragmented slides will fill your screen with a montage of half recognizable broken images. Place this type of slide in an Edmund Projection Kaleidoscope to multiply the effect.

Shapes can also be photographed using high contrast film placed between the discs to provide white images against a contrasting white background. Stark black and white slide discs are often enhanced by using a color wheel in front of the projection lens.

COLOR WHEELS

Similar techniques can be used to make color wheels. These are made to rotate in front of the projector rather than inside of the projector gate. They can be used to vary the color tones of slides or just to vary the colors of a projected spot of light.

Most color wheels have their entire surface covered with paint or colored filter material. The filter material is usually applied in a pie wedge fashion. By placing

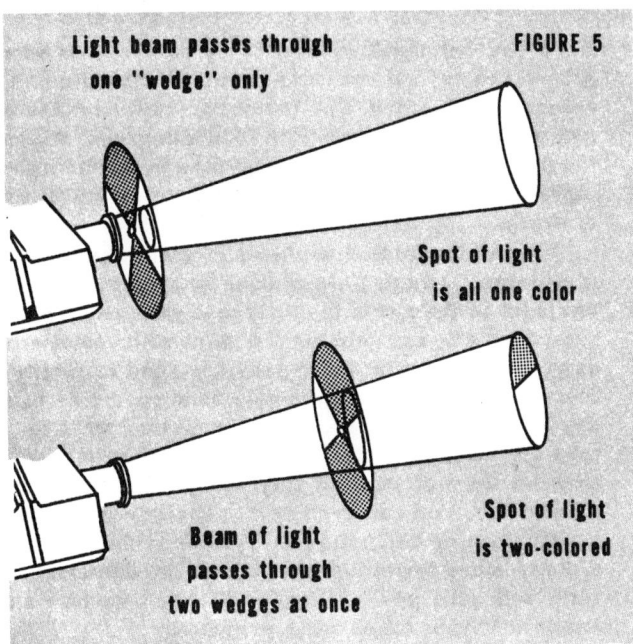

FIGURE 5

Light beam passes through one "wedge" only

Spot of light is all one color

Beam of light passes through two wedges at once

Spot of light is two-colored

a pie wedge wheel in front of a projector so that the beam of light covers one whole wedge, you can cause your spot or slide to be first one color, then two colored, then completely the second color. By moving the wheel further from the projector or light source so that the beam covers two wedges, you can make your spot or slide two toned, half one color, half another. Move the wheel further away so that the light covers three wedges and the spot or slide becomes tricolored, then two-colored again. (See Figure 5.)

If you prefer a more random color change, then apply the filter material in crazy quilt or plaid patterns, or paint the patterns using transparent paints. Cover the entire disc. Apply the paint randomly, in plaids, or waves. The paint can be sprayed on, brushed on, or dotted on with the back of a brush for disc slide flow patterns.

The color wheel can be used to vary the tones of your photographic slides, or hand painted 2 x 2 inch slides. You can also use the color wheel and the Edmund disc slide together for interesting effects. Rotate the disc

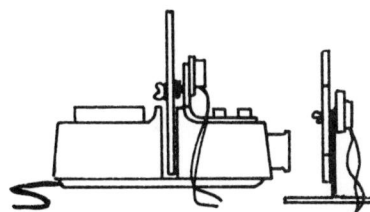

FIGURE 6
One wheel in projector gate other in front of lens

slide inside the projector gate and the color wheel in front of the projector. (Figure 6.)

With the disc slide in focus and the color wheel out, you can produce a moving, underwater effect.

POLARIZING COLOR

You can also use your clear plastic discs to make polarizing filter wheels to be rotated in front of your projector. Simply cut a sheet of polarizing filter material into semicircles the same diameter as the disc. Fasten the polarizing filters to the disc with cement or scotch tape, or sandwich them between two discs.

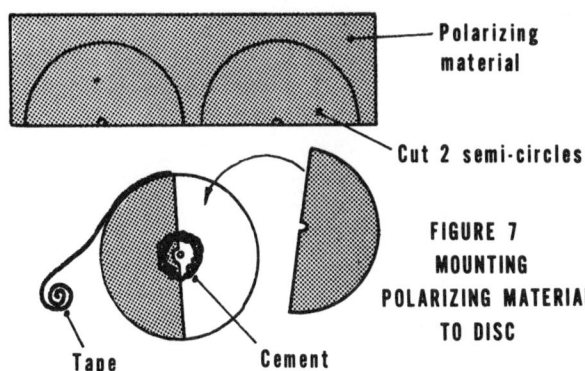

Polarizing material

Cut 2 semi-circles

FIGURE 7 MOUNTING POLARIZING MATERIAL TO DISC

Tape   Cement

Now cut more polarizing material into several 2 x 2 inch squares. Apply several layers of old style cellophane tape to one surface of each square. Apply the tape randomly on one or two squares; apply it in checkerboard patterns on others. Place the squares into the slide magazine of your projector and rotate the polarizing wheel in front. The colors will change on the screen as the polarizing wheel turns.

A polarizing disc wheel for Edmund Visual Effects Projector can be made that will provide moving, changing colors. Start by making 2 polarizing wheels as described previously (see Figure 7), then apply Scotch tape to one of the polarizing wheels, layer upon layer, in a random pattern. Rotate this wheel in the projector gate with the taped side facing the projection lens. Use the plain polarizing wheel rotating in front of the projector (see Figure 8).

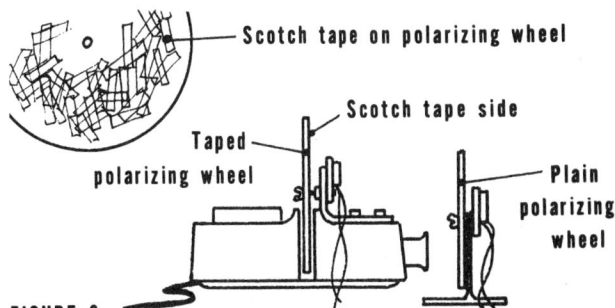

Scotch tape on polarizing wheel

Scotch tape side

Taped polarizing wheel

Plain polarizing wheel

FIGURE 8

VERSATILE SPOTLIGHT
AND
ADJUSTABLE APERTURE

The Versatile Spotlight consists of an Edmund Visual Effects Projector complete with Adjustable Aperture (No. 41,210), mounting bracket, and base. The Adjustable Aperture is sold separately for those who already own a Visual Effects Projector and want to use it as a spotlight.

How To Insert Aperture

Remove the projection lens and sight through to see if iris diaphragm is centered in aperture or gate of projector.

Applications

The No. 41,210 Adjustable Aperture can also be used in conjunction with the No. 71,057 or 71,248 Visual Effects Projectors or No. 71,212 Visual Effects Projector Set. Any combination gives you a 500-watt, sharp-imaging spotlight which may be used as a (an):

1. Theatrical spotlight (pin spot, follow spot, fixed spot, color spot)
2. Light source for Music Vision
3. Accent light for photographic work.

Maximum and minimum image diameter at various projection distances using No. 41,210 Adjustable Aperture and the Edmund Visual Effects Projector with 3" lens.

	PROJECTION DISTANCE			
Aperture Dia.	10'	20'	30'	40'
Minimum (1/8")	3.5"	6"	9"	12"
Maximum (1-5/8")	50"	108"	135"	195"

Longer Throw

Greater brilliance can be achieved with "long throw lenses" such as Edmund No. 60,799 to 60,802. These will utilize more of the light available, focusing it more efficiently at the greater distance, instead of merely masking off part of the total light area, as with a shorter F.L. (focal length) lens.

While the spot size with the supplied standard 3" F.L. lens can be varied from a spot diameter of 4 inches to 8 feet at a throw length of 15 ft., a 5" F.L. long throw lens will give this range at 42 feet, and a 8" F.L. lens at 66 ft. See complete data on various lenses on sheet enclosed, "How to Select a Lens".

For broad floodlighting, you may find it advantageous to remove the projection lens completely.

Color Spots

To color your spot, all you have to do is place a simple color filter sheet in front of the lens. A piece of aluminum, bent roughly as shown at right, will allow you to attach a square of color filter with a common spring-type clip.

PROJECTION KALEIDOSCOPES

Decorative lighting devices are quickly gaining popularity across the country and around the world in discotheques, theaters, home light shows, and parties. Among the most intriguing of these are the Edmund Projection Kaleidoscopes, No. 71,106 and No. 71,121. These devices essentially consist of a 500 watt projection lamp, a condensing lens system, a rotating pattern wheel, and a 3" F.L. anastigmatic kaleidoscopic projection lens. (See Figure "A".) The entire instrument "is" larger than a 35mm projector, weighs less than six pounds and plugs into any standard household 105 - 125 V, 60 cycle A.C. power outlet.

Moving kaleidoscopic patterns can now be projected on walls, ceilings, floors, or even dancing girls. Hexagonal patterns formed from revolving pattern wheels will cover surfaces of 20 to 2,000 square feet at projection distances of 5 to 100 feet.

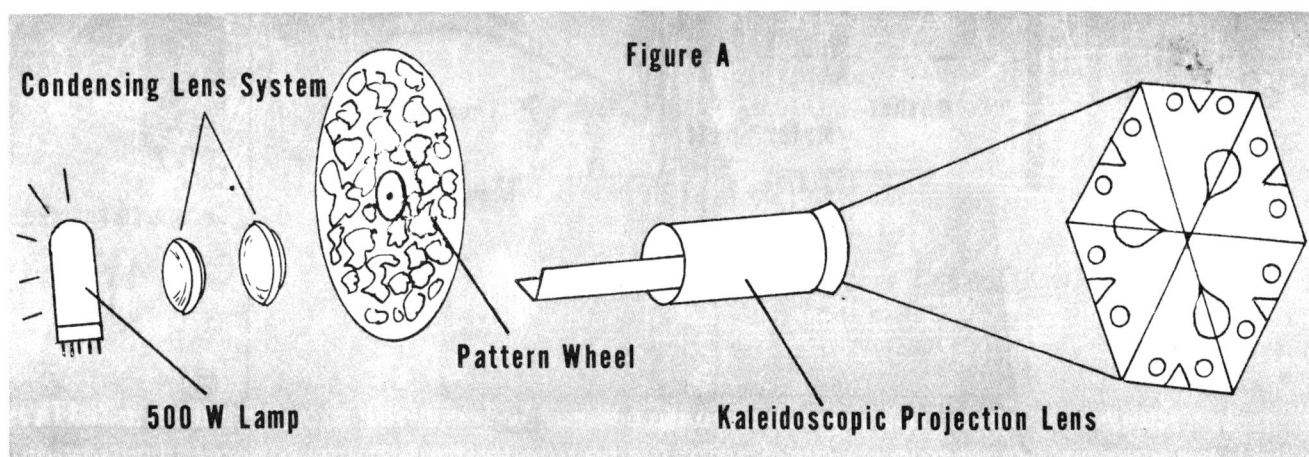

Figure A — Condensing Lens System — 500 W Lamp — Pattern Wheel — Kaleidoscopic Projection Lens

A "dry" pattern wheel is supplied with the No. 71,106 kaleidoscope. It produces hundreds of figures in a sequence which repeats itself each 60 seconds. A "wet wheel," which consists of colored plastic particles floating in a liquid, is provided with No. 71,121 Liquid Projection Kaleidoscope. As these pieces slip past one another, they combine to form a truly endless array of non-repeating patterns. Each pattern wheel is available separately for those who wish different effects or for replacement purposes. For our artistically inclined customers, blank glass discs to fit the projection kaleidoscope are available under stock number P-71,087 (set of 2) which can be painted using Edmund Transparent Paints No. 71,067. Many other user-prepared pattern wheels can be fabricated, including montage wheels prepared by cutting up pieces of colored filter material, old slides, or movie film, and sandwiching them between glass or plastic discs. (2 plastic discs available under stock number P-70,996.) A polarized color pattern wheel and spinner will provide changing colors within the kaleidoscopic pattern but the image will be relatively dim due to the light absorption of the polarizing material. If you wish to try this technique, the pattern wheel can be made using the materials provided in our Polarized Color Wheel Kit No. 71,100. The spinner can be assembled from No. 71,099 Polarizing Disc, No. 60,763 - 30 R.P.M. Motor. The spinner can be attached to the kaleidoscope with No. P-60,748 "L" Brackets.

Mounting the Pattern Wheel:

1. Using the hardware provided fasten the motor (found in cord compartment Fig. D) to the "L" bracket as shown in Figure B.
2. Attach pattern wheel to motor shaft using wing nut and washers.
3. Place entire "L" bracket with motor and wheel onto projector and secure under thumb nuts. (See Figure C.)

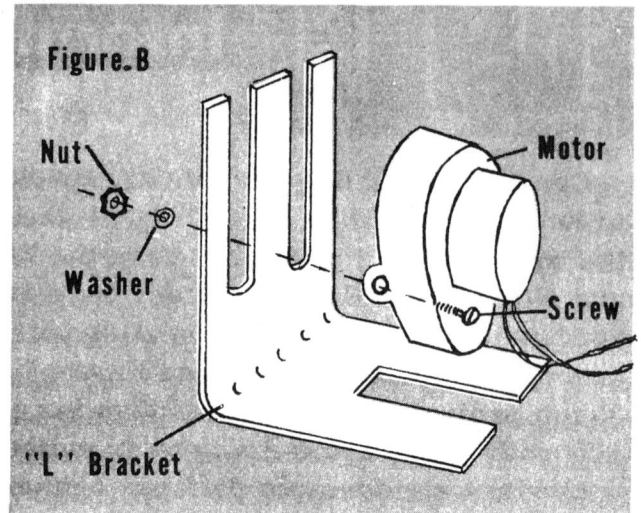

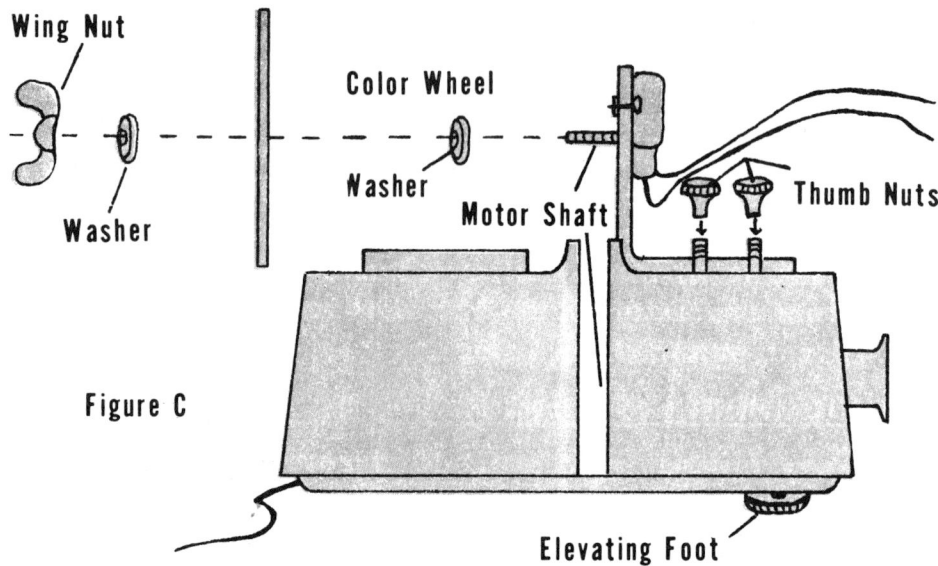

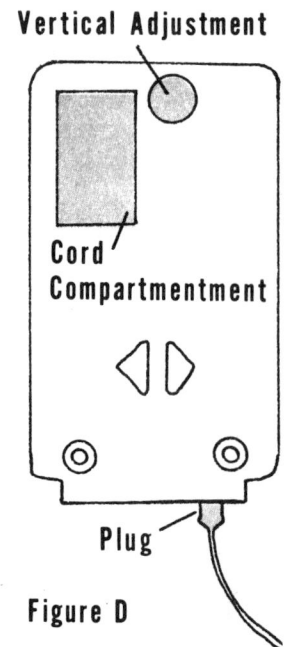

Figure B

Nut

Washer

Motor

Screw

"L" Bracket

Wing Nut

Washer

Color Wheel

Washer

Motor Shaft

Thumb Nuts

Figure C

Elevating Foot

Vertical Adjustment

Cord Compartmentment

Plug

Figure D

Readying the Projector:

1. Turn projector on its side and remove the 8 ft. power cord housed in the cord compartment. (See Figure D.) Plug one end of the power cord into the rear receptacle of the projector, and plug the other end into a 120 volt, A.C. outlet.
2. Plug the cord from the pattern wheel driving motor into a 120 volt A.C. outlet.
3. Turn on the projector by pushing the power switch (located on the base at the rear of the projector) to the right. The first notch actuates the fan only and insures cooling after the lamp is off. The second notch turns on the lamp while maintaining ventilation.

   The fan is a very important part of your kaleidoscope projector. Without it, your color wheel and the projector itself would melt under the intense heat created by the 500 watt lamp. Your kaleidoscope projector is wired so that the cooling fan runs at all times while the lamp is on. Make certain that the exhaust vent on the top and intake vent on the side of the projector are kept clear to prevent the projector from overheating. If mounted near a ceiling, leave enough space for proper ventilation. ALWAYS ALLOW THE FAN ALONE TO OPERATE FOR AT LEAST THREE MINUTES AFTER THE LAMP IS TURNED OFF.

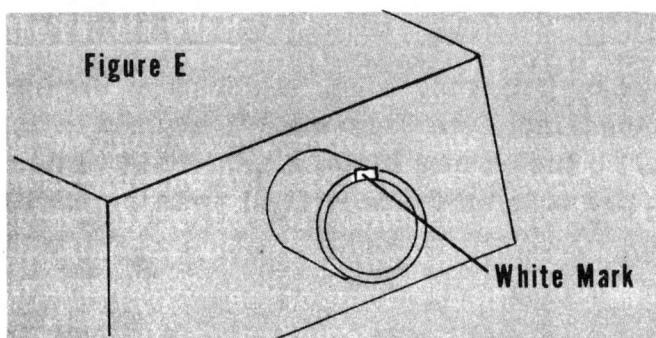

Figure E

White Mark

4. Even with the fan operating, your projector will become very warm. Therefore, it is a good idea to always have the pattern wheel rotating while the lamp is on. If you are using the Edmund "wet-wheel," which is constructed of plastic, this precaution will be added insurance against warping, bending, or melting.

5. Focusing your projection lens is done manually. Start by making sure the lens is placed in the projector case with the white mark on top. (See Figure E.) Push or pull the lens in and out until the projected image is sharply defined on the screen, wall, or ceiling. Turn the elevating foot on the front of the projector base for vertical adjustment. To adjust the horizontal position, simply move the projector itself. If the projected image does not form an evenly segmented hexagon, rotate the lens slightly in its mount until an even-sided hexagon is achieved.

6. It is possible that the pattern wheel has been mounted either too high or too low in the projector gate. If the pattern wheel does not move, or occasionly sticks, loosen the screws holding the motor in place on its bracket and raise the motor and pattern wheel until it moves freely without restriction. If the edge of the pattern wheel is visible in the projected image, loosen the motor mounting screws and lower the motor and pattern wheel until this edge can no longer be seen in the image.

Special Note for Wet Pattern Wheels:

When the wet wheel has been stopped for any period of time, such as overnight storage, the particles will sink to the bottom. These particles can be evenly dispersed in their suspending fluid by allowing the wheel to rotate for a period of 15 minutes. If a wet-wheel equipped projection kaleidoscope is to be used infrequently during a light show or in any of its other numerous applications, it is suggested that the wheel be kept revolving continuously and the lamp turned on only when desired.

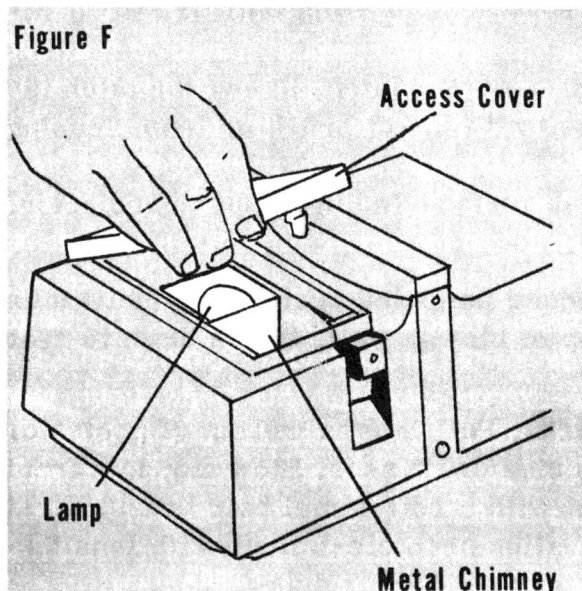

Figure F

Access Cover

Lamp

Metal Chimney

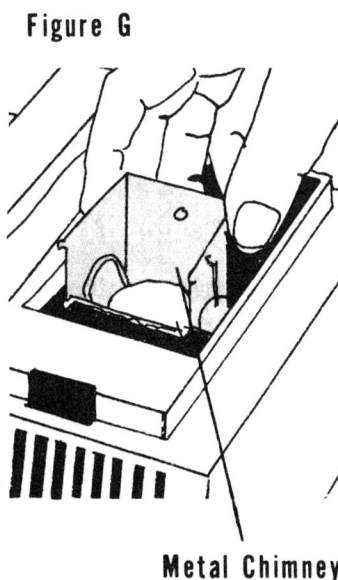

Figure G

Metal Chimney

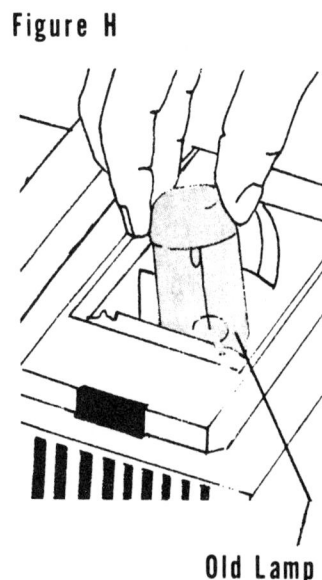

Figure H

Old Lamp

POLARIZING COLOR DISC KIT

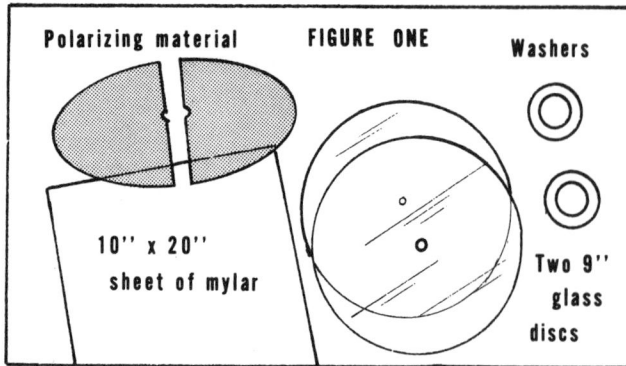

Polarizing material   FIGURE ONE   Washers

10'' x 20''
sheet of mylar

Two 9''
glass
discs

2. Place both semi-circles of polarizing filter material on top of the disc as shown in the illustration. Apply a few drops of adhesive near the center of the glass disc to hold the polarizing filter material in place.
3. Next, cut a nine-inch diameter circle out of the sheet of Mylar enclosed and set it aside.
4. Cut the remaining Mylar into strips, squares, circles, and triangles. Place the sections of Mylar on top of the polarizing material.

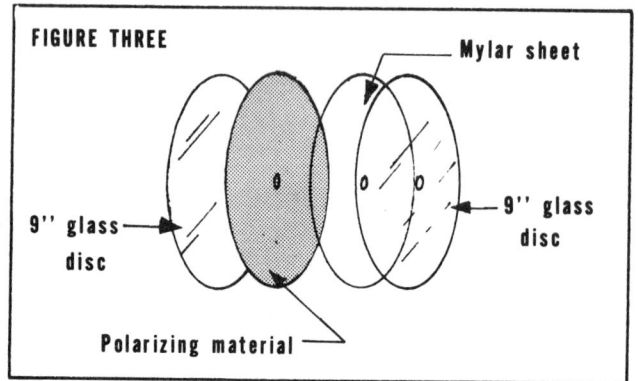

FIGURE THREE   Mylar sheet

9'' glass disc

9'' glass disc

Polarizing material

POLARIZED COLOR

Mylar has the property of birefringence. When sandwiched between two sheets of polarizing material, it changes and recombines rays of polarized light to create pastel colors. You can prove it yourself by placing the enclosed sheet of Mylar between the two polarizing semi-circles provided. Hold the materials up to the light and you will see colors that weren't there before.

Once assembled, the Mylar wheel should attach easily to your Edmund Polarizing Color Projector or Visual Effects Projector. With it, you can use the colors produced by polarized light to decorate your home, discotheque, tavern, or merchandising display. Simply follow the assembly instructions below.

5. Now place the second glass disc over the first.
6. Use the polarizing filter disc attached to your Edmund Polarized color projector to view the Mylar colors. After looking at the fragments of Mylar between two polarizing filters, remove the glass disc that was placed over the Mylar sections.

Now place the circle of Mylar you cut out on top of the Mylar sections. Place the glass on top. Tape the discs together and view the results with the polarizing spinner. Choose the effect you want for your Mylar wheel. When you are satisfied with the results, tape the edges of the discs together with adhesive or slide binding tape.

MAKING A MYLAR POLARIZING COLOR WHEEL

To Make a Mylar Polarizing Color Wheel . . . .
1. Put one of the two nine-inch glass discs on a flat table.

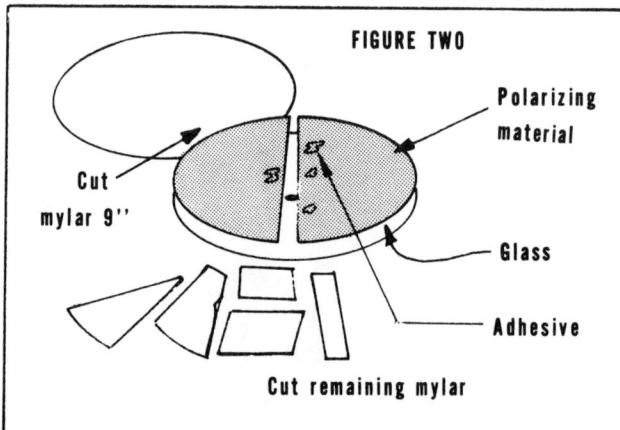

FIGURE TWO

Polarizing material

Cut mylar 9''

Glass

Adhesive

Cut remaining mylar

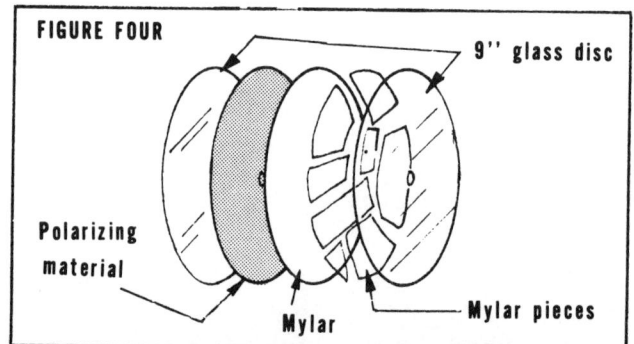

FIGURE FOUR   9'' glass disc

Polarizing material

Mylar

Mylar pieces

The instructions with your Edmund Visual Effects Projector or your Edmund Polarizing Color Projector will tell you how to mount the Mylar wheel. Keep in mind that the Mylar must always face the front of the projector and a second polarizing filter must be rotating in front of it.

POLARIZING SPINNER WHEEL

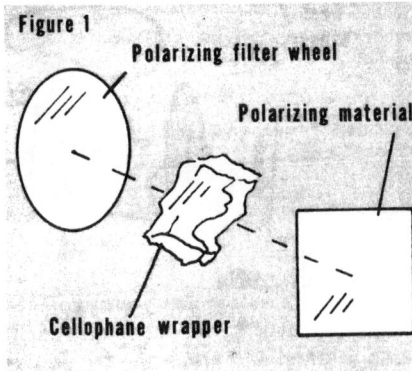

Figure 1 — Polarizing filter wheel, Polarizing material, Cellophane wrapper

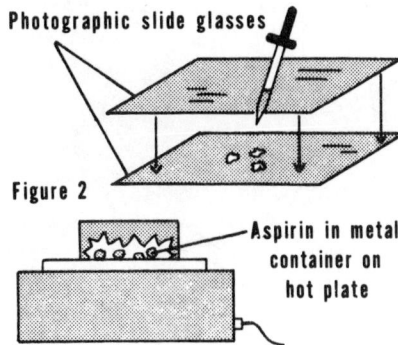

Figure 2 — Photographic slide glasses, Aspirin in metal container on hot plate

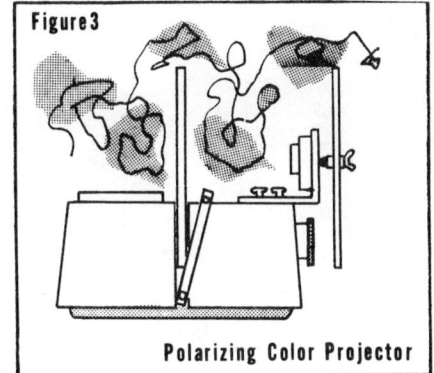

Figure 3 — Polarizing Color Projector

IT'S A COLOR WHEEL even though it doesn't look like one. You can use your polarizing spinner wheel to create a wide variety of colors. Prove it yourself. Crumple a cellophane cigarette wrapper between the polarizing filter wheel and another sheet of polarizing material (Figure 1). Turn the wheel and watch the colors change. Clear cellophane is no longer colorless when viewed between pieces of polarizing material. It becomes multi-colored. Transparent materials that take on color when placed between polarizers are called birefringent materials. Cellophane probably isn't the only birefringent material in your home. Stretched, transparent polyethylene plastic becomes multi-colored between polarizing filters. Mylar and cellophane tape are also birefringent. Melted aspirins crystallize and become birefringent when placed between photographic slide cover glasses (Figure 2). Why not try all of these materials and examine the colors produced between polarizing filters? And, if you have an Edmund Polarizing Color Projector, you can project the effects and cover entire walls with patterns of constantly changing color (Figure 3).

If you have an Edmund Visual Effects Projector, you can mount the wheel easily by using an L-bracket (S.N. 60,748; set of 2) as shown in Figure 4. If you have an ordinary 35mm projector, you can still project birefringent slides. Mount the polarizing wheel on a spinner. The spinner is only a motor-driven polarizing disc mounted on a stand. You can make your own polarizing spinner with an Edmund motor and a wood or metal book end (Figure 6), or you can buy a motor stand (S. N. 71,118). The spinner must be rotated in front of the projector for the colors to change.

POLARIZING SLIDES can be made to fit your slide disc or slide tray. You may purchase Edmund 2 x 2-inch polarizing squares (S.N. P-41,168; pkg. of 20) or cut your own squares from larger sheets (Figure 8). Apply cellophane tape to a square and place it in the projector with the taped side facing the front. You can also tape Mylar to the square and obtain additional, polarized-color effects.

Edmund Photo Motion material can be used to make interesting slides for overhead projectors or 35mm background slides. Cut 2 x 2-inch squares and project them with the spinner disc rotating in front of the projector.

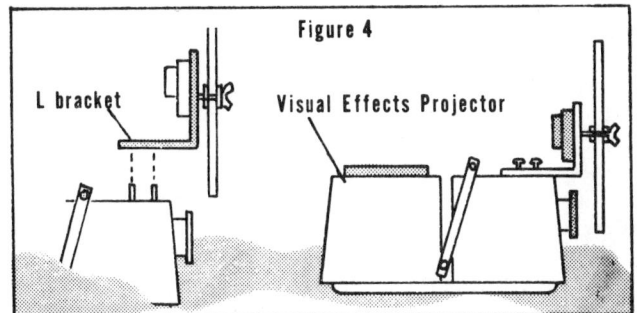

Figure 4 — L bracket, Visual Effects Projector

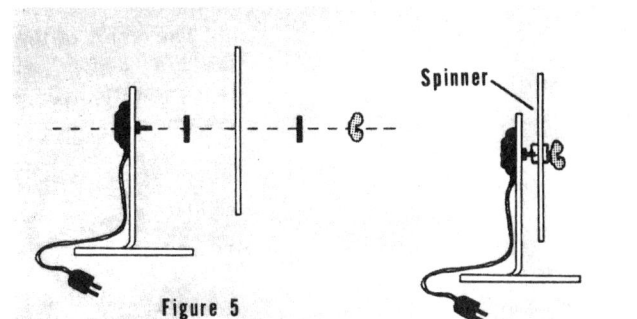

Figure 5 — Spinner

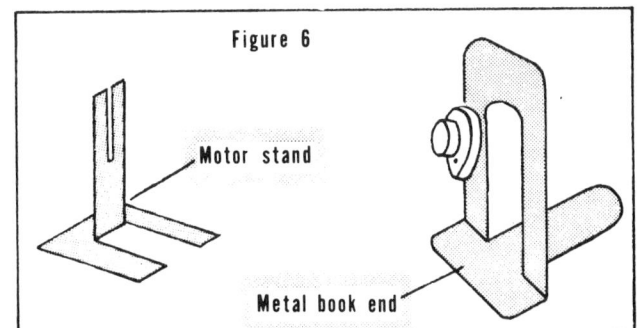

Figure 6 — Motor stand, Metal book end

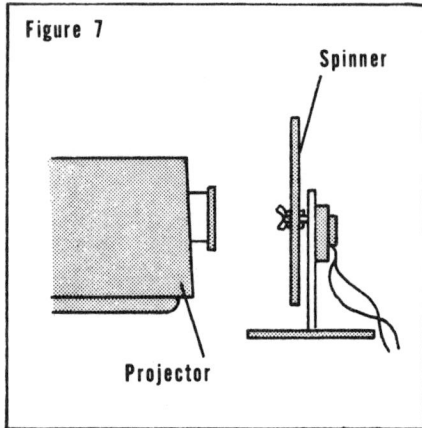

Figure 7

Spinner

Projector

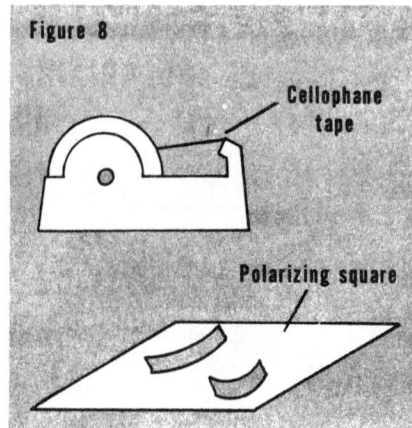

Figure 8

Cellophane tape

Polarizing square

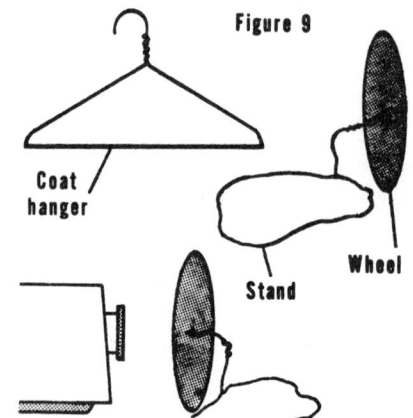

Figure 9

Coat hanger

Stand

Wheel

MATCH THE MOTOR SPEED of your polarizing spinner to the slide you are projecting. As a rule of thumb, the more faceted and detailed the polarizing slides, the slower the spinner motor used. The slower motor brings slower, more subtle color changes to the screen and gives the viewer more time to study the picture details before they change. Slow motors, as slow as one rpm, are often used with melted aspirin or other slides. Edmund polarized action or geometric pattern slides and slides made of Mylar, cellophane tape, or cigarette wrappers often seem interesting with faster motors (30 or 60 rpm). Here the high-speed color change causes a flashing effect.

Before you purchase a motor for your projector or spinner stand, experiment with different speeds. Twist a coat hanger into a stand and place the wheel over it (Figure 9). Place the hanger in front of the projector. Spin the wheel slowly for a smooth subtle color change. Then, give the wheel a good hard spin and watch the slide change color. Purchase the motors that most closely approximate your favorite spinning speeds. Mount them, with the polarized color wheel, in front of your projector. Then sit back and watch the colors change. The jagged edges of polarized cellophane will prick your imagination, rippling polarized Mylar will tickle it. Welcome to the Edmund world of color!

MusicVision Sets

MusicVision is sound that you can see. It's a technique for translating audible vibrations into visible light patterns.

Your MusicVision set will bring you hours of fun at home. It can fascinate your friends. Used in a store window, it can attract attention and customers. Used in the theater, it can provide excellent special scenic effects that change shape with the dialogue. Used in the discotheque, it lends visible emphasis to the sounds of psychedelia.

Follow these simple instructions and your Music-Vision set will enthrall you with the sight of sound.

Connecting The Motiondizer

Music motiondizers are sold in two varieties. Motiondizer 'A' features round, front-surface mirrors attached directly to the membrane. This type of mirror attachment permits the motiondizer to interpret sound in orbital patterns. Motiondizer "B" uses mirrors attached to strings. The strings are attached to the flexible membrane, allowing the mirrors more room to bounce. Motiondizer "B" interprets sound as a series of wavy lines and bouncing spots of light.

Your music motiondizer has already been assembled. All you have to do is connect it to an audio source. A tape recorder, a phonograph, or a radio will supply the sound you need.

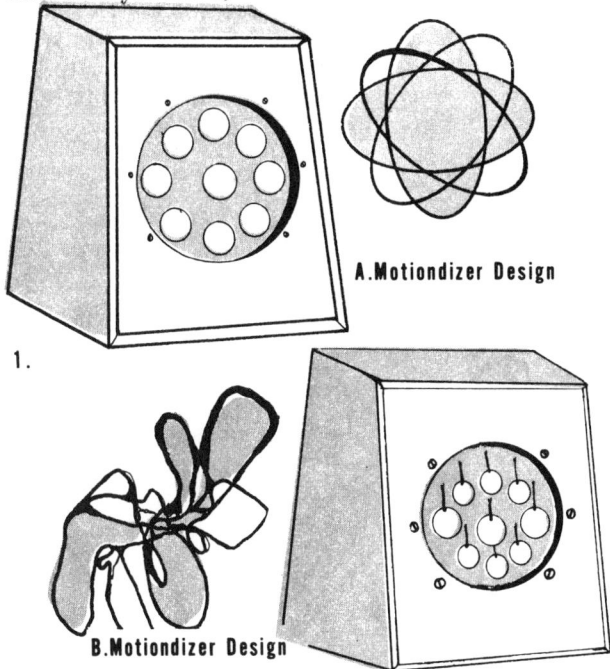

A. Motiondizer Design

B. Motiondizer Design

1.

Your audio source might have an output jack installed by the manufacturer. The jack may be marked "output," "speaker," or "extra speaker." Now select a length of audio cable. Six to eight feet of cable should give you more than enough to work with. One end of the cable should have either a 1/4" phone plug or an RCA-type pin plug. Insert the plug into the output jack of your radio, tape recorder, or phonograph.

Phone Plug

1 a.

R.C.A. Pin Plug

Now, strip the insulation from the other end of the cable. Wrap the wires around the terminals at the back of your motiondizer and tighten the screws.

Your audio source may have no output jack or terminal screws. This is likely to be the case with many portable record players and radios. If your record player or radio is of this type, use a six to eight-foot length of lamp cord and alligator clips to attach one end of the lamp cord to the terminals of your speaker. You can find these in a radio by removing the back of the speaker housing. The terminals are usually near the speaker magnet.

Your stereo record player may use RCA-type pin plugs to connect separate speakers to the turntable amplifier unit. If it does, you can use a "Y" connector to let you plug the motiondizer and speaker into the same jack. Connect the male branch of the "Y" to the turntable unit. Connect the second branch to the stereo speaker. And connect the third to the motiondizer.

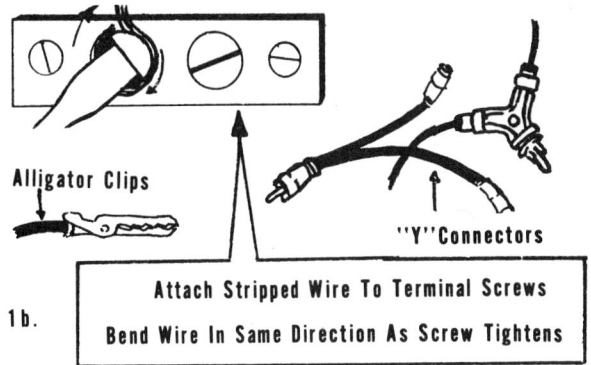

Alligator Clips

"Y" Connectors

Attach Stripped Wire To Terminal Screws
Bend Wire In Same Direction As Screw Tightens

1 b.

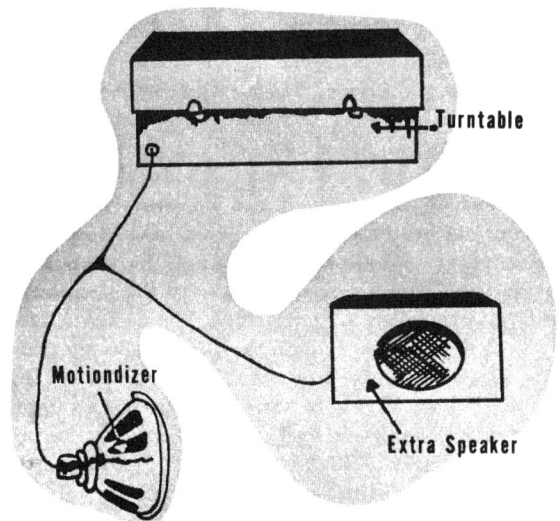

Turntable

Motiondizer

Extra Speaker

To connect the motiondizer to a stereo record player with no jack, remove the back from one of the speaker units. Use ordinary lamp cord and solder both of the conductors to the terminals or attach wires using alligator clips.

If you have a component Hi-Fi or stereo system, you will probably find terminal screws behind the amplifier. If this is the case, simply attach the cable to the amplifier the same way you attached it to the motiondizer. Strip the insulation from the wires and wrap them around the terminal screws. Tighten the screws again.

Matching Impedance

Keep in mind that the motiondizer has an eight-ohm impedance. With most modern, transistorized amplifiers, it should be possible to connect the motiondizer directly across the output (in parallel with your regular speakers). Older, tube amplifiers with multiple impedance outputs necessitate closer impedance matching. Treat the motiondizer as an extension speaker and refer to the amplifier manual for specific details.

Larger Applications

For commercial applications using constant voltage lines, a line-matching transformer is necessary. This is especially true of juke boxes and public address systems using multiple speakers. Connect the audio source to the transformer and connect the transformer to the motiondizer.

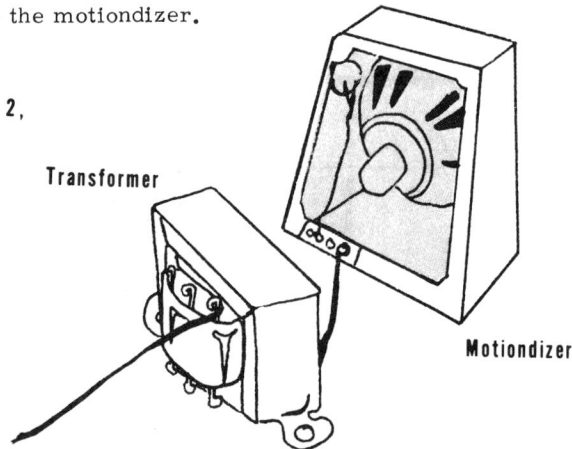

2,

Transformer

Motiondizer

Special Fusing Precautions

No special fusing is required with most ordinary audio sources. However, with extra-powerful sources such as the electric guitar amplifers used by modern "acid rock" groups those juke boxes and Hi-Fi systems capable of peak outputs in excess of 25 watts, the connection between audio source and motiondizer should be fused to protect the motiondizer speaker and control. Sufficient for the purpose will be a 1-ampere fuse of the common automotive type (Buss or Littelfuse Type 3AG, 1 amp; not SLO-BLO), connected in series to the motiondizer. This is accomplished by merely fusing one of the pair of connecting wires to the input terminal lugs. For those who construct their own motiondizers or self-contained MUSICVISION systems, it should be pointed out that this series fuse should precede both speaker and L-pad (volume-pattern control).

Assembling The Color Wheel

Now, assemble the parts of your color wheel kit. They include the pie-wedge color wheel, the motor on a stand with cord and plug, two washers, and one wingnut. Put one of the washers on the threaded adapter as shown in the illustration. Next, put the wheel on the adapter. Follow the wheel with the second washer and finger-tighten the wing nut. Plug the wheel into any convenient 120-volt receptacle.

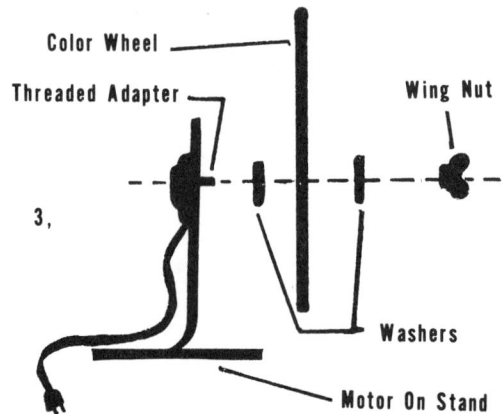

Color Wheel
Threaded Adapter
Wing Nut
3,
Washers
Motor On Stand

Aside from the motiondizer, there are three other components necessary for a good MusicVision light show. A collimated, or slightly-divergent light source is necessary. A 35mm projector makes an excellent light source for this application. You will also need a screen surface on which to project the MusicVision shapes. If you don't have a screen, a sheet or even a white wall will suffice. Next, you will need your color wheel, already assembled. This will be necessary for coloring the swirls of light.

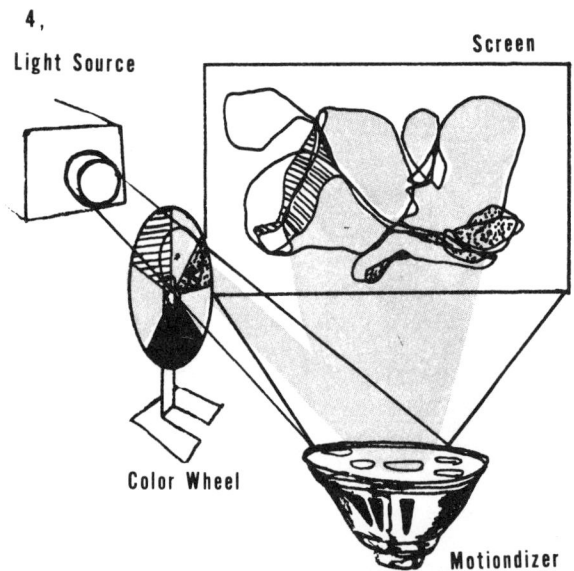

4,
Light Source
Screen
Color Wheel
Motiondizer

Now, arrange the MusicVision elements as shown in the illustration. Note that they form a triangle. Your arrangement should approximate this. Since the angle of incidence equals the angle of reflection, light will reflect from the mirror onto the screen at the same angle at which it strikes the mirrors. Now turn on the projector light. Select the aperture plate with the largest hole from among the three furnished. Place it in the projector gate to narrow the light beam. Now train the beam on the motiondizer so that it covers all of the mirrors and as little else as possible. If the beam seems too wide, narrow it with a smaller aperture. To calculate the size of aperture, see the Aperture Guide Chart (next page). Make sure that the reflection of each mirror appears on the screen. Focus the projector so that the reflected spots appear sharp. If any of the spots are off the screen, adjust the angle of the motiondizer.

Next, place the color wheel between light source and the motiondizer so that the beam covers one full pie wedge.

Plug in the wheel and start it rotating. Note that all of the spots change colors at once. Move the wheel closer to the MusicVision speaker so that the light beam covers two pie wedges. Half the reflected spots on the screen are one color, half another. Place the color wheel at the position between the light source and motiondizer that gives you the best scheme of color change.

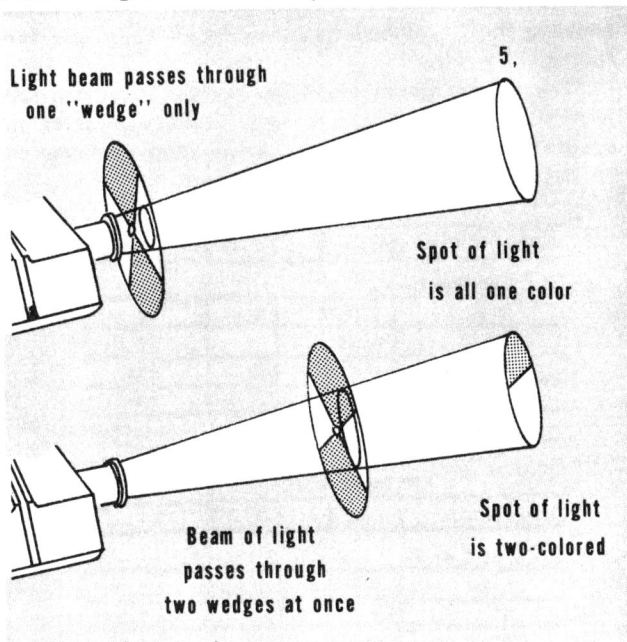

Light beam passes through one "wedge" only

5,

Spot of light is all one color

Beam of light passes through two wedges at once

Spot of light is two-colored

Turn down your house lights and turn up your audio source to the normal listening level. Next, turn the knob on the motiondizer marked "audio level" until the patterns on your screen are as large as you want them. Caution: Don't try to increase the activity on your screen by turning up the volume of your audio source to extremes. This can burn out both the motiondizer speaker and the audio control. Set your listening level first and then adjust the activity on your screen by turning the audio control knob on your motiondizer.

Details For Ceiling Mount:

You may decide to mount your motiondizer and light source on shelves or beams close to the ceiling. The advantage here is obvious. It saves space on the floor for spectators, chairs, or possibly other lighting equipment. If you choose to ceiling-mount your MusicVision equipment, the same principles apply. Once again, the angle of incidence equals of the angle rebound. The projector is placed on a hanging shelf very close to the ceiling. The motiondizer is hung from a tier somewhat below and in front of the projector. Again arrange both so that the angled beam will hit the wall below.

Details For Fixed-Mirror Motiondizer:

You must first determine how far from your ceiling you wish to hang the motiondizer, and from the Aperture Guide Chart what projection distance you will use. The motiondizer with attached mirrors does not require critical positioning of the projector because it can be tilted and fixed in position to reflect the incident light to almost any part of your wall or screen. Thus, it is necessary to place the projector only slightly above the level of the motiondizer. The color wheel motor and stand can be attached to a support extending from the ceiling.

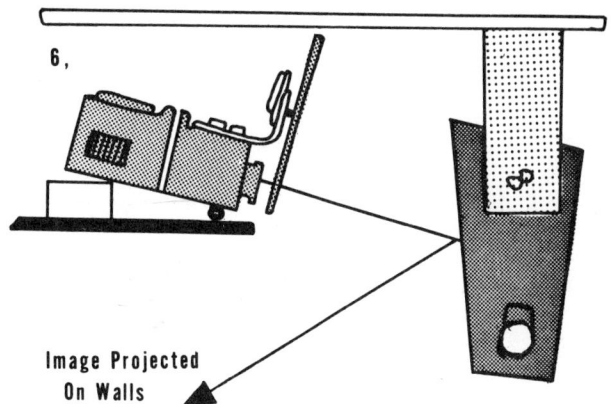

6,

Image Projected On Walls

Hanging-Mirror Motiondizers:

The mirrors should not lie flat against the rubber diaphragm. The motiondizer should be angled so that the mirrors hang slightly in front of the membrane and maintain only a light contact. It is very important to remember, in positioning the projector, that the hanging mirrors should never form an angle of less than 90° with the floor as is possible with the fixed mirrors. Thus, in order to obtain the patterns where desired on your wall, it may be necessary to position the projector above or below the motiondizer to obtain the proper angle of reflection (See Fig. 7). If space does not permit moving the projector higher or lower, a similar result may be achieved by moving the projector closer to the motiondizer while keeping it as far above it as possible. As the projector is moved closer, a larger aperture will be required to cover the mirrors completely. (See Fig. 8)

500W 35MM VISUAL EFFECTS PROJECTORS

Both manual and remote-controlled models include:
1. Basic projector featuring:
   a. 500W, fan-cooled light source,
   b. high-resolution, f/3.5, 3-inch focal length anastigmatic projection lens,
   c. efficient condenser system with heat-absorbing lens for slide protection,
   d. 3-position switch for separate control of lamp and fan,
   e. detachable line cord; self-storing cord compartment,
   f. impact-resistant, molded case with carrying handle and non-marring rubber feet,
   g. lever-operated, manual slide changer,
   h. full operation and service instructions;
2. Twelve-slide carrier disc;
3. Set of 3 aperture plates to allow use of projector as a spotlight or as a MUSICVISION light source;
4. Accessory-mounting bracket studs (2);
5. Nuts, bolts, etc., for mounting drive motors.

In addition, No. 71,002 Remote Control Model has a powered slide changer controlled by a switch with 7-ft. cord.

Either model can be used as a colored or multi-colored controlled-beam light source, conventional projector, "wet" slide projector, etc. With the proper accessories, you can project free-form color patterns (organics), crystal formations, colored montages, polarized animation slides, and polarized color slides of constantly-changing hue and pattern. Equipped with a multi-colored wheel (No. 71,116; 9-inch diam.), your Visual Effects Projector is unsurpassed as a MUSIC-VISION light source. The Polarized Color Projector, No. 71,098, is a Manual Control Model fully equipped with polarized color wheel, polarizing spinner wheel, drive motors, mounting brackets, and necessary hardware.

ATTACHING THE ACCESSORY—MOUNTING BRACKETS

Accessory-mounting brackets (Edmund No. 60,748; pkg. of 2) are used in three ways (depending on accessories used and effects desired):
1. Single bracket, rear (gate)-mounted
   a. Remove knurled thumb-nuts and washers from threaded studs.
   b. Lift projector handle.
   c. Hold the bracket by the slotted side with slotted side uppermost; pass the drilled side under the handle until slotted side is flush with handle. Drilled holes should be centered...in line with the studs. (See Figure A.)

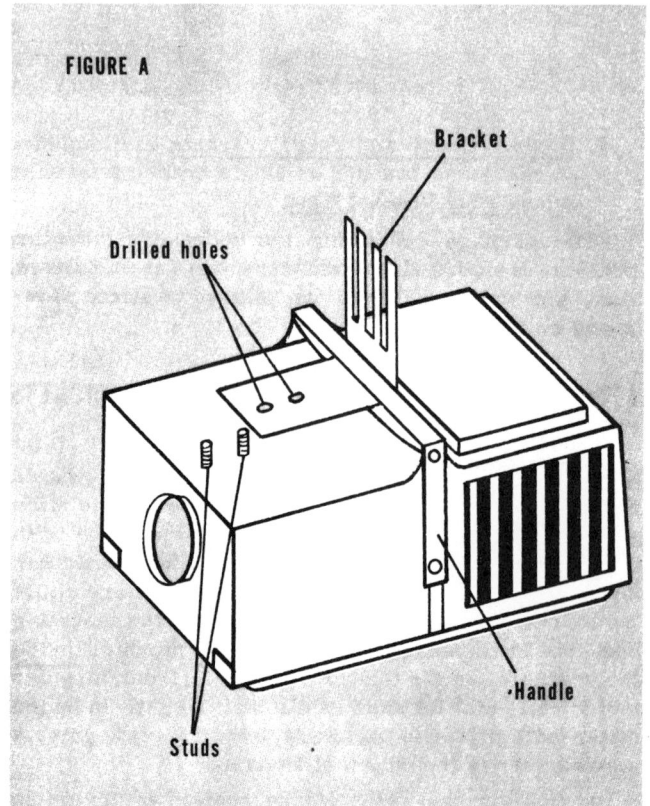

FIGURE A

   d. Push handle straight down to rest on the bracket.
   e. Holding slotted portion, push forward to bring holes down over studs. Handle will pivot forward to expose slide gate. (See Figure B.)
   f. Replace washers and tighten thumb-nuts on studs.
2. Single bracket, front-mounted
   a. Remove thumb-nuts from studs.
   b. Holding slotted portion of bracket uppermost, put holes over studs.
   c. Replace washers and tighten thumb-nuts.

(Page 21)

FIGURE B — Drilled holes, Bracket, Slotted portion, Studs, Handle

FIGURE C — Motor, Mounting hole, Thumb nuts, Shaft

FIGURE D — Outer slots, Nut, Washer, Motor, Mounting hole, Screw

3. Double (front and rear) brackets are mounted in the same manner as single brackets (above); mount rear bracket first.

The package containing the accessory-mounting brackets includes also an envelope with 4 each, screws, nuts, and washers. These can be used to attach slow-speed motors to the brackets.

ATTACHING SLOW—SPEED MOTORS TO THE BRACKETS

The purpose of the brackets is to support slow-speed motor drives for various accessory wheels either in front of the projection lens or in the slide gate. Several such motors are available, each with different speed of rotation and each for particular visual effect purposes, as shown later. All are similar in form, however, and are attached to the mounting brackets identically. Motors are always mounted inside the brackets, so the threaded shaft of a front-mounted motor will point forward, while that of a gate-mounted motor will protrude backward, over the slide gate. A screwdriver is the only tool required.

a. Holding the body of the motor as shown in Fig. C, slide the unthreaded base of the shaft down into the middle slot of the bracket.

b. Align the mounting holes on the motor with the outer slots of the bracket.

c. Using the small screws (No. 6-32 X 5/16 r.h.), nuts, and washers furnished with the bracket, attach the motor as shown in Fig. D and fasten firmly. Note that the motor can be adjusted vertically, allowing plenty of clearance for table-top use of front-mounted accessory wheels up to 14/1/2 inches diameter. Gate-mounted wheels can be as small as 7 inches in diameter.

d. Attach cord and plug of desired length to motor lead wires.

MOUNTING VISUAL EFFECTS ACCESSORY WHEELS

1. Front-mounted accessory wheel
   a. Remove wing-nut and one washer from the threaded shaft of the motor, leaving one washer on the shaft.
   b. Put center hole of accessory wheel over threaded shaft.
   c. Replace washer and screw wing-nut down firmly (See Fig. E).

2. Gate-mounted accessory wheel
   Mounting of wheel on shaft will be same as for front-mounted wheels. It will be necessary, however, to provide clerance for insertion of the wheel into the slide gate by loosening the motor-mounting screws and raising or removing the motor.

3. For Thin Wheels
   a. Raise motor till mounting screws are at the top of the bracket.
   b. Put wheel into slide gate and onto threaded shaft simultaneously.
   c. Lower the motor to desired position
   d. Make sure the wheel can turn freely in the gate; tighten motor-mounting screws.
   e. Tighten washer and wing-nut on threaded shaft of motor.

4. For thick or double (sandwich) wheels
   a. Remove motor from mounting bracket.
   b. Put the wheel onto the threaded shaft.
   c. Lower the assembly, wheel into slide gate and motor shaft into bracket slot.
   d. Make sure the wheel can turn freely in the gate; tighten motor-mounting screws.
   e. Tighten washer and wing-nut on threaded shaft of motor.

FIGURE E

Washer — Motor

Threaded shaft

Bracket

Wing nut

Washer

Accessory wheel

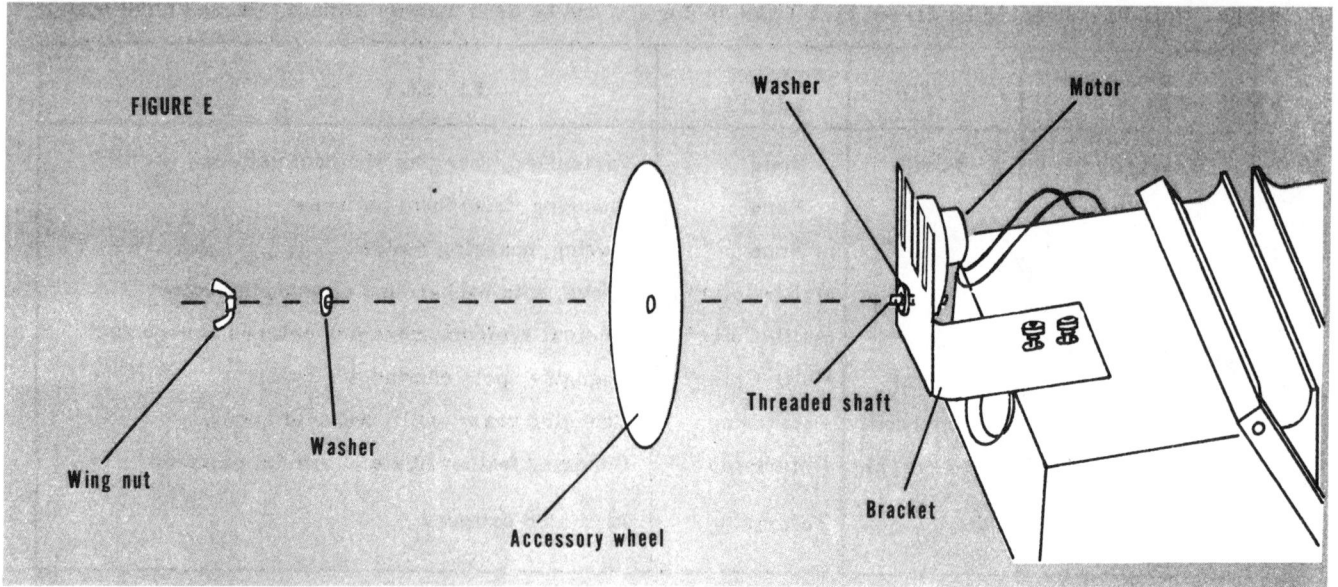

Note: For frequent use of thick wheels, the above procedure may be eliminated by removing the handle from the projector. Without the handle, the motor and bracket can be manipulated as a unit, without need to demount the motor.

Once the accessory-mounting brackets are attached, there is no need to remove them, even when only one is in use.

DIFFERENT PROJECTION EFFECTS

Material to be projected can be categorized as either Slides or Discs. The following tables summarize the visual effects resulting from certain equipment combinations.

SLIDES: Used alone or with powered front discs.

35mm Color slides in slide holder

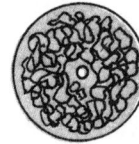

Multi-color wheel

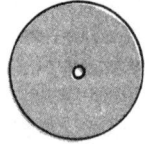

Polarizing wheel

SLIDE	MOTOR	FRONT WHEEL	EFFECT
Conventional	None	None	Conventional slide projection
Conventional	12 rpm*	Multi-Color*	Above, but with changing colors
Montage	None	None	Variegated, abstract patterns
Montage	12 rpm*	Multi-Color*	Above, but with changing colors
Moiré	None	None	Moiré "psychedelic" patterns
Moiré	12 rpm*	Multi-Color*	Above, but with changing background color
Aperture	None	None	Controlled-beam light source
Aperture	12 rpm*	Multi-Color*	Changing colored light beam
Birefringent	30 or 60 rpm	Polarizing	Crazy-quilt pattern; rapidly changing hues
Crystal	3 to 12 rpm	Polarizing	Intricate, feather-like patterns, slowly changing hues
Polarized Motion	30 or 60 rpm	Polarizing	Predetermined, selected motion patterns

*If one color only is desired, a piece of colored plastic filter sheet can be taped over the lens; front color wheel and motor will not be necessary.

DISCS: Gate Discs should be driven by a 1rpm motor and can be used with or without powered front wheels.

REAR DISC	MOTOR	FRONT WHEEL	EFFECT
Montage	None	None	Variegated, changing abstract patterns
Land-Painted	None	None	Changing, free-form patterns
Moire	None	None	Moving, changing moire
Moire	12 rpm*	Multi-Color*	Above, with background of changing color
Music	12 rpm*	Multi-Color*	Musical symbols, changing colored background
Aperture	12 rpm*	Multi-Color*	Changing spots of changing color
Birefringent	30 or 60 rpm	Polarizing	Changing crazy-quilt; delicate hues
Crystal	3 to 12 rpm	Polarizing	Changing feather like and crystal patterns
Polarized Motion	30 or 60 rpm	Polarizing	Animated patterns

POLARIZING EFFECTS

Visual effects caused by polarized light deserve special attention because they are of great interest and are little understood by the amateur. For a good explanation of the scientific principles of polarization, we recommend our pocket-sized booklet "Polarization of Light," Stock No. 9206. But here we are concerned with the effects we can obtain: color and motion.

COLOR. Certain substances, known as birefringent materials impart color and color change to the light beam when introduced between two polarizers. Some of these are: Mylar plastic film; "old style" cellophane tape; mica; benzoic acid crystals. Such materials can be applied to a sheet of polarizing material in single or several layers and will exhibit changing hues and intensities quite beautiful to see. Such a wheel is supplied as standard equipment with S. N. 71,098 Polarized Color Projector, but you can make your own from a kit (S. N. 71,100) or from materials available separately in the Edmund Catalog. Glass, plastic, and polarizing wheels are all listed in the Unique Lighting section of the catalog; birefringent materials can be obtained locally.

MOTION. We have all seen the advertising signs which urge us to eat or drink at Joe's, Moe's, or Flo's. Lest we overlook just where to find our genial host, an illuminated arrow points the way to our nourishment, the series of individual lamps in the arrow lighting progressively to reinforce the direction: A similar illusion of motion can be obtained by passing light through two polarizing layers, the second of which is the ordinary "spinner" in front of the projection lens. The first layer is more complex, consisting of specially oriented materials not readily made by the amateur. Such materials are used in preparing the sets of mounted polarized slides listed in the Edmund Catalog. We do offer this type of material, though, for use in making your own slides. It is available in a variety of motion types, such as linear, circular, turbulence, etc.; see Photo Motion, also in the Unique Lighting Section. With care, very small amounts of these can be used.

*If one color only is desired, a piece of colored plastic filter sheet can be taped over the lens; front color wheel and motor will not be necessary.

FIBER OPTICS KIT

IMPORTANT:
Read instructions thoroughly before using your Fiber Optics Kit. This kit contains glass fibers which should be kept out of the reach of small children and pets.

Punctures from these glass fibers are painful and dangerous, but they can be avoided if care is used during handling.

DO NOT work with glass fibers in areas where food is prepared and/or served. Work on paper and be sure to vacuum work area when finished.

Procedure for Constructing a Glass Fiber Optics Light Guide from Unjacketed Fibers

While the following steps refer to the construction of a fiber optics light guide from the unjacketed glass fibers supplied with this kit, they also apply to making a finished light guide out of the jacketed fiber optics bundle supplied. (Note that the basic difference is in Step 1: After cutting jacketed bundle to desired length

For your information

In fiber optics, there are different types of fibers as well as different ways of manufacturing them. One method of manufacturing a single glass fiber is as follows:

A piece of core glass surrounded by a different-quality glass sleeve (called cladding) is lowered at a controlled rate into the center of a circular, high-temperature heating element which melts the core and cladding, forming a fine glass fiber. This fiber, which is now capable of optimumly transmitting light due to thousands of internal reflections per foot, is cooled and wound on a moving drum or wheel at high speed. (Figure 2)

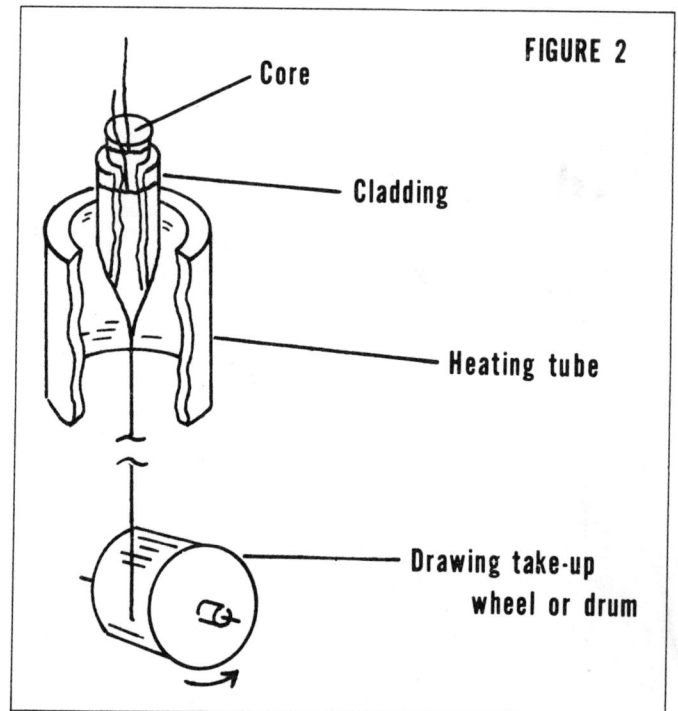

FIGURE 2

Core

Cladding

Heating tube

Drawing take-up wheel or drum

Some Basic Classes of Fiber Optics Arrangements Are:

1. Flexible light carriers...transmit light but not readable images (non-coherent bundles).
2. Flexible image carriers...transmit readable images (coherent bundles).
3. Fiber optics face plates...transmit images.
4. Fused tapered bundles...magnify or reduce images.
5. Focusing fiber optics (e.g., "Selfoc" ...latest Japanese invention).

with a razor blade, hit the bundle against a hard surface until the fibers emerge. Pull the fibers out of the jacket two inches, cut an inch off the other end of the jacket only, and push the fiber bundle back. Then proceed to Step 2.)

Step 1. Lay a bundle of glass fibers on a sheet of black paper. Using a large needle, stroke the bundle until it lays flat and straight. (Figure 3)

Step 2. Wet one end of the bundle with alcohol and move all the stray fibers back into the bundle with a stroking motion of the needle (Figure 4). When the bundle is compact, slip a 3/4" section of heat-shrink tubing over one end, leaving 1/4" of fibers showing. (Figure 5)

Step 3. Allow the alcohol to air dry and then shrink the end tubing using a soldering iron or match. (Figure 6) DO NOT touch the tubing with the soldering iron or hold the match too close. This will destroy the tubing and cause the fibers to melt. (Repeat Steps 2 and 3 for other end.)

Step 4. Using Edmund's Clear Epoxy (No. 40,674), Duco, or other clear epoxy, dip a needle into the epoxy and apply to each end of the light guide. Maximum distribution is assured if the needle is repeatedly pushed through the fibers about 1/4" from the end. (Figure 7)

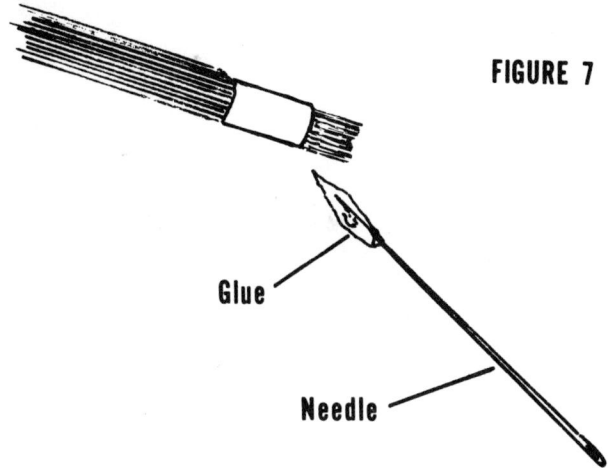

FIGURE 7

Glue

Needle

Step 5. Continue the process described in Step 4 until the bundle end is saturated with epoxy. This can by checked by holding the end in contact with the needle. (Figure 8) When the needle can be observed from the other side, enough epoxy has been applied. Let the epoxy cure per manufacturer's recommendations before starting Step 6.

Step 6. After curing the epoxy, cut the excess fibers off 1/16" from the end of the heat-shrink tubing.

FIGURE 3

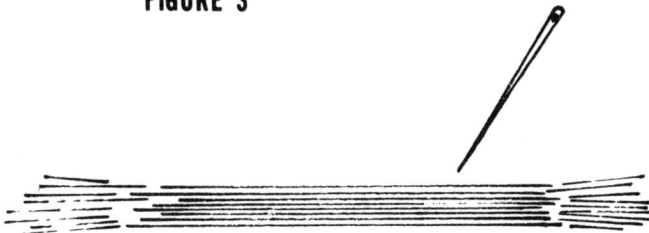

FIGURE 4

FIGURE 5

FIGURE 6

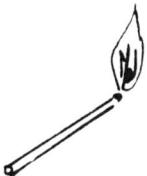

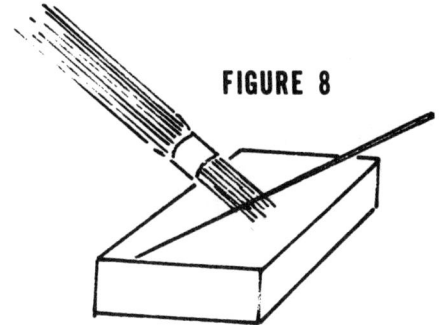

FIGURE 8

FIGURE 9

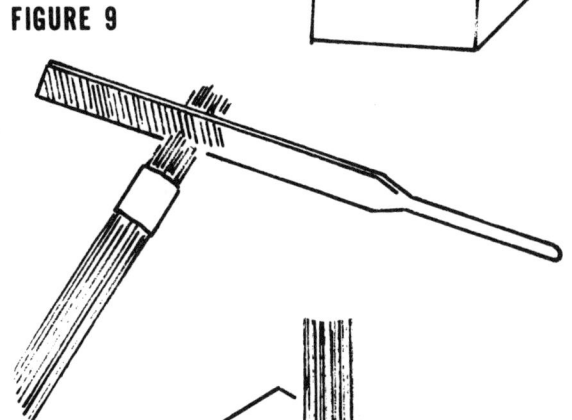

FIGURE 10

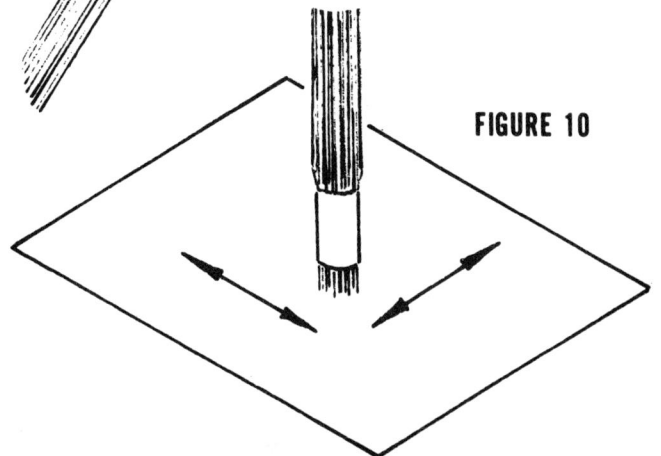

Using a jeweler's file and a gentle sawing action assures a smooth cut with minimum breakage of fibers. (Figure 9)

Step 7. Hold the fibers in an upright position, sand the cut ends smooth using No. 600-grit, waterproof emery paper (available from auto body supply shops). (Figure 10) Add a few drops of water to assure a fine finish and sand the excess fibers flush with the heat-shrink tubing.

Step 8. For a light guide offering maximum transmission, the ends of the fiber optics bundle can be polished. This is accomplished by turning the emery paper over and using the back side of a polishing pad. Add toothpaste as a grinding compound. Holding the bundle perpendicular to the pad, polish the end by moving it in a "figure-8" motion. (Figure 11) This is a time-consuming process, so do not get discouraged. Continue the polishing until the surface appears smooth and shiny when viewed at an angle.

Step 9. Repeat Steps 4 through 8 for other end. Your glass fiber optics light guide is now complete and can be used in the experiments described below or in some of your own.

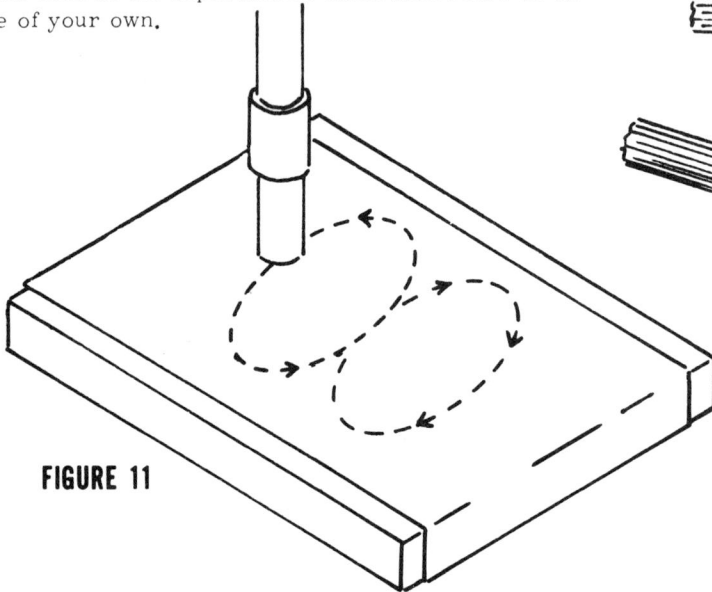

FIGURE 11

Procedure for Constructing a Plastic Fiber Optics Light Guide

Step 1. Lay the plastic fibers on a clean surface, aligning the individual fibers as shown in Figure 12. Wrap a 1"-wide piece of tissue paper around one end as shown in Figure 13, overlapping the end 1/8".

Step 2. Crimp a 2"-wide strip of aluminum foil over the tissue-wrapped end. (Figure 14)

Step 3. Slip a 3/4" section of heat-shrink tubing (Figure 15) over the foil and position it 1/2" from the end. Using a match or soldering iron, apply heat until the shrink-tubing reduces in diameter and firmly grips the bundle. (DO NOT touch the flame or soldering

FIGURE 12

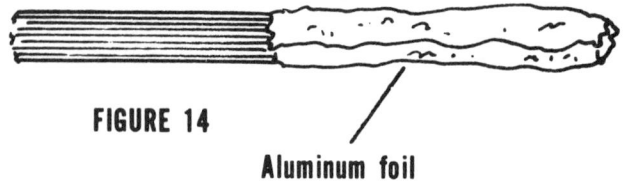

FIGURE 13

Tissue paper

FIGURE 14

Aluminum foil

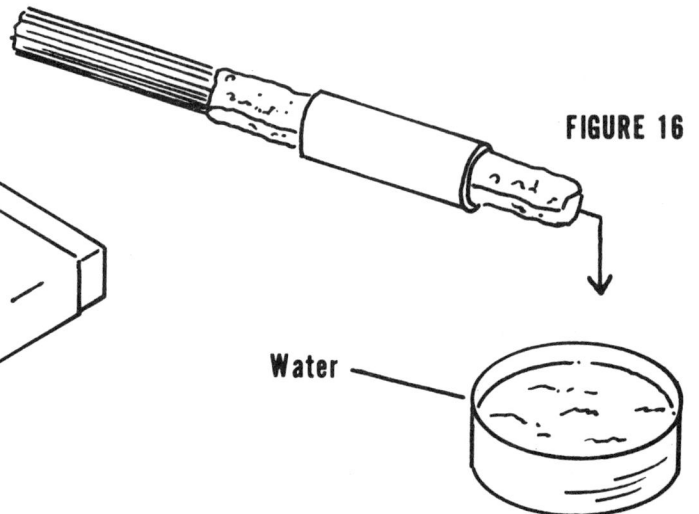

FIGURE 15

Heat-shrink tubing

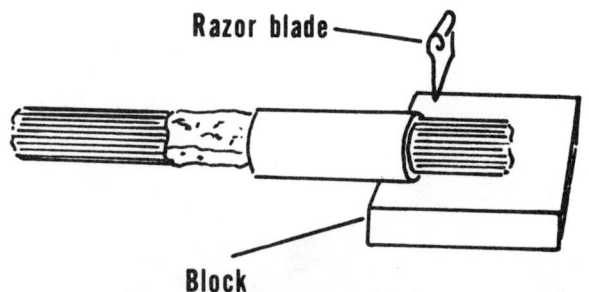

FIGURE 16

Water

iron directly to tubing.) Immediately dip the end of the tubing into water to cool the aluminum foil, which acts as a heat shield for the plastic tubing. (Figure 16)

Step 4. Using a single-edge safety razor blade, cut off the aluminum foil and excess fiber ends so that they are flush with the tubing. (Figure 17)

FIGURE 17

Razor blade

Block

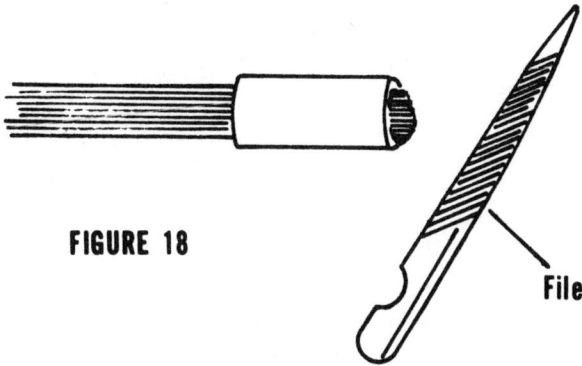

FIGURE 18

Step 5. Using a nail file or other fine file, gently file the end until the surface is smooth to the touch. (Figure 18)

Step 6. (Optional) For maximum light transmission, the end can be polished with toothpaste, bond typewriter paper, and a piece of glass. Squeeze a small amount of toothpaste onto the bond paper which has been placed on the glass. Holding the fiber bundle vertically to the paper, move the end in a "figure-8" motion. The abrasive action of the toothpaste and paper will assure a fine finish. Continue this procedure until the end appears smooth.

Step 7. Repeat Steps 2 through 6 for the other end of the bundle.

Light Guide Experiments and Variations

1. Take your finished light guide (glass or plastic fibers) and hook up one end to the penlight using the supplied lamp adapter (Item "F"). Now turn the light on and note that a beam is emitted from opposite end of the light guide. This demonstrates the possibilities of illuminating remote areas when a light guide can be hooked up directly to a light source. (Figure 19). However, in a situation where the light source is also remote, a plano-convex lens can be used to focus the beam onto the "receiving end" (either end can receive) of the light guide. You can demonstrate this by positioning the plano-convex lens in this kit approximately 7" from light source (no adapter needed) or until you get a point of focused light approximately 1-1/2" beyond lens. This is where you place the "receiving end" of

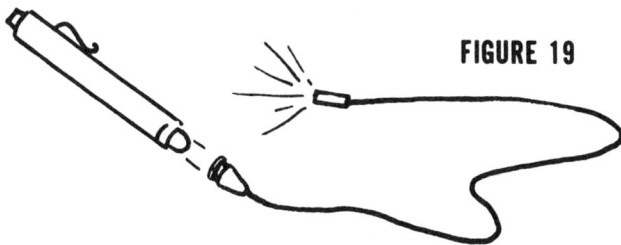

FIGURE 19

FIGURE 20

your light guide and note the beam of light then transmitted out the other end. (Figure 20)

2. Besides illuminating areas that are merely remote, light guides, because of their flexibility without loss to light transmission, can be used to illuminate areas

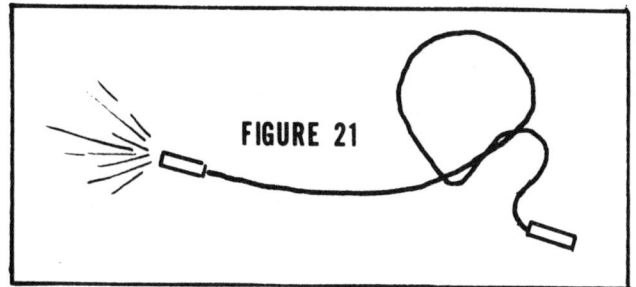

FIGURE 21

that are virtually inaccessible by other means. You can demonstrate this by repeating the first portions of Experiment No.1 above. However, this time make a loop in your light guide and note that the beam is still transmitted. You can even tie your light guide in a loose knot (Figure 21)...but do so with extreme care as the bundle may break (its bend-tolerance is determined by the bundle diameter, length, fiber size, construction of light guide, etc.).

3. There are many applications in industry where many points of light from a single light source would be most desirable (e.g., instrument panels). Here again fiber optics come into play with specially constructed light guides that have a single "receiving end" and branch into two or more "transmitting ends". You can make a single, "2-branched" (bifurcated) light guide by finishing one end of a bundle as you would a regular light guide (glass or plastic), splitting the fibers where you want the branch to begin (regular tape can secure this juncture), and then finishing the end of each branch individually. (Figure 22)

FIGURE 22

Tape

Common end

4. Aside from its many practical applications in industry, medicine, etc., fiber optics is also a "natural" for unique lighting effects in the home and office. A fiber optics "tree", for example, is certainly beautiful to behold. You can make a small one using the glass fibers in this kit (cut to about 4"). Finish one end of the bundle as described above. Place a colored piece of glass or plastic at the finished end and illuminate with penlight or other light source. The fibers can then be spread by applying a drop of Duco cement as shown in Figure 23. Before the cement hardens,

Positioning glue

FIGURE 23

Polish end

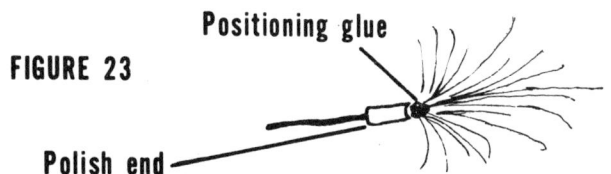

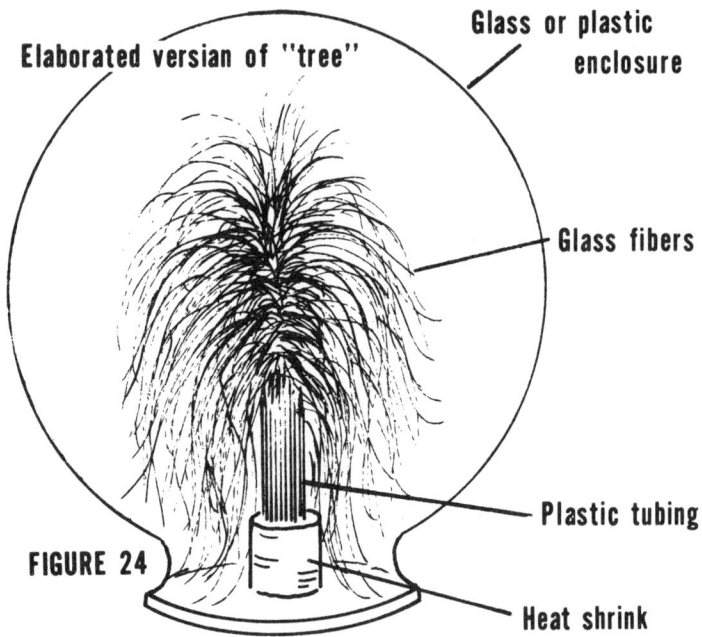

Elaborated version of "tree"

Glass or plastic enclosure

Glass fibers

Plastic tubing

Heat shrink

FIGURE 24

spread the fibers with a toothpick to the desired shape. (Note: Since glass fibers tend to splinter at the ends, it would be wise to enclose your fiber optics tree under a glass or plastic dome. Figure 24)

Fiber Optics Image Guide

A fiber optics image guide, as opposed to light guide, transmits actual images from "receiving end" (again, either end may receive) to the other end. This is accomplished using the same basic principle of fiber optics...that of transmitting light from one end of each fiber to the other. However, the key difference in an "image guide" is that the fibers are arranged within the bundle in such a way that each individual

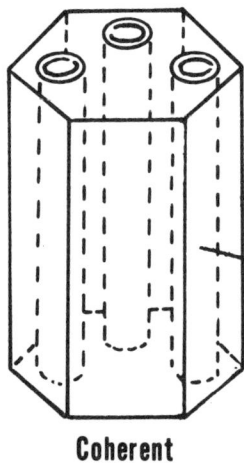

FIGURE 25

Fibers enlarged to show principle

Coherent

FIGURE 26

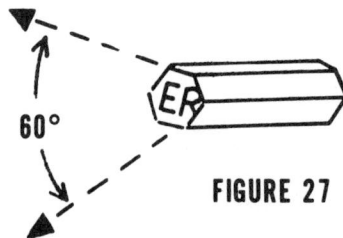

60°

FIGURE 27

fiber is located at the same geometric position at either end of the guide. This type of arrangement in fiber optics is called "coherent". (Figure 25) Since the image at the "receiving end" is broken down into dots of light and transmitted to the other end, you get a reproduction of the image directly on the surface of the other end (much like in a halftone photograph, although you may need a magnifier to see the individual dots at transmitting end). This entire concept can be demonstrated with the 1-1/2" rigid image guide (glass fibers) included in this kit. Touch one end of the guide directly to one of the words in this paragraph. Note how each letter appears at the top of the guide, (Figure 26) and can therefore be viewed from angles as great as 60° from off-center looking down (Figure 27). For comparison, take the 1-1/2" plain glass rod also included and place the rod on a word and look down into the rod. Note that the letters appear at the bottom of the rod...and then only when you are directly over rod. (Figure 28) Think of the advantages of fiber optics image guides in reading numbers, symbols, etc. from areas that are normally inaccessible to the eye. (Repeat this experiment with the coherent fiber optics face plate and clear glass plate provided.)

Before Proceeding Further: Since you only have one image guide, we suggest that you put off any of the following experiments that involve heating, bending, or twisting the image guide until you have performed the other experiments.

FIGURE 29

FIGURE 28

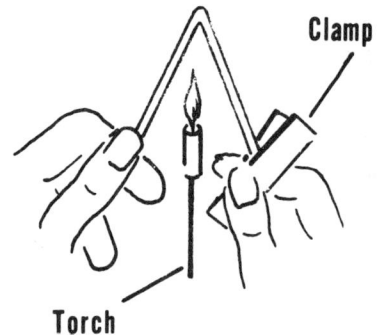

Clamp

Torch

Image guides need not be confined to straight rigid rods. Just as your light guide transmitted light even when looped or knotted, a flexible image guide can be made to do the same thing...while still transmitting the image. If you have the proper tools, this can be demonstrated with the 1-1/2" image guide. Hold one end of your image guide in a heat insulated clamp. Apply a small gas flame to the center of the guide and slowly bend it approx. 45°. (Figure 29) DO NOT OVERHEAT or the image guide may melt. Now touch it again to a letter on this page...the letter is still clearly visible at opposite end.

Another fascinating experiment with your image guide involves twisting it (using heat as above). You will note that when you twist the "receiving end" a certain amount of degrees in one direction, that the image at the other end is rotated that same number of degrees in the opposite direction. For example, twist the "receiving end" 30° clockwise, the image at the other end will rotate 30° counterclockwise...and a 180° rotation at the "receiving end" will turn the image upside-down at other end (valuable in righting an already-inverted image).

Just as you focused a beam of light from a remote light source onto the "receiving end" of your light guide, you can also focus an image onto the "receiving end" of your image guide and have the image transmitted to the other end. This can be demonstrated by first setting up a high-contrast viewing area (a black arrow on a 8-1/2 x 11" white piece of paper tacked to wall will do). Step back approximately 15 feet, hold lens at arm's length, and focus image onto the lens. Now position your image guide between your eye and the lens (about 1-1/2" from lens) until you can see image at near end of the guide. (Figure 30) Now try the same thing with the clear glass rod...if you can pick up an image at all, you will note that it is at the far end of the rod. [In this particular experiment, the lens inverts the image and this same inverted image appears at end of the image guide. By using the twisted image guide (as described above), you can turn this image right side up.] Repeat this experiment with the fiber optics face plate and clear glass plate provided.

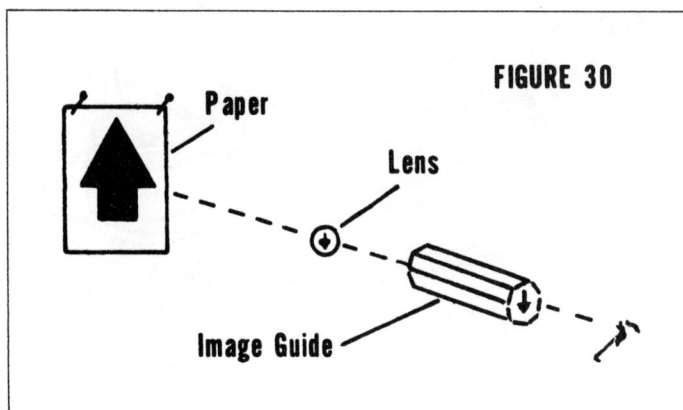

FIGURE 30

Paper

Lens

Image Guide

RIPPLING COLOR ACCESSORY

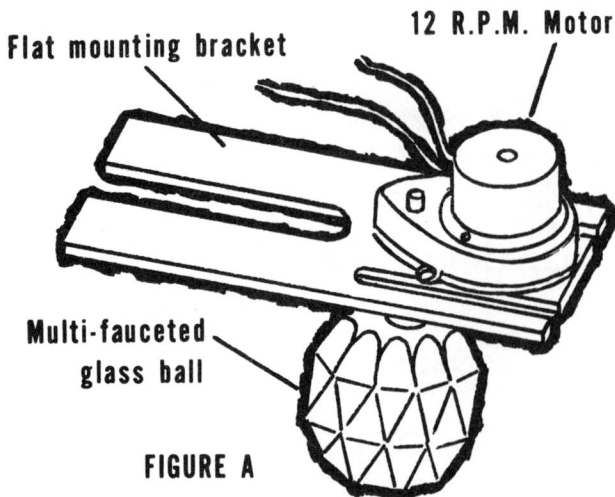

FIGURE A

This accessory is an assembled unit consisting of a multi-faceted glass ball, a 12 R.P.M. motor and a flat mounting bracket. The Rippling Color Accessory is designed to be used in conjunction with:

1. Visual Effects Projector, No's 71,057, 71,002.
2. One R.P.M. Motor, No. 60,734.
3. Motor Mounting Bracket, No. P-60,748 (pkg. of 2).
4. Wheels, Color Pattern, No. 71,122, Liquid Wheel, No. 71,107 or homemade wheels.

THE BASIC IDEA

A 1 R.P.M. motor causes an image wheel to rotate in the gate area of the projector while the multi-faceted ball is rotated at 12 R.P.M. in front of the beam (either with or without the projector lens barrel assembly in place). This produces the effect of covering the projection surface with rippling, undulating, changing amorphous color.

REMOVAL OF PROJECTOR CARRYING HANDLE

Removal of the carrying handle is recommended for frequent use with thick wheels or discs. We feel that it would be to your advantage to remove the handle for techniques discussed here. Therefore, proceed as follows:

1. Both front and rear housings must be removed as well as the handle. With a small Phillips screwdriver, remove the slide advance knob and the two retaining screws on the bottom of the projector base holding the rear housing. See Figure B.

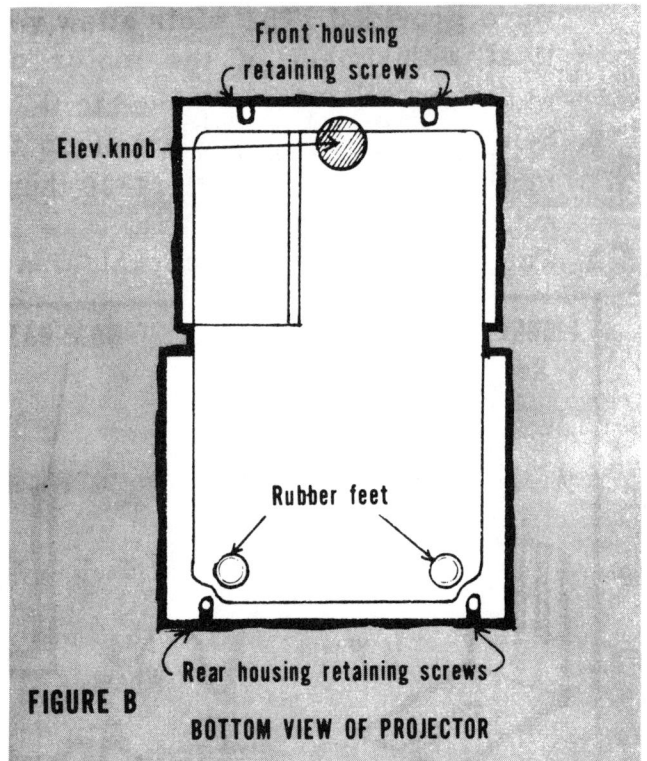

FIGURE B

BOTTOM VIEW OF PROJECTOR

2. Remove the two retaining screws on the bottom side of the projector base which hold the front housing.
3. Now hold the base steady with one hand and guide the handle hinge pins and retainers out of the bottom of the slots.
4. Replace front and rear housing and slide advance knob. Make sure that the two lugs on both housings are inserted under their respective metal retaining lips. See Figure C.

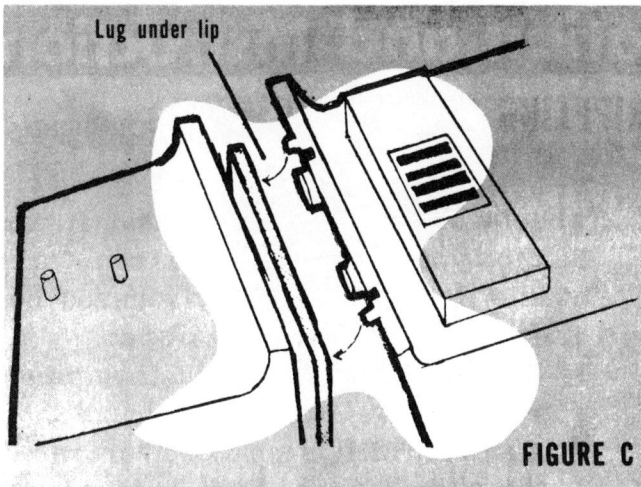

Lug under lip

FIGURE C

INSTALLATION AND USE

1. Mount the 1 R.P.M. motor to one P-60,748 bracket using the No. 6 hardware provided. The slots allow vertical adjustment of the motor and wheel which will be attached to it.
2. Select a wheel and mount it on the motor hub with the No. 1/4-20 thumb nut and washer.
3. The wheel, motor and bracket form an assembly, which is mounted as a unit on top of the projector body with two No. 1/4-20 thumb nuts and washers. You may find that the wheel binds in the bottom of the gate area or is too high for complete illumination. In either case, adjust the height as described in 1.
4. Slip the Rippling Color Bracket onto the studs on top of the projector body over the motor bracket and under the No.1/4-20 nuts and washers as shown in Figure D.
5. You may or may not wish to use the projector lens barrel. In either case, move the ball close to either the front end of the projector lens barrel or close to the opening in the projector housing to create whichever version of the effect you prefer.

Have ball as close to the lens or opening in the projector as possible, without the ball touching the lens or projector.

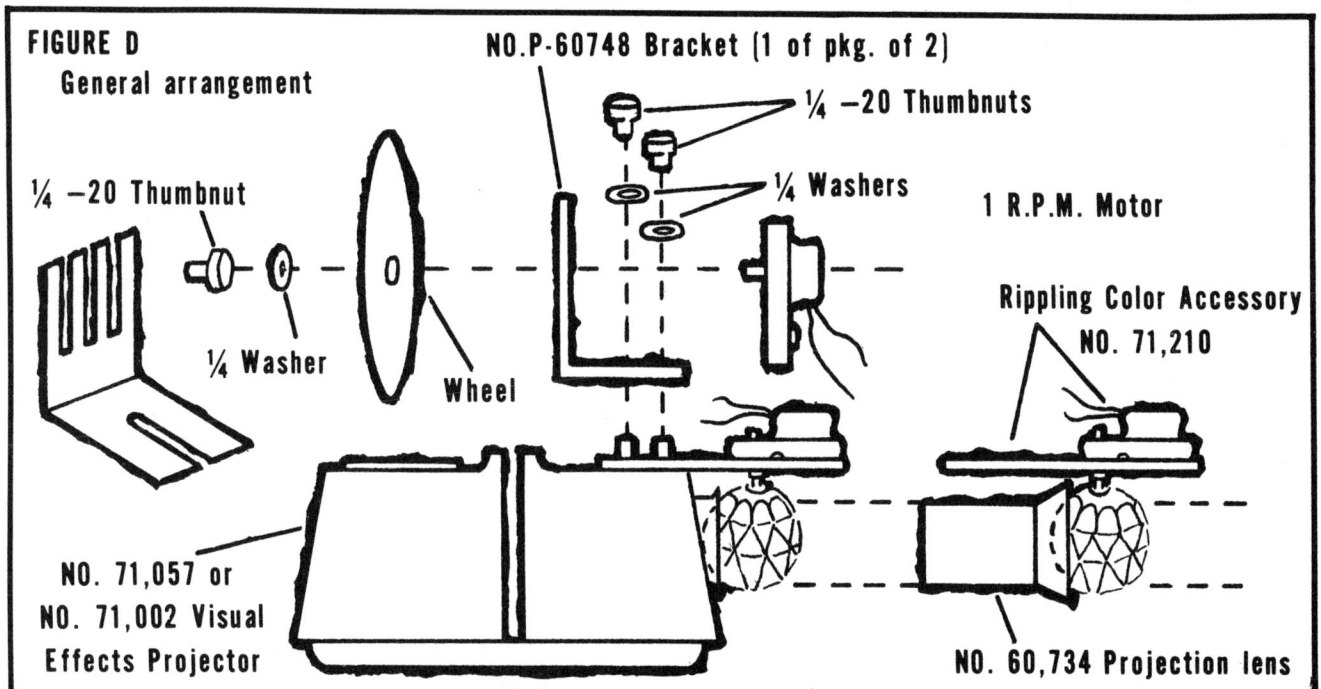

FIGURE D
General arrangement

NO.P-60748 Bracket (1 of pkg. of 2)
1/4 -20 Thumbnuts
1/4 Washers
1 R.P.M. Motor
Rippling Color Accessory NO. 71,210
1/4 -20 Thumbnut
1/4 Washer
Wheel
NO. 71,057 or NO. 71,002 Visual Effects Projector
NO. 60,734 Projection lens

6" POLARIZING SPINNER AND STAND

FIG. 1

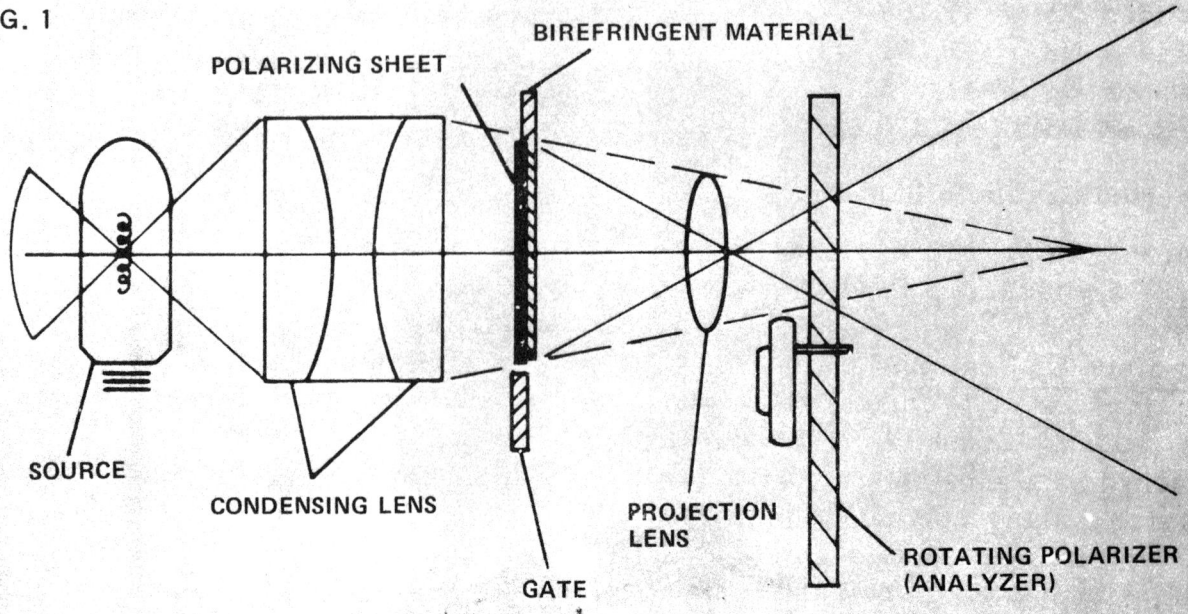

Operation:
Any slide containing birefringent material (such as cellophane, Mylar, split Iceland spar, ephedrine crystal, ammonium chloride, citric acid, and many others) can be used to show various shapes in beautifull colors, even though it has no color at all when viewed in normal light. To achieve this effect, polarizing material is placed between the condensing lens of a projector and the birefringent material. Then a polarizing disc (analyzer) is rotated in front of the projection lens as in Figure 1.

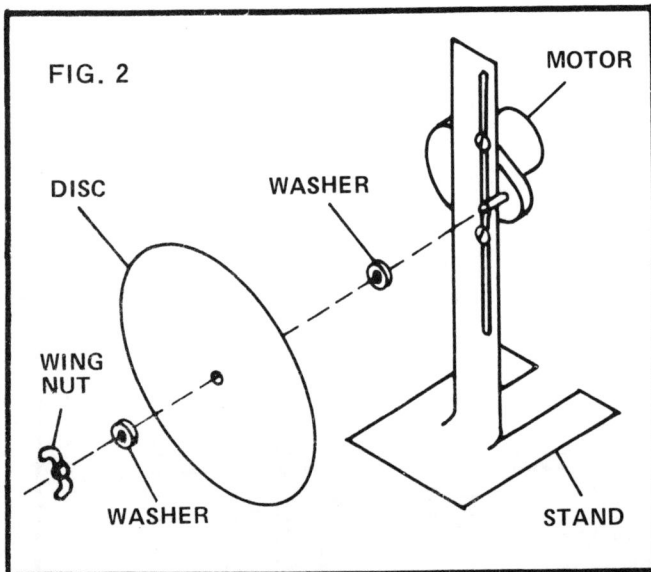

Assembly:
Mount the disc on the motor hub using the two washers and the wingnut pro - vided as shown in Figure 2.

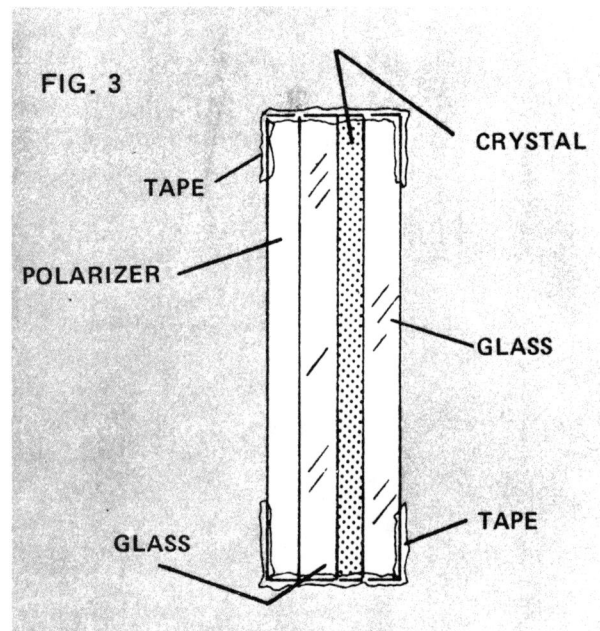

Parts check list:
1-30 rpm motor and stand assembly
1-6" polarized disc with ¼" hole
1-¼" standard wing nut
2-¼" standard washers

VISUAL EFFECTS PROJECTOR SET

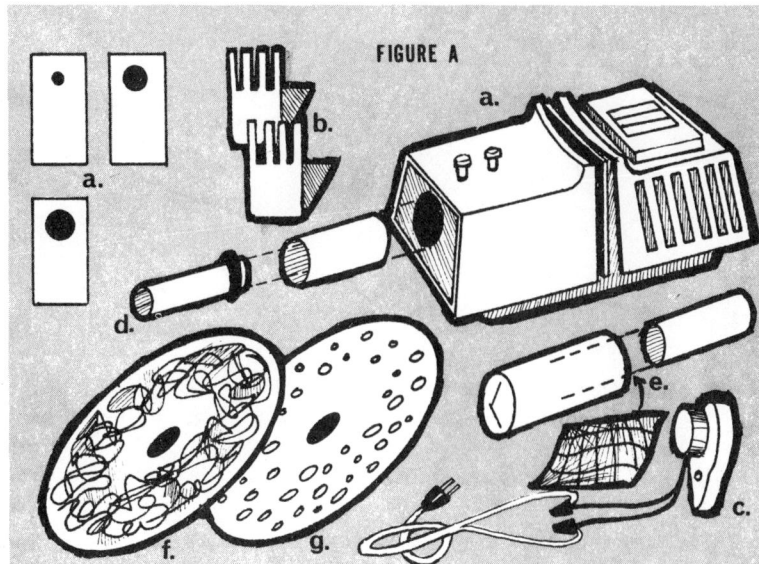

FIGURE A

THE BASIC IDEA

With the Visual Effects Projector Set you are now able to create an almost endless variety of unique chromatic lighting displays.

Basically, the motor causes an image wheel to rotate in the gate area of the projector while the projection lens is either supplemented or replaced by specialized optical projection devices. Let's see how we can get a number of specific effects using the components in our set.

HEXIDOSCOPE EFFECTS

All Hexidoscope effects use the Hexidoscope Accessary which is a phenolic tube with 6 internally mounted mirrors and a rubber friction lock externally mounted. The lock holds the accessory firmly in the forward part of the modified projection lens barrel as in Fig.E. Fig. B shows standard and modified barrel.

NOTE: On page 3 of Instruction Sheet 711264, the removal of the carry handle is recommended for

frequent use with thick wheels or discs. We feel that it would be to your advantage to remove the handle for techniques discussed here. Therefore, proceed as follows:

1. Both front and rear housings must be removed as well as the handle. With a small Phillips screwdriver, remove the slide advance knob and the two retaining screws on the bottom of the projector base holding the rear housing. See Figure C.

2. Remove the two retaining screws which hold the front housing; they are located on the bottom side of the projector base. Remove the housings.

3. Now hold the base steady with one hand and guide the handle hinge pins and retainers out of the bottom of the slots.

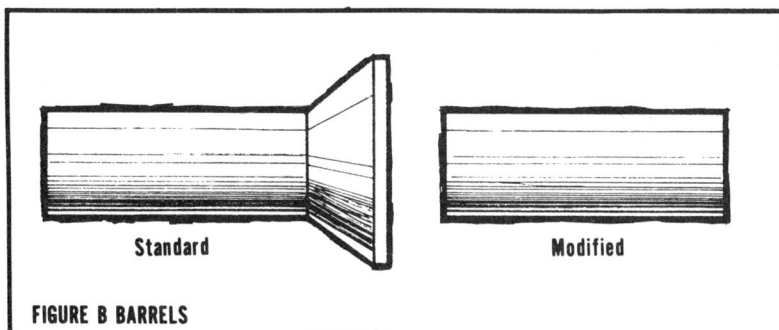

FIGURE B BARRELS

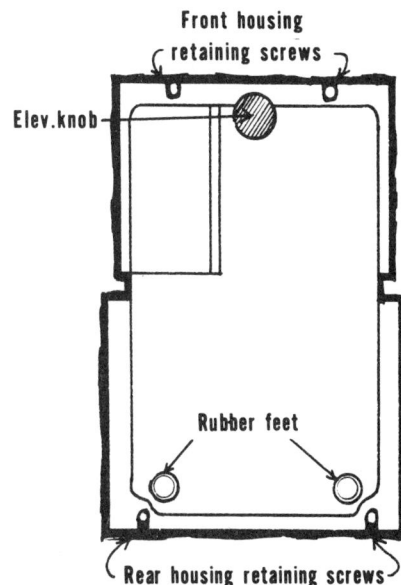

BOTTOM VIEW OF PROJECTOR   FIGURE C

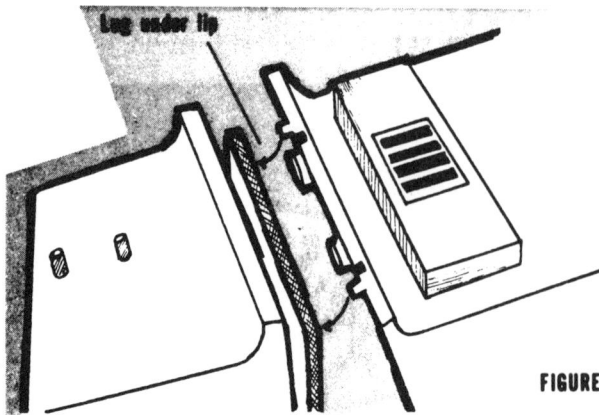

Lug under lip

FIGURE D

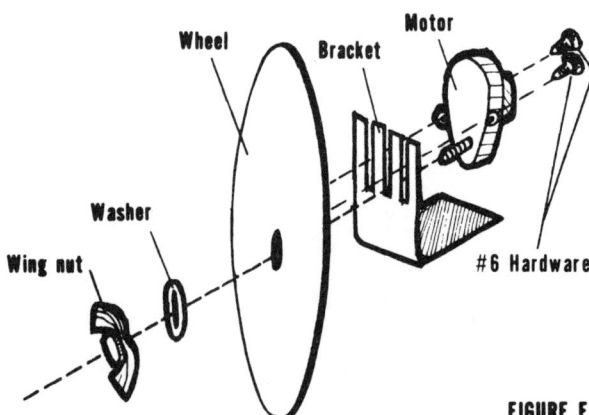

Modified barrel

Friction lock

Hexidoscope accessory

FIGURE E

4. Replace front and rear housing and slide advance knob. Make sure that the two lugs on both housings are inserted under their respective metal retaining lips. See Figure D.

To use the Hexidoscope Accessory, proceed as follows:

(1) Twist and push the Hexidoscope Accessory into the modified projection lens barrel with one hand while holding the barrel with the other hand. See Figure E.

(2) Mount the 1 R.P.M. motor to the bracket as shown using the #6 hardware provided. The slots allow vertical adjustment of the motor and the wheel which will be attached to it. See Figure F.

(3) Select one of the wheels and attach it to the motor hub with the 1/4-20 nut and washer. See Figure F.

(4) The wheel, motor and bracket form an assembly which is mounted as a unit on top of the projector body with two 1/4-20 nuts and washers. You may find that the wheel binds in the bottom of the gate area or is too high for complete illumination from the lamp. In either case, adjust the height as described in 2.

(5) Note that the projector cord is stored in a compartment in the bottom of the projector and can be removed and connected to the 2-pin plug at the rear of the projector. Plug both the motor and projector cords into a 110-120 VAC outlet.

(6) Now turn on the projector switch so that both fan and lamp operate. The motor will start to rotate the image wheel immediately since no switching is required.

(7) You may focus to suit by moving the combined modified lens barrel-Hexidoscope Accessory in or out within the projector housing.

(8) To change wheels, remove the two 1/4-20 nuts and washers retaining the bracket to the top of the projector housing and lift off the wheel-motor-bracket assembly. Change the wheel and reinstall the assembly.

D. COLORED CLOUD

All Colored Cloud effects are achieved using the Colored Cloud Accessory (C.C.A.) with either the modified projection lens barrel or the 4" extension tube. The Colored Cloud Accessory is a phenolic tube with folded metalized mylar inside and a conical lens at the forward end. See Figure G.

To operate, proceed as follows:

(1) All instructions above regarding wheels, motors, cords and brackets still apply.

(2) The Colored Cloud Accessory has its own support bracket which holds it onto the projector body. First install either the 4" extension tube or the forward end of the modified projection lens barrel into the rear portion of the Colored Cloud Accessory. It is suggested that the barrel be removed from the projector to accomplish this. Slip the C.C.A. support bracket over the motor bracket and under the 1/4-20 nuts and washers while guiding the cylindrical portion of the modified projection lens (4" extension + C.C.A. or modified lens barrel + C.C.A.) into the projector housing. Focusing is accomplished by moving the modified projection lens in or out and then locking the 1/4-20 nuts when a satisfactory adjustment has been reached. See Figure H.

NOTE: Alternate image wheels may be purchased or, if you prefer to make your own, we are offering 9" plastic or glass discs, paints, etc. Please see the list of related products at the end of this instruction sheet.

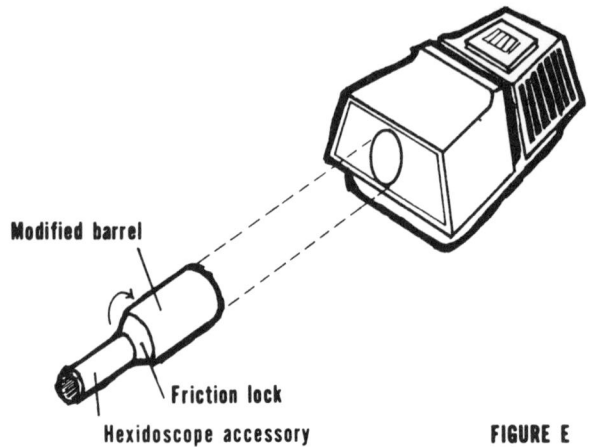

Wheel

Bracket

Motor

Washer

Wing nut

#6 Hardware

FIGURE F

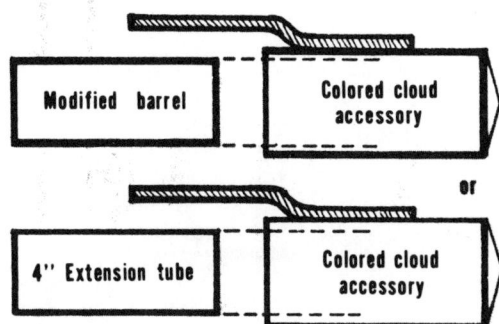

FIGURE G

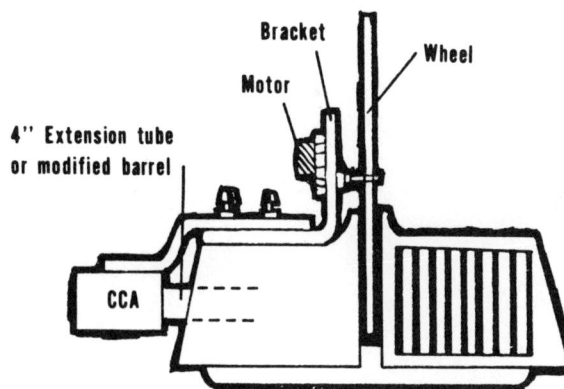

COLORED CLOUD ACCESSORY SET-UP FIGURE H

E. TABULATION

	Accessory	Wheel	Effect
1.	Hexidoscope No. 60,797	Hexidoscope Wheel No. 71,211	Symphony of Spheres: Colored spheres glide by—floating in space, sometimes colliding, sometimes sliding past each other, contrasting and blending hues in continuous, semi-kaleidoscopic array.
2.	Hexidoscope No. 60,797	Color Wheel No. 71,122	Calico Collage: Continuous, free-form patterns in bright colors and white remind of splashy calico prints. At times, becomes strongly bio-morphous-suggesting stained microslides. A real Techni-color Rorschach.
3.	Colored Cloud & 4"Ext.(no barrel) No. 71,208	No. 71,211	Crystal Starburst: Incredibly beautiful display of intense, fiery, central color bursting into fine, crystalline, "needle-like" splinters of delicate hue.
4.	Colored Cloud & 4" Ext. (no barrel) No. 71,208	No. 71,122	Morning Glory: Pale hues blush across a screen del-icately dominated by the rising,out-of-focus solar disc.
5.	Colored Cloud & Barrel (no ext.) No. 71,208	No. 71,122	Tinted Glacier: Imagine the Aurora Borealis —those splen-did Northern Lights - and the pure, intense colors of the rainbow captured in layers of frosty, translucent ice. One look and you'll be captured too!
6.	Colored Cloud & Barrel (no ext.) No. 71,208	No. 71,211	Chromatic Starbursts: Ex-ploding colored nuclei in the vast cold blackness of inter-galactic space. Bursting rock-ets in the warm summer air.

NOTE: Further variation may be achieved by purchasing a 71,107 Liquid Wheel.

FIGURE I

Ceiling

Table base

Theatrical pipe mount

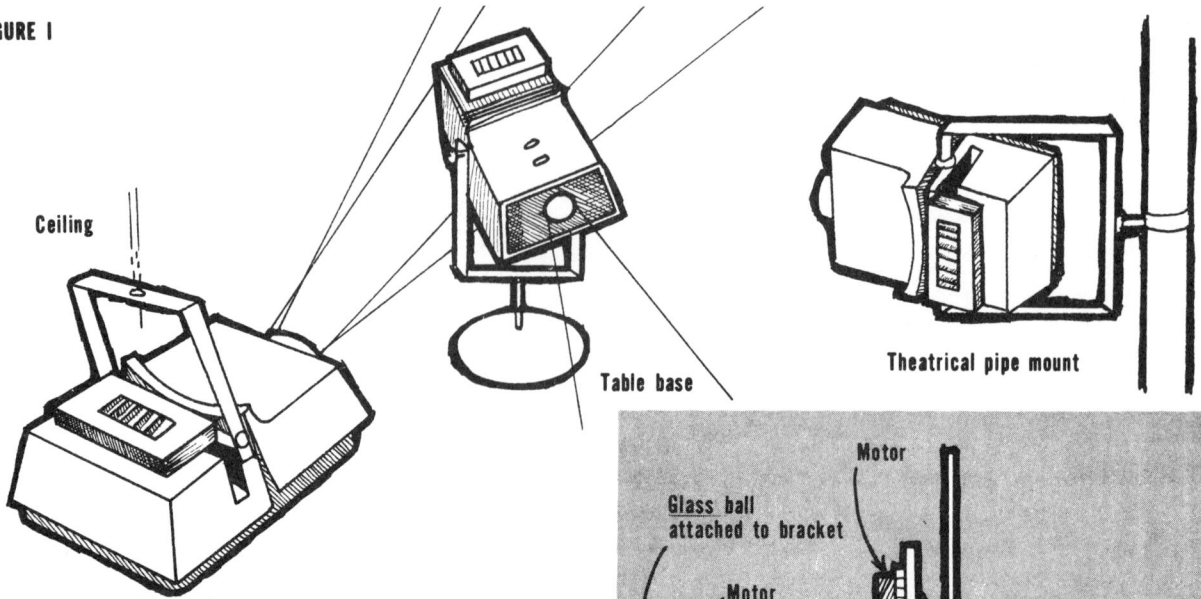

5. See No. 711264 for information regarding polarizing spinning disc No. 71,099 .

6. See No. 711264 for information regarding musical note wheel No. 71,097 .

7. We have a range of low R.P.M. motors listed. This is necessitated by the wide variety of applications which the V.E.P. can accommodate.

8. Rippling color effect using No. 71,210 . (Fig. J)

9. By applying transparent paint No. 71,067 to a clear, 9'' plastic disc No. P-70,996 you may create your own color image wheels and vary the effects to suit yourself.

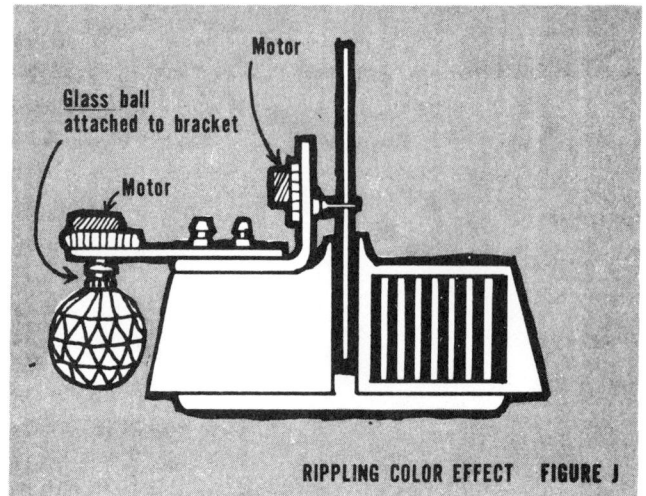

Motor

Glass ball attached to bracket

Motor

RIPPLING COLOR EFFECT   FIGURE J

Chapter 2

PHOTOGRAPHY UNUSUAL

Have you been using a camera and film just to take pictures?
There's nothing wrong with this, for that's what a camera is
for ... Or is it? Perhaps after reading through this section,
you'll find some new ways to use your camera, photographic
film, and perhaps you'll develop an entirely-new attitude
about photography in general!

KIRLIAN ELECTROPHOTOGRAPHY KIT
WITH PIEZOELECTRIC POWER SUPPLY

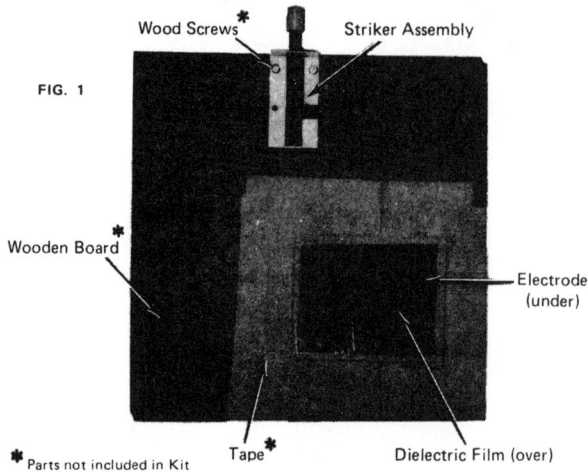

FIG. 1

Wood Screws* Striker Assembly

Wooden Board*

Electrode (under)

* Parts not included in Kit Tape* Dielectric Film (over)

Fig. 1 - Electrophotography Equipment Setup

Photograph "energy life forces" like this begonia leaf.

HISTORY

The bluish flames of quiet electrical discharges apparently have been with us from the dawn of time. A reference to miraculous fire appears in Exodus 3:2, where Moses describes the burning bush on Mount Sinai which was never consumed. Another biblical reference to the blue flames accurs in Acts 2:3, where the flames are described as appearing on the twelve Apostles on the day of Pentecost.

This energy was associated with life forces in the legends and histories of many ancient civilizations. The Egyptians called it "ka", the Chinese "ch'i", and the Hindus "prana". It naturally was regarded with religious awe and became a part of the healing rituals of the Shaman, the Witch Doctor and the High Priest. Perhaps the halos painted about the heads of holy men by Renaissance artists were attempts to record this mysterious phenomenon.

St. Elmo's Fire has been observed and recorded by mariners for centuries. It usually appeared around or on sharp painted objects such as the masts and yardarms of ships, church steeples or similar structures. This bluish discharge was named after St. Elmo, the patron saint of sailors. It has also been called the Dioscuri, the Corpusant and Fermies Fire.

The first man-made St. Elmo's Fire resulted from the work of Nikola Tesla and his experiments in man-made lightning. His discovery of the high frequency resonant transformer, or Tesla coil, made this possible for the first time. When this coil was coupled to a human being, the high voltage ionized the air about him and the subject was surrounded with the unearthly blue glow of a corona discharge. Tesla, himself, took photographs of several of his associates surrounded by the spectacular glow of electrical discharges produced by his high voltage equipment.

Perhaps the first successful attempt to use these quiet flames to expose photographic material occurred in Russia. In 1898, Yakov Narkevich-Todco exhibited "electrographic" photographs at the Fifth Photographic Exhibition sponsored by the Russian Technical Society. The photographs were the hit of the show; they were considered interesting and spectacular, but there was no suggestion of the future potential of the new techniques displayed.

The first effort to apply this effect to the field of diagnostic medicine occurred in London. Dr. Walter J. Kilner, a member of the Royal Academy of Physicians, reported the existance of the human aura. He was in charge of electro-therapy at St. Thomas Hospital--the first hospital to give a practical demonstration of roentgen rays in 1896.

Dr. Kilner experimented with various dyes, including dicyanin, which made certain ultra-violet radiations visible. He used coated glass screens which enabled him to see the aura around the human body. He contended that fatigue, changes in mood, or disease could effect the size and characteristics of the aura. He described his methods in the book "The Human Atmosphere" published in 1911. In addition, he made a set of slides available which illustrated his studies.

In the 1930's, the method of electro-imaging was discovered by accident when a high voltage wire sparked across a piece of photographic material. This occurred in the laboratory of Semyon and Valentina Kirlian. The equipment consisted of a Tesla coil connected to two metallic plates. When S. Kirlian placed his hand next to a photographic film, he obtained an image which amazed him. He described it as "a spectacular panorama of colors, whole galazies of lights, blue, gold, green, violet, all shining and twinkling". Succeeding work by this dedicated pair of Russian scientists was responsible for the development of interest in this area.

During recent years this research has continued at Kazakh State University in the U. S. S. R. The first Western Hemiphere conference on Kirlian Photography, Acupuncture and the Human Aura was held in New York City in 1972. This conference stimulated research by various students and universities. Much of the serious research in the U.S. dates from that period. From those small beginnings in the mid 1930's the interest in Kirlian photography has grown to the point where it has sparked the public imagination, as well as that of the scientific community.

Corona discharge or "Kirlian" effect can be produced in a form which is easily photographed by applying high-voltage, high-frequency AC to the subject under study. This is normally done by making the subject one plate of a two-plate capacitor, isolated from the other plate by a dielectric capable of withstanding the applied voltage. The high-voltages involved in this experiment are completely harmless to a living specimen because the currents supplied by the crystal are miniscule. This is due to a characteristic of high-frequency AC, known as the "skin effect". High-frequency AC voltages and currents tend to travel on the surface of a conductor. In the case of a human subject, the vital organs of the body are not affected at all because all of the high-voltage travels harmlessly over the skin. (Remember Dr. Tesla and his experiments!)

Most of the applied power is dissipated in the corona, which is caused when electron and gas molecules in the air interact. This radiation expresses itself in a wide range of radiation energy. Radiation components from ultra-violet through visible light, infra-red and other portions of the electro-magnetic spectrum (used for television and radio), are included in this electrical discharge. This discharge evidences itself by a glowing ring of light around the subject.

This corona pattern may be recorded with a simple camera or by simply observing with a pair of blue spectacles. However, it is more generally recorded using the direct method. In this case, the two-plate capacitor mentioned above is modified by placing a sheet of photographic paper on top of the dielectric and first electrode. The subject (forming the other plate of the capacitor) is then placed on top of the film, in direct contact with it, and the radiation energy is allowed to act upon the film directly.

Early black and white photographic materials have now been replaced by materials capable of recording color by most researchers. The complete significance of the various colors is yet to be determined. Blue of course predominates but yellows, whites and greens are also common. The occasional red is the mystery color. It does not appear to fit the pattern of the appearance of the other colors. It may be the key to the interpretation of the pattern.

Many researchers believe they are photographically recording a form of energy which they call Bio-Energy. They believe that Bio-Energy is generated by all living organisms. This energy has been observed and recorded by electro-physiological means and has also been captured by non-conventional photographic means. There are others who will take exception to the word "energy" when describing these observations and results. They would rather say "conditions".

In the case of the polygraph, or lie detector, for instance, skin resistance is one of the variables that is monitored when the subject's honesty is being evaluated. Skin resistance varies because activity of the sweat glands is influenced by the psychophysiological conditions of the subject. Since the electrical discharge properties of any subject whether living or inanimate will be influenced by the amount and the distribution of moisture present at the time of the observation--perhaps "condition" is more accurate. This implies situations where control is exercised over externally applied energy, rather than the generation of energy itself. Externally applied energy might be the electrode potentials in the case of the polygraph or electro-encephlograph or the high voltage, high frequency potentials used in electro-photography methods.

Some researchers have claimed that the electro-photographic images are simply recordings of imperfections in the emulsion surfaces that have created paths

of least resistance. Others believe that all living organisms emit minute quantities of various gases from their pores. They use this argument to explain odors --- all the way from the delicate fragrance of a tender flower to the miasma that hangs over a foul-smelling bog. They further contend that this envelope of gas, which surrounds all things, changes with the physio-psychological conditions of living things. This change, they believe, is responsible for the variations in the aura which, in turn controls the energy present in the corona.

The "Kirlian" photographic method has generated interest in researchers throughout the world. To differentiate their work from that of the Kirlians', some workers have developed their own names for this high voltage, high frequency process. For example, the Czechoslovakians call their process "electrography"; some American researchers call their experiments a "photo-electrographic" process.

In the words of Kirlian and Kirlian (1959) these new studies "put at the disposal of science and technology a new means of laboratory investigations which reveal enticing prospects in the study of nature through the effect of the electrical state of an object".

The piezoelectric power supply is the heart of this simple Kirlian photography system. Inside the black plastic casing is a special crystal — a "Piezoelectric" crystal. When this type of crystal is subjected to mechanical stress, such as squeezing, an electrical voltage will be produced between the two sides of the crystal. The harder the crystal is squeezed, the greater is the voltage produced. If the crystal is struck a sharp blow from a small hammer, a very short, very high-voltage pulse will be generated by the crystal. Because the pulse is so short, it contains many high-frequency AC components. This device provides a simple and safe way to produce the high-voltage, high-frequency AC necessary for Kirlian photography.

The Kirlian Power Supply is Shown in Fig. 1 & 2

```
┌─────────────────────────────────────┐
│             CAUTION                  │
│ (a) This equipment should not be used│
│     by children or anyone not        │
│     familiar with normal safety      │
│     precautions to be used around    │
│     electrical equipment.            │
│ (b) The power output of this         │
│     equipment is insufficient to     │
│     cause paralysis or injury to any │
│     healthy normal person.           │
│ (c) Do not operate the apparatus in  │
│     the presence of anyone with      │
│     implanted inductive devices or   │
│     electrodes such as heart pacer   │
│     equipment.                       │
│ (d) Use a pair of glass lensed       │
│     sunglasses when viewing the      │
│     corona if you do not wear        │
│     glasses—common glass absorbs the │
│     short wave ultra violet rays     │
│     which can cause eye irritation.  │
└─────────────────────────────────────┘
```

How To Set Up The Edmund Piezoelectric Kirlian Power Supply (See Fig. 1)

1. Remove equipment from carton and check it against the equipment list.
2. Select a suitable working area. Ideally, this might be a photographic dark room. If a dark room is not available, any clear, dry, well-ventilated room that can be darkened is suitable.
3. A piece of 3/8" plywood is ideal for the setup. However, the cardboard shipping carton may be used instead of plywood.
4. Attach the piezoelectric crystal striker assembly to the wood support with the wood screws provided.
5. Attach the lead wire with the lug on one end to the striker assembly as shown in Figure 2.

6. Strip off about 1" of insulation and place the other end of the lead under the 4 x 5" high voltage electrode. Place the clear plastic dielectric over the electrode and tape all the edges securely to the support.
7. Strip the ends off the other lead wire and attach one end to one of the wood screws so that it makes a good electrical connection with the base of the striker assembly. Leave the other end free. The equipment is now ready to operate. Figure 1 shows the entire set up.

HOW TO MAKE KIRLIAN PHOTOGRAPHS

The film is partially exposed each time a pulse is sent through the circuit from the piezoelectric crystal. It will take a number of pulses to produce an exposure of the proper intensity, however. To produce a pulse, depress the button on the striker until you hear a loud click. This is the hammer striking the crystal. At first, it will be necessary to take several exposures of the same object, each exposure made with a different number of pulses (say 5, 10, 25 and 50) so that you can see approximately how many pulses you will need to properly expose the film. In our laboratory, we found that we needed 13 pulses to make a good exposure, if the film speed rating was ASA 400.

A. Kirlian Photographs of Coins

1. Place whatever type of film you are using (see following sections) emul-

sion side up on the clear plastic dielectric.

2. Place the coin directly on top of the film. At first you will want to make about four exposures with a different number of pulses each time, so position the coin on the film so that there will be room to make the other three exposures.
3. Place the free end of the second lead wire on the coin and hold it there with your finger. Make an exposure using five pulses.
4. Move the coin to a new position on the film and expose using ten pulses.
5. Make two other exposures of 25 and 50 pulses respectively.
6. Develop the film and you should see your first electrophotograph! The image which appears the clearest corresponds to the approximate number of pulses it takes to make a proper exposure.
7. Now you can begin photographing objects of your choice using the number of pulses as determined above to make the exposures.

B. Kirlian Photographs of Fingers

1. Place the film as before, emulsion side up, on the plastic dielectric.
2. Hold the base of the striker assembly with two fingers so that you can squeeze the button on the striker assembly with the thumb of the same hand. Place the free end of the second lead wire under your thumb between it and the striker button. Make sure your hands are clean.
3. Put a finger of your other hand directly on the film. Expose using five pulses.
4. Make three other exposures on the same piece of film of 10, 25 and 50 pulses respectively.
5. Develop the film and determine by the relative clarity of the images the approximate number of pulses it takes to make a clear exposure of a finger.

NOTE: If you make an exposure of more than one finger at a time, you will need more pulses to adequately expose the film. In general, the more objects exposed at one time, the more pulses that are needed.

USE OF KODABROMIDE® ENLARGING PAPER

1. Obtain Kodabromide® Single Weight Glossy Enlarging Paper size 2-1/2 x 3-1/2 inches. Kodabromide® makes black and white prints.
2. You will need developing chemicals. The Kodak Tri-Chem Pack provides the necessary materials in one package.
3. In the dark, remove a sheet of Kodabromide® paper and place it slick side up on the plastic dielectric.
4. To determine the number of pulses necessary to properly expose the paper, first follow the procedures outlined in the section "How to Make Kirlian Photographs".
5. To develop the paper, follow the instructions included in the Tri-Chem Pack for prints.

NOTE: You will have to mix up the chemicals before you begin taking pictures. After the chemicals have been mixed, they will only last about a day if left in the open. Covering the solutions with plastic kitchen wrap will slightly extend their lifetime. Also, the solutions will only develop about 25 prints. For these reasons, it is a good idea to have clear in your mind what objects you wish to photograph. Have them all assembled in a logical order so that you can find them in the dark. If you wish, a dim-amber darkroom safelight can be used with the Kodabromide® paper. Be prepared to take all your pictures at one time (or in several sessions during one day) in order to maximize the use of the solutions.

6. When you have determined the number of pulses necessary to properly expose the Kodabromide® paper, then you can begin taking pictures of your experimental objects.

USE OF POLAROID® 4x5 SHEET FILM TYPE 58

Most of our electrophotography experiments were made on this material. It is ideal for this purpose because of its convenience and instant development. We are assuming that most workers who have the film available will also have the Polaroid® Land Film Holder #500 or 545 for developing the film.

The procedure to be used with this film is as follows:

1. Place the type 58 film on the plastic dielectric directly over the metal electrode. Make sure the side marked "This Side Toward Lens" is upward.
2. Tape down the metal strip at the bottom of the film to the plastic dielectric.
3. Measure 14 inches up from the metal strip and fasten something at that point that will serve as a stop. A block of wood or any solid object that can be felt in the dark will do.
4. You are now ready to try your first exposure. In the dark, pull the protective sleeve of the film out to the stop described in Step 3. This uncovers the film.
5. Place your objects directly on the film - if they are coins or leaves or anything small, provide a ground by placing your finger on the object.
6. To determine exposure times, follow the suggestions in the previous section.
7. Shove the protective sleeve back toward the metal strip.

NOTE: If you do not have the Land Film Back you can omit steps 8 through 10 and do steps 11 and 12 instead.

8. Make sure the Land Film Holder is in the "Load" position, remove the film from the plastic and tape, and insert the end with the metal tip into the film holder.
9. Put the film holder into the "Process" position and remove the film from the holder with a steady regular pull.
10. This starts the developing cycle; wait the specified period, then strip the print from its protective paper sleeve and you should see your first electrophotograph!

For developing without the Back:

11. Using a rubber print roller, starting at the tab end of the film, carefully and evenly, with steady firm pressure, roll the roller toward the bottom of the film (the metal strip end). This distributes the developing chemicals from the pods of the film assembly.
12. See Step 10.

The same methods can be used for the black and white versions of the Polaroid® sheet film (Types 51, 52 and 55) making proper allowances for the different films' speeds by varying the exposure times.

35MM FILM

Suitable photographic films for electrophotography in color are High Speed Ektachrome, Kodachrome X and, in black and white, Tri-X pan. A suggested method of using these films, in the readily available 35mm cassettes, is shown in Figure 3.

1. Tape the magazine to the clear plastic dielectric. Secure the leader to the spool of a 35mm cassette designed for reloading from bulk film. (Available from most good camera stores.)

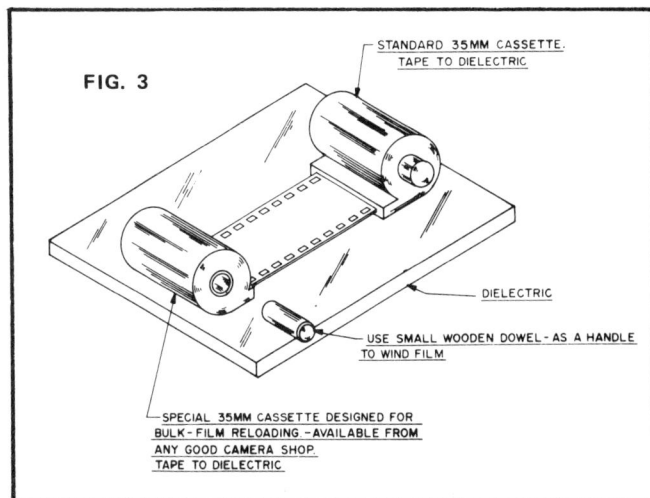
FIG. 3

2. Assemble and close the cassette housing around the spool and attached 35mm leader.

3. Tape bulk film cassette to clear plastic dielectric, taking care that about a two inch length of film leader is exposed between the two cassettes.

4. Use a small length of a 3/8" wooden dowel, with its end tapered to fit the film spool of the bulk film cassette, as a handle.

5. In a darkroom now, make about 5 clockwise turns of the spool handle of the bulk film cassette which will withdraw unexposed film from the storage cassette.

6. Expose the film for the lengths of time listed in Table 1 as a starter. Later you may want to experiment with longer or shorter times. See the suggestions concerning exposure times in the section on making Kirlian Photographs.

Table I

METHOD OF USING 35MM FILM

Suggested Exposures	Film Type
15 seconds	High Speed Ektachrome
25 seconds	Kodachrome X
8 seconds	Tri-X Pan

7. Turn the bulk film spool (by means of its wooden dowel handle) three turns to pull the exposed film into the bulk film cassette.

8. Repeat steps 6 and 7 until definite resistance to film movement is encountered indicating that you have reached the end of the roll. Stop at this point, being careful not to tear the end of the film from its anchorage.

9. Transfer the wooden dowel to the supply spool and rewind film back into supply spool.

10. Remove the supply cassette and process the film.

Specific recommendations are not being made concerning film to be used in your "Kirlian" experiments. Naturally the results will be more meaningful if color materials are used but it is not mandatory — interesting results can be achieved in black and white.

It is assumed that anyone who purchases this kit will have some basic knowledge of photography. For those of you who are new to electrophotography, suggested starting exposures are listed in Table 1.

PHOTOMICROGRAPHY WITH A PEN MICROSCOPE

To be able to reproduce faithfully and brilliantly all the details of an image as seen under a Microscope is indeed a rich experience. Many enjoyable hours may be spent hunting for specimens, indoors and outdoors, mounting and finally reproducing them as accurately as possible.

Photomicrography is generally considered an expensive hobby, but with the aid of the small 50 power vest-pocket Microscope, the expense is no more than that of ordinary photography. Excellent photomicrographs may be taken with such a Microscope and a suitable camera. The Microscope has a chrome concave reflector attached to the objective lens which directs the proper light onto the subject.

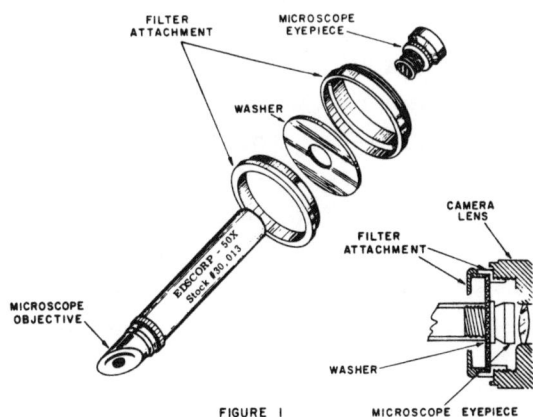

FIGURE I

As illustrated in Figure 1, a washer is made with an inside diameter cut to fit tightly over the threads of the Microscope eye-piece. This diameter is important and it must be smaller than the outside diameter of the Microscope tube. It is advisable to cut the hole smaller than necessary and file it to the correct diameter with a small rat-tail file. The outside diameter of the washer is cut to fit the camera's filter holder, and the Microscope is attached as illustrated. As some camera lenses are mounted shallow in their lens barrels, a series of filter holders may be used in order to allow clearance for the Microscope eye-piece.

If the camera used is a single lens reflex or press camera, focusing may be accomplished directly through the Microscope by means of the ground glass. The camera is mounted either vertically or horizontally, with the light source at one side as shown in Figure 2. The horizontal arrangement is recommended because of its advantages or rigidity and adaptability, although vertical mounting is necessary for specimens that are suspended in liquids. If the camera to be used is not a ground glass focusing type, then a stand must be used.

With a stand, the correct camera position for a sharp focusing is determined beforehand. A vertical stand as illustrated in Figure 3 is typical. The correct camera position is determined by using a piece of ground glass fastened in the film plane of the camera. The camera lens is set on infinity and the aperture is used at its maximum f stop. The camera is then moved up and down until the image of a specimen located on the object stage is in accurate focus on the ground glass. A circle should

be drawn on the object stage to indicate the proper specimen position and the maximum field of view. The camera and object stage are then fastened firmly in position and specimens to be photographed are then always in focus when placed on the stage. The depth of field of any Microscope is quite small, and extreme care must be taken to make the specimens to be photographed as thin as possible. However, with careful preparation, excellent results may be obtained by using this method.

In order to prevent the waste of material, it pays to sacrifice a few films in making test exposures, as is done when enlarging a negative. Exposure time should be carefully noted, along with the size bulb used, the dis-

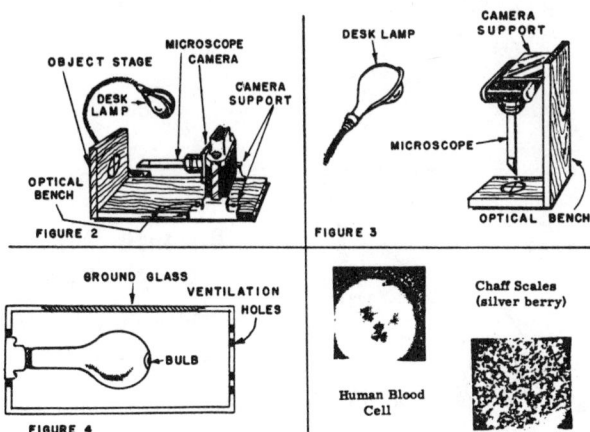

tance between the light source and the specimen, and the type film used. For black and white film, a 100 watt bulb, mounted in a desk lamp is a good light source. If color film is used, particular attention must be paid to the correct color temperature of the light source in order that the colors may be reproduced exactly as they are seen. In this case, commercial photo-flood bulbs must be used in conjunction with color film that is properly balanced for use with tungsten light. A good example is Kodak Kodachrome, type B. It must be remembered that only after a great deal of experience will the amateur be able to visually gauge the correct exposure.

Since it would be foolish to destroy good work by using coarse-grained film, all films used for photomicrography must be fine-grain type. Thus, Verichrome or plus X would be better than Super XX. A good rule to follow when choosing film is always to put fine grain before high sensitivity, even though long exposures may be necessary. High-speed film should only be used when it is desired to photograph living organisms, and must be developed slowly to prevent undue graininess.

For making photomicrographs of transparent objects, the object stage must be illuminated from below. A 100 watt bulb mounted in a well-ventilated box, which has a piece of ground glass secured to the top, may be used as an efficient object stage and is illustrated in Figure 4. The stage should have a clamping arrangement similar to that found in a standard Microscope stage so that glass slides may be held firmly in place. Typical Photomicrographs taken with the 50 power Microscope are shown in Figure 5. These were taken with the use of the stand described above, and an illuminated stage.

SPECIAL EFFECTS AND TRICK PHOTOGRAPHY KIT

A LITTLE BACKGROUND

No matter what you call it, "trick photography," "special effects photography," etc., it is actually "doing your own thing." The items in your kit are merely props and can be used in many ways. We suggest you copy your photos with the prop in front of the camera as shown in the basic set-up, Figure 1. This is the easiest and the least expensive way. After you get the idea, try

famous paintings, sculptures, photos of friends and relatives, scenes, etc.

Many books have been written on this subject but almost all of them keep many of the technical details secret and leave much to wasteful and needless experiments; some even retouch the photos. We have attempted to show all details on how we made the pictures illustrated here. (Your set-up may vary slightly from ours due to different lighting, cameras, photos, etc.) None of the photos here were retouched. However some have been cropped to exclude glass holders or other undesirable items outside the edges of the photos.

EQUIPMENT USED TO MAKE THE PHOTOS

All photos except the diffraction grating effects were made with 35mm "TRI-X" film and were commercially developed and enlarged; grating photos were made with Kodachrome II slide film. Unfortunately we cannot show in black and white the beautiful chromatic effects that can be achieved utilizing the grating in front of your camera. We can only tell you how to get these effects.

The camera used was a single lens reflex camera equipped with a +3 diopter close-up lens. If your pictures are large, you may not need the close-up lens. Light readings were taken with a Weston Master IV light meter. The lights used were two 250 watt photoflood bulbs.

TECHNIQUES
A. Patterned Glass Effects

The basic set-up in Figure 1 was used to achieve these effects. Shutter speeds, "F" numbers, and glass types are listed below each photo. Each piece of glass will produce different effects depending upon

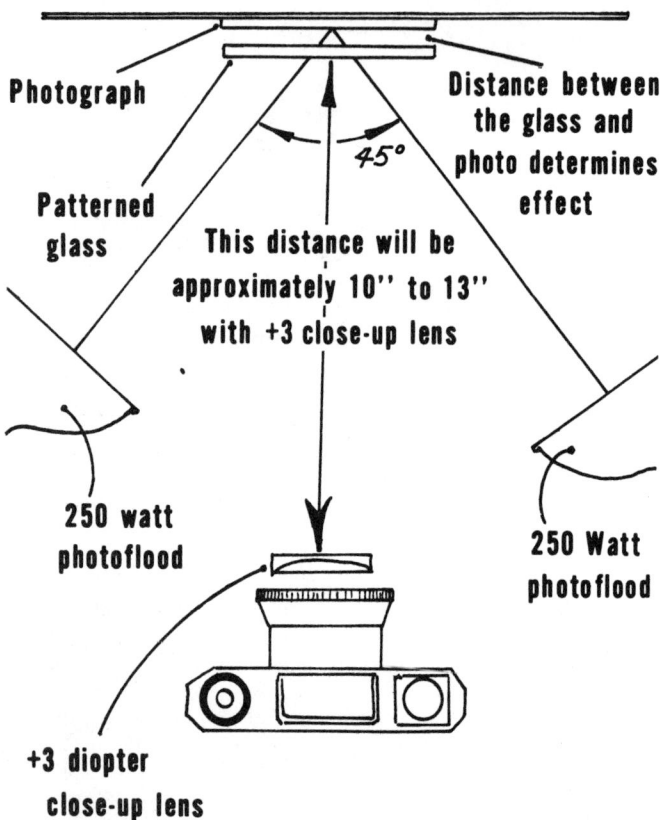

Photograph

Distance between the glass and photo determines effect

45°

Patterned glass

This distance will be approximately 10'' to 13'' with +3 close-up lens

250 watt photoflood

250 Watt photoflood

+3 diopter close-up lens

FIGURE 1   THE BASIC SET-UP

the distance between the glass and the photo. After you have your camera and lights set up, hold the glass near the photo and notice the effect in the ground glass of your camera. Then slowly move the glass away from the photo until you get the effect you want. If you are artistically inclined print your effect on photo linen and paint in the style of Van Gogh or other artists. To hold the glass upright in front of the photo, we used a small "C" clamp. As a rule you will need a close-up lens unless your photo or picture is large. Try to completely fill the ground glass of your camera; in this way you will have the largest picture possible and very little to crop. To prevent cuts and accidents we suggest that you cover the edges of each

FIGURE 3

Vertical format best for most portraits

of your 3 pieces of glass with adhesive tape or masking tape. Our photo (Fig.2) shows a patterned glass effects.

Please note that the Linex patterned glass can also be used vertically for a different effect. If you have a small table-top camera or universal clamp tripod, you can use your camera vertically for photos that have a vertical format. (Fig. 3) Of course, for subjects that have a horizontal format, the camera can be held normally. Using the +3 close-up lens, the field of view is approximately 4-3/4" x 6-1/2" at 12"lens-to-copy distance.

B. Psychedelic Slides

Here's your chance to be really creative. Make a light box as shown in Figure 4. Buy some transparent colored paints

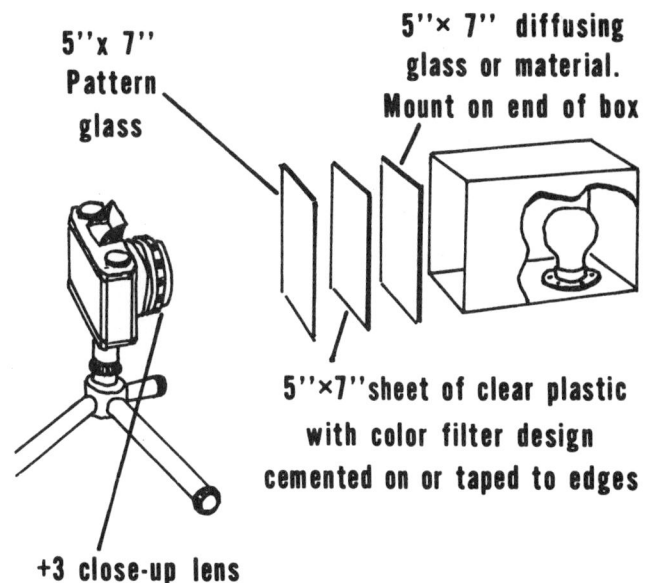

FIGURE 2

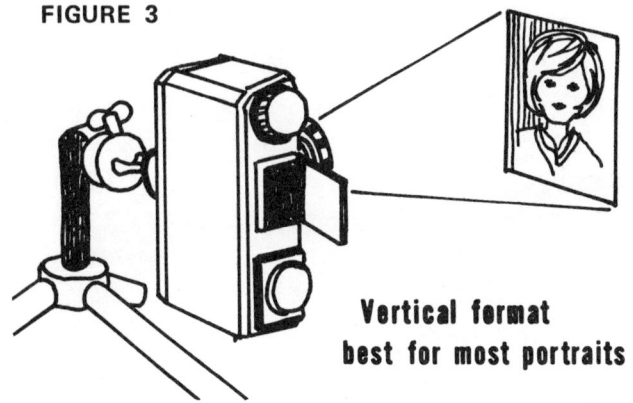

5"x 7" Pattern glass

5"× 7" diffusing glass or material. Mount on end of box

5"×7"sheet of clear plastic with color filter design cemented on or taped to edges

+3 close-up lens

FIGURE 4

and apply your own psychedelic design to a piece of clear plastic. Place this between the diffusing screen and the patterned glass. The color design can be fastened with cellulose tape to the diffusing material. By moving the patterned glass away from the design you can vary the effects according to the separation distance. You are limited only by your imagination! Don't be afraid to combine the different patterns or even to rotate the glass horizontally or vertically. Now, for the slides! Load your camera with color slide film and put on your +3 close-up lens. Focus the camera to make sure that the design only is shown in the ground glass. If the edges of the glass show, move the camera closer to the patterned glass and refocus. One plastic filter design can be the source of many different colorful slides by just changing or moving the patterned glass. Try using a moiré pattern in front of the color design. Have your film made into slides and project them on a screen with your projector.

C. Kaleidoscope Photos

This is probably the most difficult photo effect to achieve, but if you are careful you can produce some highly fascinating kaleidoscope pictures. The most important thing is to arrange the "V" of the 2 mirrors to exactly 30°, 45°, 60°. If the mirrors are as little as 1° off, the photo will not be symmetrical. Important! The kaleidoscope mirrors in your kit are front surface aluminized and must be handled with care. When mounting your mirrors, it's best to handle the mirrors with a soft cloth or wear thin cotton gloves.

How To Make The Kaleidoscope Mirrors:

An easy way to tell which side of the mirror is the reflecting side is to place a pencil point lightly on the glass surface. If the pencil points touch, this is the reflecting surface (see Figure 5). To arrange the mirrors, place a soft cloth or tissue

on the table; space the mirrors at their thickness apart. Then take a piece of adhesive tape and carefully tape the mirrors together (Figure 6). You cut a "V" in a box or cut out a "V" in 2 pieces of cardboard (Figure 7) to hold the mirrors at either 30°, 45°, or 60°. Check this with a protractor before you take your pictures; if "V" angle is off even slightly, use adhesive tape to hold them at the correct angle. Note that the camera is tilted slightly toward the "V" in the mirror (place a small piece of tape at the end of each mirror to

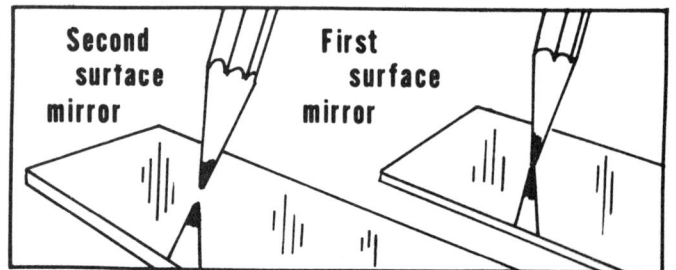

Second surface mirror **First surface mirror**

FIGURE 5

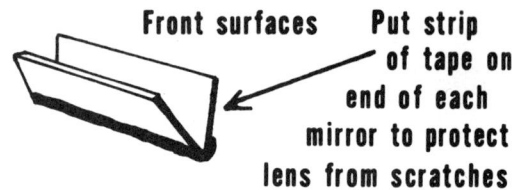

Front surfaces **Put strip of tape on end of each mirror to protect lens from scratches**

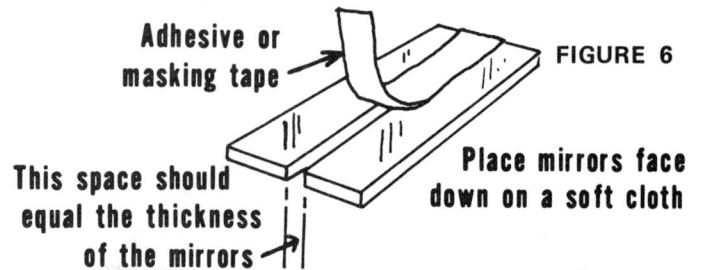

Adhesive or masking tape **FIGURE 6**

This space should equal the thickness of the mirrors

Place mirrors face down on a soft cloth

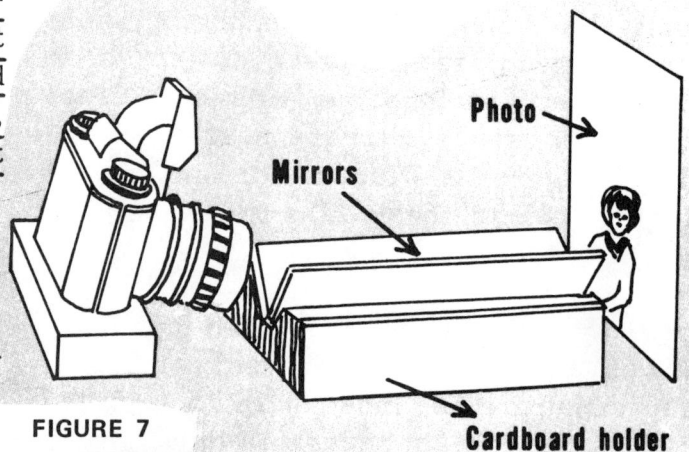

Photo

Mirrors

Cardboard holder

FIGURE 7

Kaleidoscope set-up

protect the camera lens) and that your subject or photo will be approximately 2" from
the end of the mirror. Check the ground
glass image carefully before you shoot,
and make sure the design is symmetrical.
You can also use your mirrors in front of
your camera for outdoor shots, but getting
a symmetrical image is almost impossible.

D. Kaleidoscope Slides

Attractive colored kaleidoscopic pictures can be made from your 35mm slide.
An arrangement similar to Figure 4 is
used here and the dimensions are essentially the same. Instead of a photographic
print set-up, take a piece of ground or
opal glass and tape the slide to it. Erect
the kaleidoscope mirrors near the slide
as in Figure 7. Place a No. 1 photoflood
lamp about 16" behind the ground or opal
glass. You may use your +3 diopter close-
up lens. The camera should be as close as
possible to the mirrors. When taping the
edges of the mirrors to avoid scratching
the camera lens, make sure to trim the
tape so it will not appear on the edges of
the kaleidoscopic segments in your photograph.

E. Mirror Tricks

A 5" x 7" front surface mirror is supplied in your kit. This type of mirror can
be used for many photographic gimmicks.

1. Horizontal Mirror

Shooting across the mirror with the
horizontal set-up, as in Figure 8, you
can put a beard on your favorite girl
(Figure 8a) or take a photo of your
house, etc. with water up to the second
floor. The house will have inverted
reflection similar to flooded house.
Make a rainy scene on a bright sunny
day. Mirror will represent wet street.

2. Vertical Mirror

Which way is he going? Figure 9a
(normal photo and trick photo) was
done by holding the mirror in the vertical set-up.

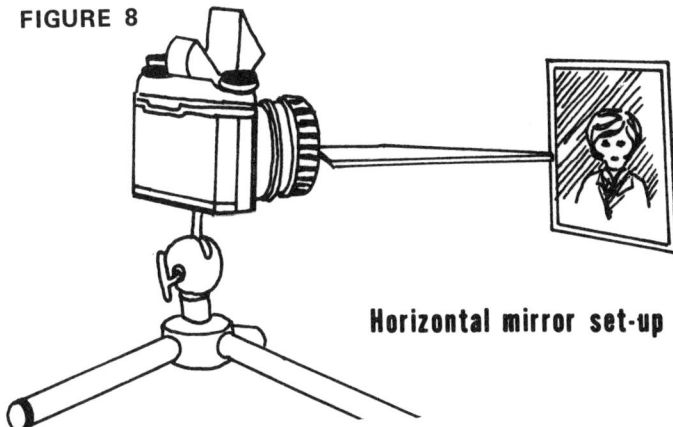

FIGURE 8

Horizontal mirror set-up

FIGURE 8a

3. Right Angle Mirror

This type of mirror can be used to shoot pictures to left, right, up or down without being seen. (Figure 10)

F. Bent Plastic Effects, Photos

This is probably the most creative and the most fun of all the special effect photos. With very little effort you can produce hilarious caricatures of friends, relatives, famous persons, etc. Your favorite magazine is a good source material. First you'll need some bent plastic to work with.

Included in your kit is piece of 5' x 7" plastic. Remove the protective covering by just peeling it off. (Try to keep finger prints or dirt off the plastic.) Place the plastic in a cookie pan or frying pan and heat it on the stove or in the oven until it is soft (about 350° F). Pick the plastic up with the heat-resistant gloves and bend it arbitrarily with a pair of pliers. Cover the jaws of the pliers with tape to keep from scratching the plastic. You can also lay the soft plastic on a marble or pencil to produce a localized effect (such as distorting one eye, nose, teeth, etc.) After the plastic cools, the curves will remain. You can immerse it in cold water to speed the cooling. If your plastic picks up reflections put the photofloods at a flatter angle. Set up your props as in Figure 11 and watch the ground glass in your camera when you rotate or move the bent plastic. You're sure to see some bizarre pictures.

FIGURE 9a

FIGURE 9

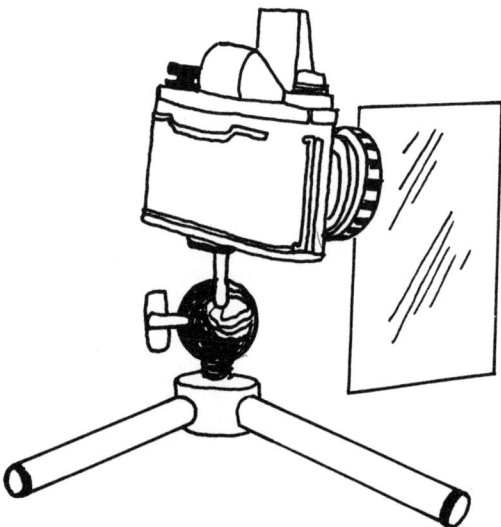

FIGURE 11   **Set-up for bent plastic photos**

FIGURE 10

Use mirror to photograph
upwards or at right angles   Mirror

Bent plastic

+3 close-up lens

Photo

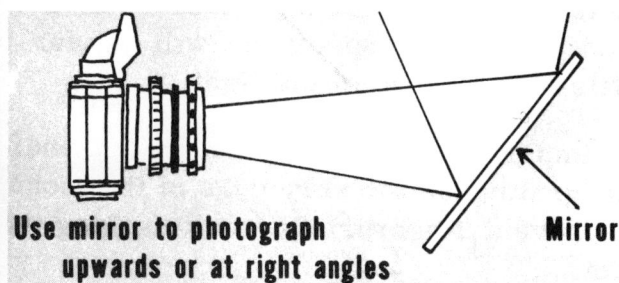

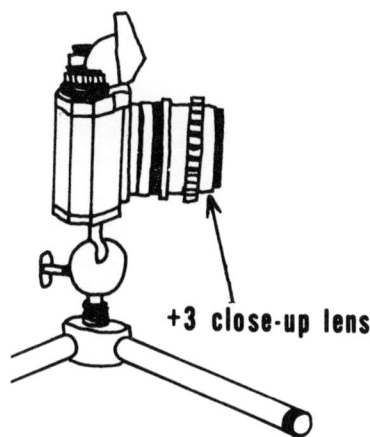

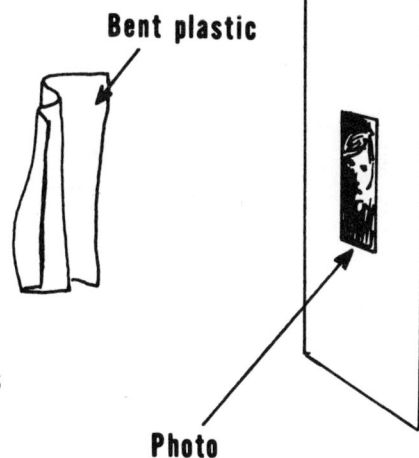

G. Diffraction Grating Slides

Included in your kit is a linear diffraction grating. At first glance, it will appear to be a piece of clear plastic, but when held up to a desk lamp or any clear small filament lamp the spectrum will appear a little to each side of the light.

Important! It is always best to handle the grating on the very edge of the mount to prevent fingerprints from marking the film.

Basically, the best spectral color slides and movies are made from brilliantly lighted subjects, with a dark background, but you will find that sunshining on sparkling water as well as other daylight scenes make colorful slides also.

The spectrum will appear next to the light. When you are ready, load your camera with color slide film and find a scene such as carnivals, picnic grounds, circuses, amusement parks, main streets of cities and towns, inside scenes such as Christmas trees, crystal chandeliers, etc. Most people place the grating in front of the camera with cellophane tape.

NOTE: As these instructions are printed in black and white, we have not attempted to give you illustrations of actual scenes because the beautiful colors of the spectrum would be lost in black and white illustrations.

H. Pattern Projection

Included in your kit are four 2" x 2" pieces of stamped pattern metal slides. These slides are put in a 35mm slide projector and the image is projected on the subject and then photographed.

A white background such as a sheet or movie screen is necessary. Place the model about 3 or 4 feet in front of the white screen (see Figure 12). In back of the model place two 250 watt photofloods. These can be set on the floor in back of the chair if your model is sitting. If your model is standing, these can be put up above and to the side so as not to appear in the picture. Do not put the lights on until you have the model and the projector ready. Select one of the four patterns

Set-up for pattern projection

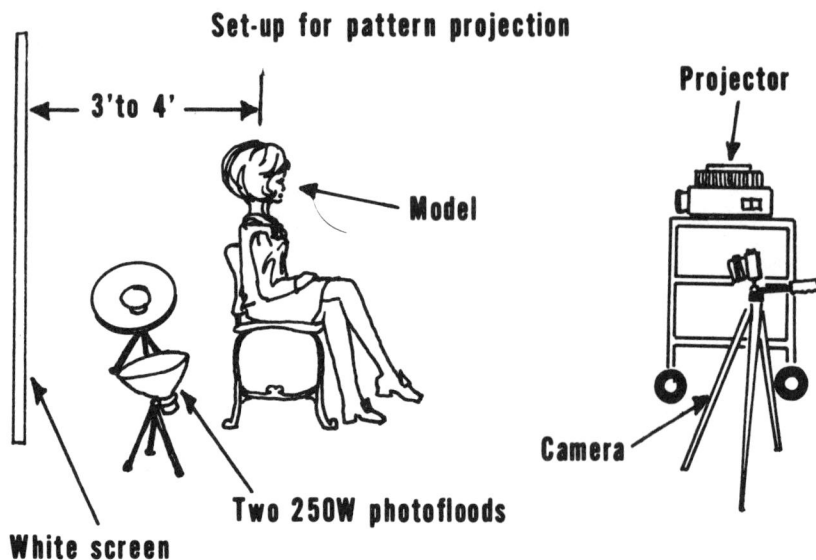

Projector

← 3'to 4' →

Model

Camera

White screen

Two 250W photofloods

FIGURE 12

Fantasy

FIGURE 13

Ripple

Ovalesque

Clover

Random

(Figure 13) and place it in the projector; project the image on the model. Try each one to see which one produces the effect you want. Next step is to set your camera along the side of the projector and as close to it as possible. If the design appears too large on the model, move the projector closer to the model.

After you have everything set up, you will notice that the design is also projected on the white screen. Shine the photoflood lights on the white screen to wash out the black patterns on the screen. Move the lights around, then observe the image in the viewing screen of the camera. Be sure that most of the pattern is obliterated and that the lights do not appear in the picture. When this is accomplished, the model will stand out from the screen.

Chapter 3

GENERAL SCIENCE

Have you not as yet decided exactly what area of science interests you the most? You aren't alone! Lots of people find each and every aspect of this fascinating field to hold vast interests for them. In this section, you will be introduced to some of the areas of specialization that have no specific category. Maybe your own interest is right here!

INTRODUCTION

Say "Fresnel" (pronounced "Freh-nel") to most people and, if it rings a bell at all, they will probably think of the giant lens in a lighthouse or the lens on a spotlight that photographers use. These are Fresnel lenses---and quite expensive. Now you can buy inexpensive Fresnel lenses, made out of a plastic material called acetate butyrate. The most remarkable thing about these plastic lenses is that they appear to be absolutely flat. So, how can they be a lens?

If you look closely at one of these new plastic lenses you will see a series of concentric lines etched into the plastic. These lines are only a few thousandths of an inch apart. Each concentric line acts as <u>part</u> of a lens; but taken all together, they form the function of a true lens. That is, they will focus all light they gather into a single spot---sort of like a giant magnifying glass.

CAUTION: The Fresnel is extremely powerful. Any combustible material, such as paper or wood, will immediately burst into flame when placed at the focal point of the lens. Reflection and glare at this point are also dangerous to the eyes. Exposure can cause retinal burns causing headaches, tearing or even blindness. Dark glasses should be worn while focusing the lens.

CLEANING: Do not wash the Fresnel lens any more than is absolutely necessary. To clean the lens, first brush it with a camel's-hair brush to remove surface dust. It is best to follow these steps:

1. Brush the lens with a circular motion, following the embossed lines in the lens.

2. If fingerprints or stains are apparent after the brushing, wash the lens with a piece of absorbent cotton soaked in a mild solution of a non-gritty detergent, plus a few drops of ammonia and some warm water. Use a circular motion when washing, the same as for brushing.

3. Wash only a small portion at a time. Use a new piece of cotton frequently to prevent accumulation of gritty particles.

4. Careful. Do not let the cotton become too dry, as the lens may be scratched from a pile-up of gritty particles.

5. Rinse the lens in two changes of cool clean water.

6. Dry the lens with a large piece of clean absorbent cotton, again using a circular motion.

7. Remove any lint from the surface with the camel's hair brush.

IMAGE BRIGHTENER FOR GROUND GLASS CAMERAS

If you use a camera that employs a ground glass for focusing, such as a Speed Graphic, a view camera, or even a Rollei-type of camera, you can get a much brighter image on the ground glass by means of a Fresnel lens.

First, measure the length and width of your present ground glass. Transfer these dimensions to the Fresnel lens. Make absolutely certain that the center of the Fresnel lens will be in the center of the area you are going to cut out. A good way to cut the Fresnel is to make a sandwich.. by placing the Fresnel lens between two pieces of 1/4" plywood. The plywood will prevent splintering of the hard plastic. If you own power tools, a jigsaw, circular saw or a band saw will do a good cutting job. You can also do the job by hand. Use a finetooth coping saw for the cutting.

You will be pleasantly surprised at how much brighter the image is and how much easier it is to do the focusing. Fig. 1 shows a Fresnel lens image brightener being installed over the ground glass screen of a Speed Graphic camera. Make sure the grooved side of the Fresnel lens faces the camera lens...to prevent possible scratching of the engraved surface.

THE SOLAR FURNACE

You can make a simple solar furnace with a single Fresnel lens mounted in a wooden frame as shown in Fig. 2. The base consists of a piece of 1/2" thick plywood with rounded corners. The U-shaped frame is made out of 1 x 1-1/2" wood (these dimensions are not too critical). The frame stands 18" high and is 15-1/2" wide. Drill a hole in the bottom part of the U to pass a 1/4" bolt and wing nut. The two arms are slotted at the top to accept 1/4" bolts and wing nuts which project from the mid-point of the frame.

The frame which holds the Fresnel lens is out of the same stock used to make the U-shaped frame. Cut a groove in the middle of the four pieces of wood which make up the frame to accept the Fresnel lens. The outside dimensions of the frame measure 13-1/2 x 13-1/2". The groove cut into the wood should be deep enough to accept about 1/4" of the Fresnel lens all around its periphery. Before inserting the Fresnel lens into the frame, drill two holes at the mid-point of two of the frame sections. Through these holes pass two 1/4" bolts. These bolts, tightened with wing nuts, form the axis which will allow you to tilt the Fresnel lens up or down so that it will be perpendicular to the sun. The wing nut assembly at the bottom of the base will allow you to shift the assembly from left to right.

The next step is to insert the lens into the frame grooves. Use glue and brads to secure the four pieces of the frame together.

You are now ready to give it a try. Crumple up a sheet of newspaper, point the lens at the sun, and lo and behold...the paper will burst into flame. Be careful. You are, in effect, concentrating a disk of sunshine 13" in diameter, into an area less than an inch in diameter.

The final step in the construction of the solar furnace is the mounting of the L-shaped bracket that will hold the crucible. This bracket, also made out of the same stock used for the construction of the furnace, is fastened in place with two round-head screws to the bottom of the frame holding the Fresnel lens. The length of the bracket is determined by the focal length of the Fresnel lens---and with allowance for the height of the crucible.

The crucible can be made out of ordinary firebrick, a good grade of ceramic tile---or you can buy a small crucible, such as shown in the photograph, from a supply house specializing in products for chemistry college classes.

When you set up the furnace, make sure that the crucible is in place, otherwise you will char and burn the bracket. This furnace will develop a temperature of 2,000°F, so be careful. Do not look directly at the projected image of the sun... wear dark glasses, if you must. This hot spot is as bright as the arc in a welder's torch...and he always wears dark glasses!

The solar furnace can produce some unusual jewelry. At about 1,500°F, powdered enamel will fuse to metal, but since some enamel colors reflect and absorb heat more than others, you will get some really exotic effects because of the difference in melting rates. You can watch this operation through dark glasses.

THE CAMP COOKER

The camp cooker is really a variation of the solar furnace. Its construction is identical except for the projecting L-shaped bracket. This bracket is somewhat longer, it measures 15" in length. At its end it has a small U-shaped yoke designed to hold an ordinary can. The can is mounted with two round-head screws. The screws should be just tight enough to allow the can to move so that it is always vertical to the ground, regardless of the tilt of the Fresnel lens and assembly.

The can shown in Fig. 3 is 3-1/4" in diameter, just wide enough to accept a slightly smaller can of soup. Fill the space between the two cans with water, paint a black spot on the outside of the larger can, and you now have the equivalent of a double boiler. A two or three minute exposure to the sun will cause the water to boil, effectively warming the contents of the inner can. Many brands now offer soups which do not require dilution with water. Of course you can use this arrangement to heat up other groceries such as franks and beans,

canned corn, etc. But don't forget, open the top of the can before you start the cooking operation.

An alternate method of construction, from a safety standpoint, is to make the projecting L-shaped and U-shaped brackets out of Reynolds do-it-yourself aluminum. The aluminum will not burn if accidentally left exposed to the sun's rays. But, it will give you a nasty burn if you touch the hot surface--treat the furnace and cooker with respect and avoid an accident.

WOODSCREW & FLAT WASHER.

NOTE: 1/4 SLOT FOR LAMP ADJUSTMENT

SEE 7 3/8 DISTANCE SHOWN IN FIG 5

DOUBLE THICK WINDOW GLASS

SEE DETAIL "A" & "C"

SEE DETAIL "B"

DETAIL "B"

1/4   1 1/8

TOP

CUT OUT FOR POLE

1 1/4

6 3/4

ALL SIDES 1/4 PLYWOOD

ADJUSTMENT PLATE
#6 FLAT WASHER

6-32 HEX. NUT

REFLECTOR

6-32 MACH. SCREW.

DETAIL-A

2 1/4

11

3/8 1/8

5/8

1 7/8

1/4

1 1/4

10

10

NAIL SIDE STRIPS TO TOP PLATE WITH BRADS.

COVER

CUT OUT ACCURATELY WITH KEYHOLE SAW OR SABRE SAW.

1/4

18

1/2

14 3/4

2 3/8

C OF BULB FILAMENT.
30MM. C OF REFLECTOR.

DETAIL-C

GLASS

SPRING METAL CLIPS (4)

DETAIL-X

#8-32 HEX. HD. SCREW WITH #8 FLAT WASHER & #8-32 HEX. NUT.

FRESNEL LENS

6" VENTILATING LOUVRES (ROUND)

BOX

2 1/4

1/2

END PIECE
(BOTH END PIECES NOTCHED THE SAME)

(6) 1" DIA. HOLES PER SIDE PIECE.

9

14 1/2

1/2

1/2

1/2 1/2

SIDE
(BOTH SIDES DRILLED & NOTCHED THE SAME.)

6" DIA. HOLE
(ONE PER SIDE PIECE)

2 2 2

2 2 2

3

3 64

4 1/4

11 5/8

16

END PIECE

10 7/8

1/2

10

1 3/8

11 1/4 REF.

11 1/4

BOTTOM

5 SPACES AT 2 1/4 FOR HOLE CENTERS.

2

4 3/4 2

11 1/4

1 1/4

16

2 3/8

1 1

1

BLOCK 4 REQ.
(ONE EACH CORNER)

THE OVERHEAD PROJECTOR

A Fresnel lens, part of Edmund Kit No. 70,966, will enable you to build a professional-style 10 x 10" overhead projector. In addition to this kit you will need a lamp, socket, motor-driven fan, mirror, switches, wood, hardware, plus wire, etc. The total, including approximately $12 for the kit, should not exceed $40. You will wind up with a projector easily worth $175, capable of showing 8 x 10" color transparencies, tracings, line drawings, and even the outlines of flat objects such as keys, coins, etc.

The first step is to make the box. (For complete construction plans, see Fig. 4.) It can be made from wood or sheet metal, painted, stained, finished plywood, etc. It is important to choose well seasoned wood as the heat is liable to warp green wood and throw the projector out of alignment. 3/4" pine makes a good working base. The box should measure 12-3/4"x 16"x 11-5/8" high. Paint all inside surfaces dead black to prevent stray reflections from the light surfaces. (Note: The construction photos were taken before the inside was painted black.)

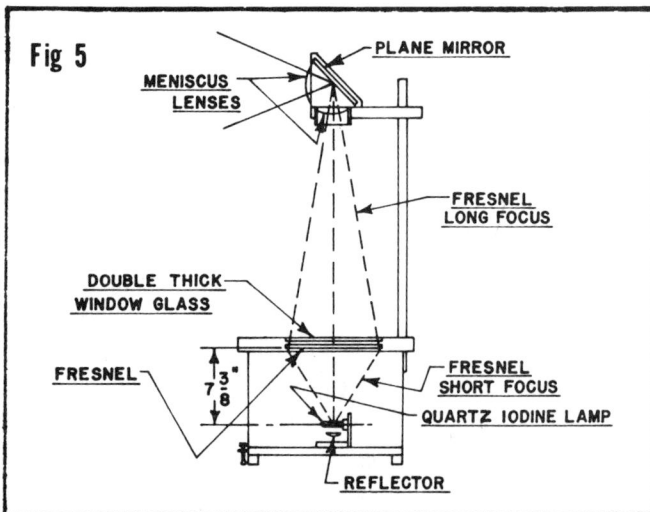

Fig 5

Ventilating Cooling Alignment. These are the most important items in building an overhead projector. Make sure the center of the bulb filament, the center of the Fresnel condenser and the center of the projection lenses are exactly in line. (See Fig. 5.) Check and recheck this using a try square and plumb line.

Ventilation. Four cutouts (see Fig. 6), one at each side of the box, raise the box 1-1/4" off the table to provide an air flow. Two louvers, each 6" in dia., face each other on the long side of the box. (See Fig. 7.)

In addition a series of 1" diameter holes near the top of the box also provide ventilation. A fan mounted opposite one of the louvers provides a forced draft (see Fig. 8). The Quartz Iodine lamp is rated at 500 watts and produces quite a large amount of heat plus intense light. Try not to look at the bulb filament when adjusting the projector; if necessary, wear dark glasses. Never run the projector without the cooling fan or blower. If you do this, the intense heat from the bulb will ruin the Fresnel condenser. See Fig. 9 for ventilating cooling diagram.

Build the bulb, socket, and reflector holder in 1 unit and wire to switches and fan according to diagram (Fig. 10). Always handle the Quartz Iodine bulb with a piece of cloth and never touch the glass with your fingers. If you do, clean the glass with alcohol or lens cleaner before lighting.

MAKING THE TOP

Your hardware store will cut you a piece of double thick window glass for the stage. This should be larger than the 10 x 10" hole in the top (see Fig. 11). Cut the wood top so the glass will be even with the top of the wood, then use metal clips to hold the glass in place. (See Fig. 4.) When cutting the 10 x 10" hole in the top, make sure the edges are neat and sharp. Use a keyhole saw or sabre saw and file smooth. If the edge is jagged, your screen image will have a jagged frame. If you can't get it accurate enough to suit, cut a sharp mask 10 x 10" out of cardboard and place this between the glass and wood. Fasten the top to the box with wood screws, then these can be removed to change bulbs or adjusting.

PLASTIC FRESNEL CONDENSER

This is actually a double plastic lens cemented together. One lens has a long focus, the other a short focus. The short focus lens must face the light bulb. These lenses are not marked, therefore, it will be necessary to try one side; if this does not work, try the other. If the long focus faces the bulb, the image on the screen will be a round circle instead of a square. Reverse the lens and all will be forgiven.

BUILDING THE HEAD

Alignment of the lenses so that they are at absolute right angles to each other, with the mirror at an exact 45° angle, is a must in order to achieve correct optical alignment. Before you fasten the lenses permanently to the wood, clean the inside lens surfaces carefully. The outside surfaces can be cleaned after permanent mounting. If you use household cement, be sure to use it sparingly and be careful it does not get on the lens surface. The mirror should be cemented to the wood; cleaned; then the wood is nailed or cemented in place. (See Fig. 12.) Paint the inside of the lens head a dead black before "locking" up. The tube that fits into the bottom of the lens head is for swiveling the lens head. For safety after inserting in the hole of the lens arm, put several rubber bands around the tube to prevent the head from coming off when carrying and moving, Fig. 13. If a larger size tube is available it can be split and pulled into correct outer diameter.

MAKING THE ARM AND POST

Be sure to drill the holes in the arm before cutting the slot, Fig. 14 and 14-A. The post can be 1-1/8" wood dowel or Reynolds 1/4" O. D. aluminum. If the latter is used, the hole in the lens arm must be made 1/4" dia. After assembly, a light coating of wax will allow easier up and down movement of the arm and head, Fig. 15.

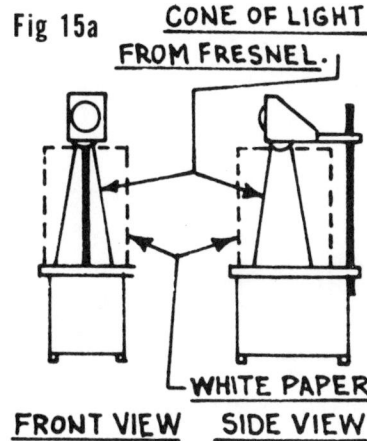

Fig 15a
CONE OF LIGHT FROM FRESNEL.
FRONT VIEW   SIDE VIEW
WHITE PAPER

CHECKING ALIGNMENT

An easy way to see if your optical system is centered and aligned is to switch your projector on with nothing on the stage and put out the room lights. Take a piece of white paper or white cardboard, approximately the size or a little smaller than the distance between the stage and the lens when in focus. Stand the paper or cardboard on its edge in the middle of the system. This will show a cone of light from the condenser on the white paper. The cone should come to the exact center of the lens. Do this from the side and front of the projector. If the cone does not point to the center of the lens, viewing from the side and front, move the Fresnel lens until it does. (See Fig. 15A.)

TESTING THE PROJECTOR

Select a projection distance of approximately 12 feet from lens to screen. Switch on the projector, the screen image should be a well lighted square approximately 8' x 8'. The edges of the square should be sharp when in focus.

ADJUSTING FOR PROJECTION DISTANCE

If the edges are blue, this means the lamp is too close to the screen. If the edges appear brown, the lamp is too far away. When the edges are not colored, the lamp is adjusted for the 12 foot distance. If you change this distance drastically, you will have to repeat the above. The metal reflector must always be at the same distance from the bulb (30 mms from the center of reflector to the center of the filament of the Quartz Iodine lamp; see Fig. 4.).

KEYSTONE EFFECT

When the projector is not square with the screen, a keystone effect will take place. Fig. 16 shows several ways to correct this. Overhead projectors should stand between 2 and 3 feet from the floor.

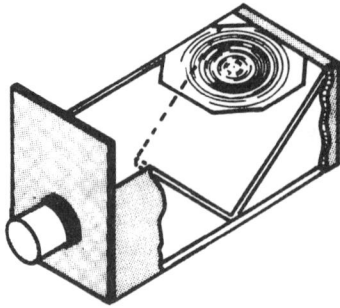

A CAMERA OBSCURA

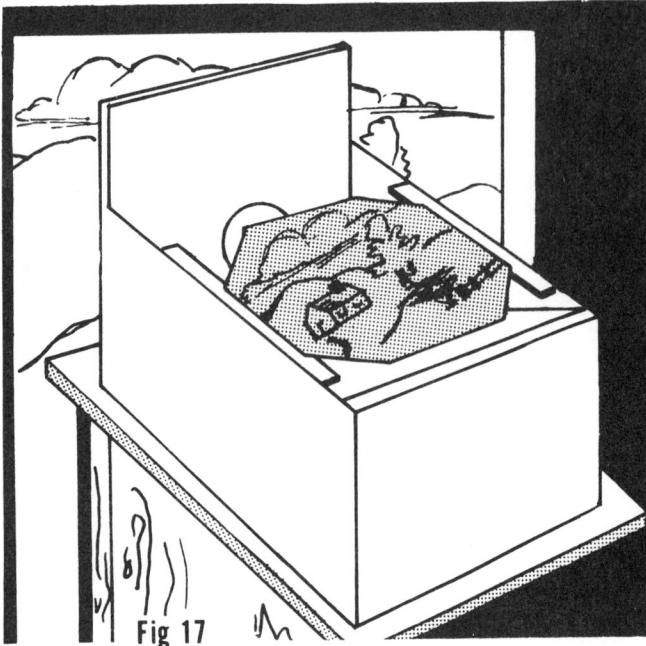

Fig 17

A camera obscura is a fascinating optical device (see Fig. 17). Make it for a child and he will enjoy hours of pleasure with it. But don't think it's just a toy. Professionals us it for making sketches, landscapes, and portraits. Thomas Jefferson had a small one at his home in Monticello. His guests were fascinated by the magic view of the landscape which they were able to view in a darkened room. Jefferson's camera obscura was a small one, yielding an image of about 5 x 5". With the Edmund Camera Obscura Kit, No. 70,881 you will have a large, brightly illuminated 12 x 12" image.

The kit contains a projection lens, a lens tube, focusing sleeve and a special 12 x 12" plastic Fresnel lens. The only other items you will need to build the camera are plywood, glue, and nails, plus a mirror which you can buy at the five-and-ten.

The first step is to buy a mirror at the five-and-ten. Get one that measures at least 10 x 12". The one used in this particular camera is 12 x 15". The size of the mirror really determines the size of the box and that is why we say, get the mirror first.

Next, make the box out of 1/2" plywood. (See Fig. 18.) Its outside dimensions are 13 x 20" and 12" high. Mount the mirror at an exact 45° angle by means of two 1/4" thick cleats glued and nailed to the sides of the box. Note that the mirror is not centered, the short side of the mirror should rest against the back of the box.

Fig 18

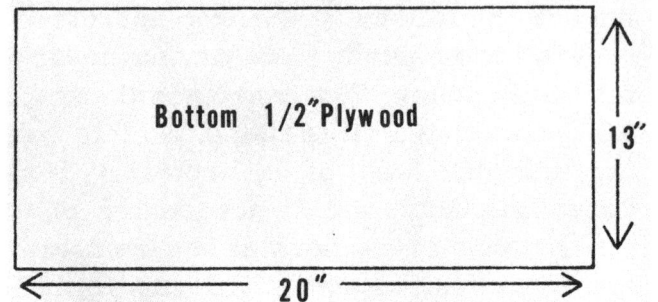

Bottom 1/2" Plywood

13"

20"

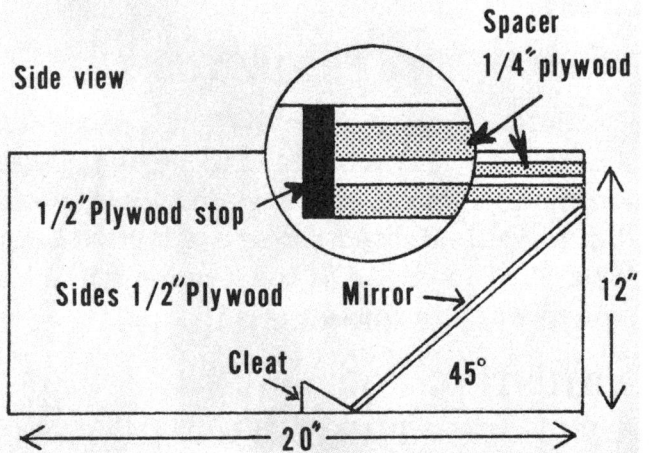

Side view

Spacer 1/4" plywood

1/2" Plywood stop

Sides 1/2" Plywood

Mirror

Cleat

45°

12"

20"

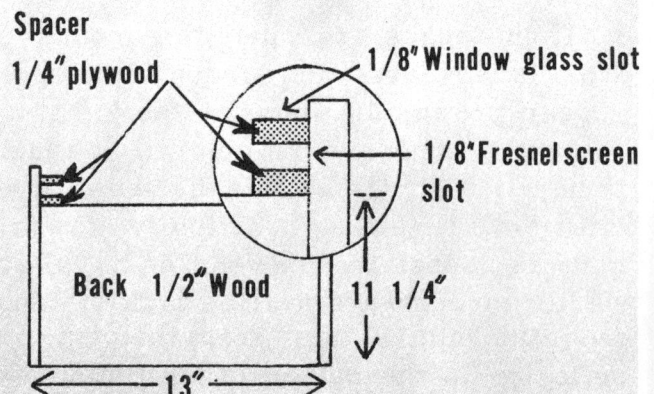

Spacer 1/4" plywood

1/8" Window glass slot

1/8" Fresnel screen slot

Back 1/2" Wood

11 1/4"

13"

Cut a hole in the exact center of the front of the box for the focusing sleeve. (See Fig. 19.) This hole should be 3-5/8" in diameter. Cement the focusing sleeve into this hole. Remove the mirror and paint all the inside surfaces a flat black. After the paint has dried, replace the mirror, secure the back of the box with flat-head screws and start the assembly of the lens. This is simple. All you need do is to glue the plano-convex lens (supplied) to the tube with a good grade of cement, such as 3M's Super Strength. Run a bead of cement around the inside of the tube, set the lens in place and add more cement to the outside. Paint the inside of the tube flat black before cementing the lens in place. If you desire, a lens shade made out of a sheet of photographic album paper may be added. It will help you get a brighter image.

The Fresnel lens should be installed with the etched or grooved side facing the lens mounted in the cardboard tube. In addition, you will need a sheet of double-thickness window glass to cover and protect the Fresnel screen. A glazier or hardware store will cut this to size for you. Cost should be about one dollar. The glass will provide a good working surface for making tracings and drawings.

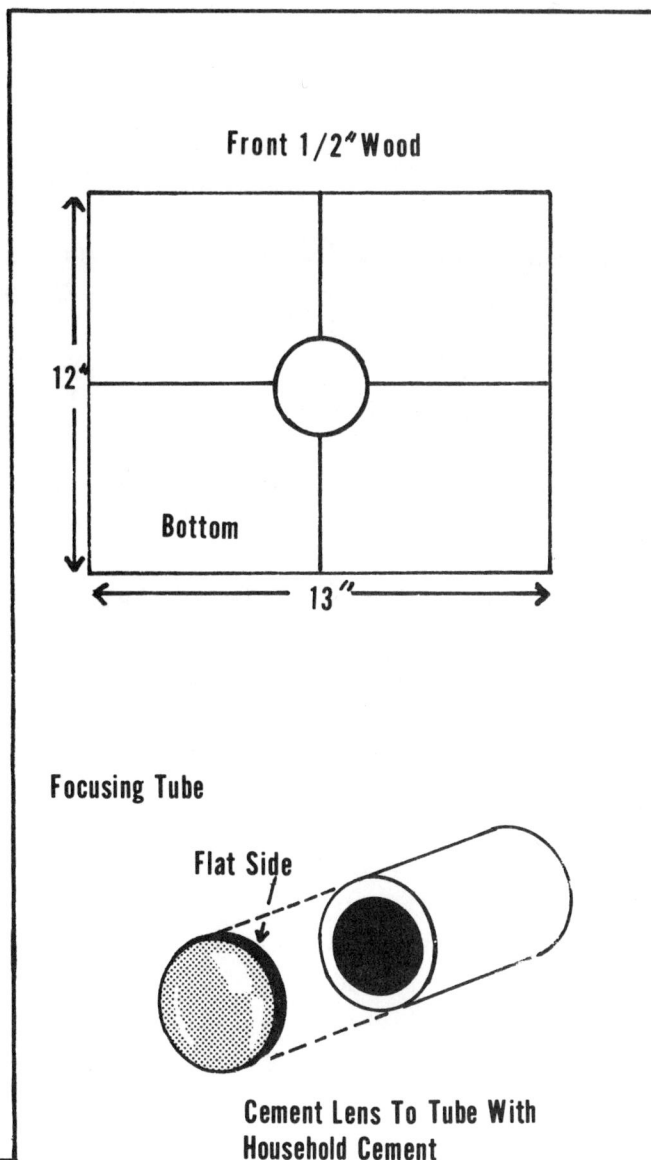

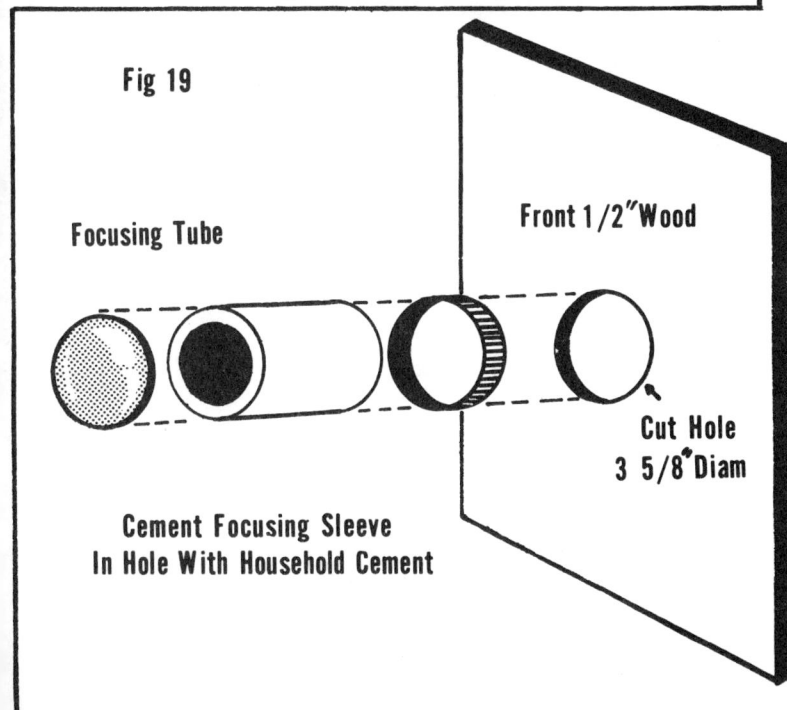

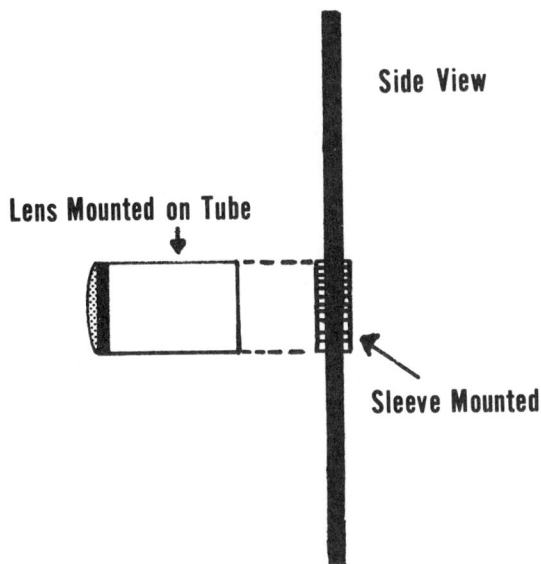

Front 1/2" Wood

12"

Bottom

13"

Focusing Tube

Flat Side

Cement Lens To Tube With Household Cement

Fig 19

Focusing Tube

Front 1/2" Wood

Cut Hole 3 5/8" Diam

Cement Focusing Sleeve In Hole With Household Cement

Side View

Lens Mounted on Tube

Sleeve Mounted

The last step in construction is the making of the triangular-shaped light shield. Cut it as shown to the dimensions indicated in the drawing out of 1/2" plywood. (Fig. 20.) Paint the inside flat black. You will be pleasantly surprised at how much the addition of the light shield adds to the brightness of the image. Glue it in place with a bead of white glue. Weight the top, wrap a strap or string around it until the glue sets. (generally overnight is sufficient).

If you find it difficult to slide the lens tube in and out of the sleeve for focusing, try coating the tube as well as the sleeve with some hard wax. This will ease the operation.

The best way to use the camera obscura is by pointing it out of a window. The darker the room the brighter the image will be on the screen. The nearer the object you are looking at, the farther out you will have to pull the lens. The image you see will be right side up, but it will be reversed from left to right, just like looking in a mirror.

OTHER APPLICATIONS

In addition to large Fresnel lenses, small Fresnel lenses are available in 8 x 10" sheets with 25 Fresnel lenses to a sheet (Edmund Stock No. 60,811). These lenses show small upright images wherever they are positioned. Opically, they are considered the same as negative lenses. However, no matter what they are, they give you some unusual effects when used for decorative purposes.

Used as part of a lamp shade, or even as a complete lamp shade, you will see a conglomeration of miniature images of the light bulb behind the shade (see Fig. 21). Most fascinating. They can also be used as part of a room divider screen; in lieu of window glass for semiprivacy; as part of the shade in a ceiling light fixture; for psychedelic light displays; and much more.

DIFFRACTION GRATING REPLICA

TWO TYPES AVAILABLE
Transmission type

This is a transparent acetate film material that has been embossed with 13,400 grooves to the inch. To see a beautiful spectrum simply hold a small piece up to your eyes and look through it. This can be done with larger panels which will be described on the following pages. If a sheet is placed on a window, etc. through which the sun is shining, a spectrum will be thrown on the floor, wall, or ceiling and will be very pleasant to see if the room is reasonably dark.

Reflecting type

This type is of the same material as above, except a thin coating of aluminum has been deposited on the grooved side in a vacuum chamber for reflecting the colors. Held close to the eyes you will see that it is approximately 10% transparent like a one-way mirror. This type lends itself beautifully to areas where you want the spectrum reflected back at you.

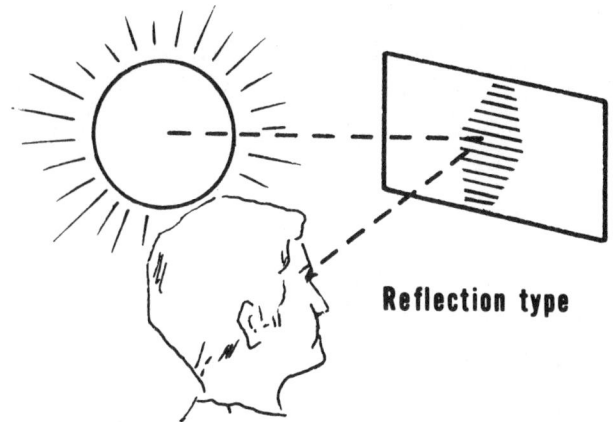

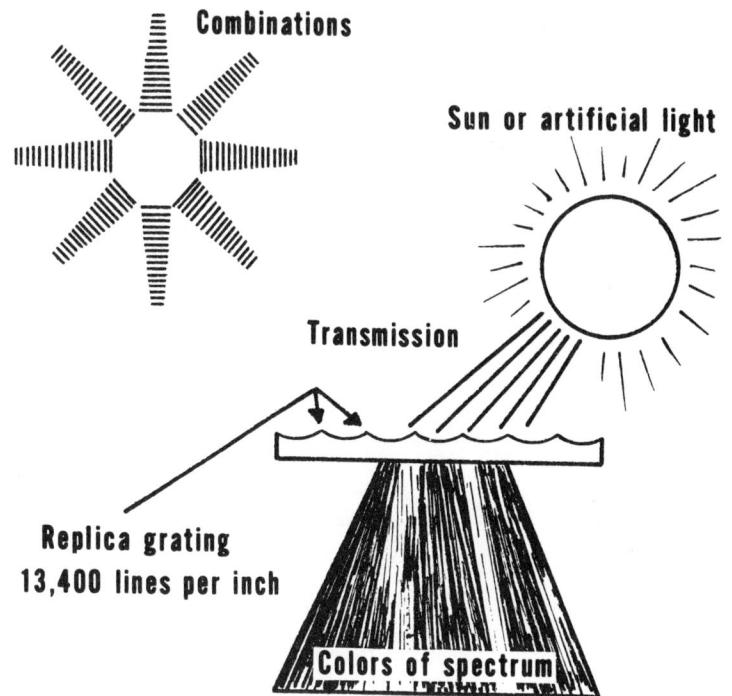

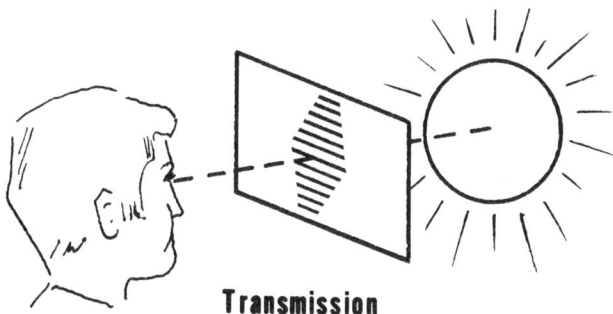

Reflection type

Combinations

Sun or artificial light

Transmission

Replica grating 13,400 lines per inch

Colors of spectrum

Transmission

Elegant table top

64

Hundreds of photo tricks

ABOUT DIFFRACTION GRATING REPLICAS

Because these are rather uncommon terms we would like first to acquaint you with their meanings.
DIFFRACTION: the bending of light around an obstacle.
GRATING: a pattern of many of these obstacles.
REPLICA: a duplicate.

DIFFRACTION GRATING REPLICA is a highly exact, acetate plastic duplicate of a master pattern having thousands of very fine, closely spaced, parallel grooves per inch. When light strikes this material at various angles, a sight more magnificent than the beautiful rainbow is produced.

SEEING THE LINES OF GRATING

Straight line gratings have 13,400 lines per inch. Seeing the lines of grating is impossible with the naked eye. And because these lines of grating are responsible for the beautiful color effects, you may wish to see exactly what you are working with.

Seeing the highly precise embossed lines of grating is readily accomplished with a microscope having a power as low as 300X; 900 power enables you to see them quite easily, while 600 power affords a very convenient workable power for the observation of these lines.

The above holds true for both the transmission and the reflecting types of grating when properly lighted. How-

ever, the reflecting type presents a much more attractive field of view and the lines are more discernible.

Diffraction grating

Lamp shade

EXPERIMENTAL

Diffraction grating

EDUCATIONAL

MAKING A STUDENT SPECTROSCOPE

Use our small pieces in mounts for chemistry, physics, or science classes. They show the spectrum beautifully. And they are so inexpensive you can have each student make a spectroscope. The only extra things you need are:
1. A piece of aluminum foil 2" x 2"
2. A 10" to 12" long paper tube (from a paper towel or wax paper roll)

Take the grating slide and cement it to the end of the paper tube by placing a small amount of cement on the tube and carefully placing the grating over it, allowing the tube to be cemented to the cardboard frame.

of the diffraction grating. If the cardboard tube is sufficiently large in diameter (at least 1-1/2"),the diffraction grating slide can be trimmed to fit the diameter of the tube. If, however, the tube is too small in diameter do not attempt to cut the cardboard slide for it will fall apart if too much is cut away. On the other end of the tube place the aluminum foil; cover the open end and fold the foil snug against the tube. With a penknife pierce the aluminum foil and draw the knife along in a straight line cutting a slit about 3/4" long, and no wider than the knife point (1/32" is amply wide).

Mounted grating *

*Lined corners indicate probable area that will be cut away to conform to shape of tube

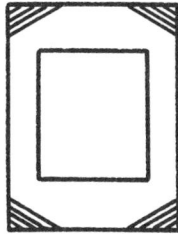

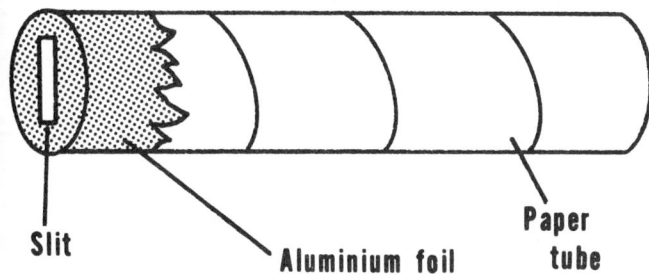

Slit   Aluminium foil   Paper tube

NOW YOU'RE READY TO EXPERIMENT

Hold the tube toward a light and incandescent lamp or fluorescent lamp, with your eye very close to the diffraction grating. You can immediately see the slit in the end of the tube. You can also see a band of color on each side of the slit. While looking at one color band rotate the aluminum foil (with the slit) holding the tube still. The color band will appear to change its shape. When the band is at its widest the spectroscope is adjusted and ready for use. Looking at a light through a spectroscope, it is possible to see that there are two spectra — one on each side of the slit. These are spectra of the first order.

Farther out from these and more difficult to see are other spectra of the second order. The red end of the spectra is away from the slit in both cases.

Applications

To use as a monochromator for microscope illumination, cover the plane mirror with a piece of grating. Focus the condenser and illuminate with parallel rays from a lamp. By tilting the grating, different portions of the spectrum will pass across the field. Useful for determination of refractive index of crystals with different wave lengths, and for changing contrast of stained specimens.

Demonstrate Abbe's diffraction theory of resolution by microscope. An inside frosted bulb will serve as light source. Focus the condenser on the grating and close its diaphragm as far as possible. Examine grating with 16mm (N.A. 0.50) objectives and a 10X or higher eyepiece. Then remove eyepiece and look at back aperture of objective. Axial beam (white) and two diffracted beams (spectra) will be seen. With the 16mm objective, only 3/4 the blue ends of the spectra will be seen, and the structure will be resolvable with blue (or white) lights, but not with red. With the 8mm objective, the grating will be easily resolved.

Viewing Various Spectra, an incandescent lamp gives a continuous spectrum. Viewing a fluorescent lamp, a bright line (or "emission") spectrum of mercury will be seen if the slit in the aluminum is narrow enough. The third type of spectra and the more difficult to see is the dark line (or "absorption") spectrum found in light. Permit sunlight to be reflected from a white card into the spectroscope. You are now ready for further experimentation.

For Science Fair Projects, our diffraction grating offers unlimited possibilities. Uses range all the way from simple demonstrations of spectra as produced by diffraction gratings to advanced studies in spectroscopy.

Art Classes will find that our diffraction grating is the ideal material for instilling a respect and full realization of color's potential. The colors as seen through our transmission grating or reflected from our reflecting grating can be used for various projects or exercises in color work.

Use as a precise microscope scale to measure size of object being observed. To get size, multiply number of spaces occupied by object by .0000746. Use to test the resolving power of microscope objective, or for checking critical illumination.

Some Facts about Common Dinosaurs of the Past

Background information regarding the various dinosaurs in your kit appears below. Pictures and additional information on each specie may be found in the included "How And Why Book of Dinosaurs".

PLATEOSAURUS

These Dinosaurs, or 'terrible lizards' were land reptiles. One of the first of the dinosaurs was the Plateosaurus. Its name means 'flat lizard' and it lived about 160,000,000 years ago. This dinosaur was 20 feet long and had a very long tail and neck. Though it walked erect on its two broad hind legs when traveling, it stood on all fours when feeding. Plateosaurus ate plants. Such animals are called Herbivores which means 'plant-eaters.'

CYNOGNATHUS

The Cynognathus lived 190,000,000 years ago. Its name means 'dog-jaws' because its head resembled the head of a dog. It was a small reptile and a very active hunter, and may have been the early ancestor of the mammal. Mammals are warm-blooded animals that nurse their young. Man is a mammal and so are dogs and most other animals we know today.

PTERANODON

The Pteranodon was not a dinosaur but a flying reptile. Its name means 'wing-without-teeth.' It had no teeth but its dagger-like beak enabled it to catch and eat fish.

Pteranodon, with a wing-spread of 27 feet, weighed only 30 pounds for its bones were hollow and paper-thin. Three tiny claws on each wing enabled it to cling to the rocky cliffs where it lived. The wings were made of membrane and Pteranodon flew with a glider-like motion. It lived about 80,000,000 years ago and its fossils have been found in Kansas.

KRONOSAURUS

This dinosaur class is part of a larger group known as the Plesiosaurs. This group consisted of marine reptiles whose habits of living were suited to the open seas, although at times they invaded swamps and shallow waters. Two types existed. Common features included flattened heads, fat, elliptical bodies, long finless tails, and legs and feet shaped like paddles. The two types were distinguished by by their long or short neck.

The Kronosaurus evolved as these two types spread beyond their original European habitat. They were further characterized by a 9 foot skull.

DIMETRODON

The Dimetrodon was another primitive reptile. It was a large animal, probably eleven feet long with sharp, dagger-like teeth and it was almost certainly an expert hunter. A giant 'sail,' supported by long spines, grew two to three feet above its back. This gave it the nickname of 'finback.' Fossils of Dimetrodon have been found in Texas.

MACRAUCHENIA

The Macrauchenia is categorized among the group known as litopterns which were descendants of primitive hoofed animals.

This species had very wide bodies. They stood about five feet in height, and their legs were very thick terminating at the three-toed hoofed foot. The head and neck resembled those of a present day camel.

STYRACOSAURUS

The Styracosaurus was a horned dinosaur about 15 feet long. The name means 'Spiked Lizard,' referring to the collar of sharp horns which it had about the neck and head. In addition, it had one long sharp horn on the nose measuring almost 2 ft. in length. A thick tough skin also served to protect this plant-eater from the attack of larger beasts. Styracosaurus lived 90,000,000 years ago. Fossils have been discovered in Montana and Alberta, Canada.

WOOLY MAMMOTH

The Wooly Mammoth reminds us of the elephant of today but it was much larger and more powerful with tremendous curved tusks. The long thick hair of its hide protected this mammal against the dense cold of the Ice Age. The bump on its back is said to have been a hump of fat on which it survived when snow covered the twigs and plants which it normally ate. Well-preserved fossils have been found in Alaska and Siberia and much of the world's ivory is said to come from their tusks.

CERATOGAULUS

The Ceratogaulus was a comparatively small but plump quadruped mammal. Its fore and hind legs resemble those of a cat, but its tail is longer and has a fairly thick fur covering as does the entire body. The head and nose are similar to those of a cow with two small horns protruding from the forehead. This mammal existed over 25,000,000 years ago and flourished in the Pacific Northwest

PARASAUROLOPHUS

Parasaurolophus means 'Lizard with a Crest,' referring to the bony extension on its head which may have served as an air storage chamber, thereby permitting this beast to graze underwater for great periods of time. A duck-billed dinosaur, the Parasaurolophus had webbed feet and was about 28 feet long. Rows of flat peg-like teeth lined its jaws to grind the soft plants on which it lived in swampy areas near Alberta, Canada, some 75,000,000 years ago.

GLYPTODON

The name of this species is attributed to the appearance of its teeth in carved patterns. The features included a deep set head, a solid shell formed by skeletal plates that had cemented together, tails covered with ringlets and solid sheets of bone with spikes protruding. Those of the Pleistocene era averaged from three to five feet larger than those of the Miocene era.

MEGATHERIUM

The Megatherium whose name means 'Giant Sloth,' was more than 24 feet in length. This bulky, slow-witted mammal had a bushy tail which helped to support his weight in the upright position when it fed on the leaves of trees. Strong, sturdy hind legs and somewhat lighter front legs were edged with sharp claws which were sometimes used to dig up bulbs and vegetables from the earth. Fossils have been found in North and South America.

DIRE WOLF

The Dire Wolf had a prominent, sturdy and weighty head. It was a carnivarous beast and was similar to, but not quite as large as, a present day timber wolf. This mammal tended to hunt in packs and feasted on carrion as well as freshly killed food.

MOSCHOPS

The Moschops was an early reptile about 7 feet in length with short, stubby legs, a bulky body and a massive head. Short peg-like teeth were suited for the plants that it ate to survive. The Moschops lived about 200,000,000 years ago along the banks of rivers in South Africa.

ANKLYOSAURUS

Roaming the land 135 million years ago, this lizard was noted for his curved armored back ribs. His strong bony tail proved quite useful in combat. This plant-eater lived on higher dry land, away from the swamps and marshes.

SMILODON

The Smilodon is better known as the 'Saber-Toothed Tiger' because of the two 6-inch tusks which jutted down from its upper jaw to stab and slash its prey like a sword. This ferocious mammal was larger and far more powerful than the tiger of today, measuring anywhere in length up to 9 feet. A blood-thirsty flesh-eater, it was probably responsible for the extinction of many of the large mammals of its era. Fossils have been uncovered in California and Argentina.

DIATRYMA

The Diatryma was a huge flightless bird. Nearly seven feet tall, this bird was slow moving and deliberate, having few enemies from which to escape. Its powerful beak and overall size were constant threats to the earliest mammals.

The structural variations prevalent in this species indicates that it was probably never able to fly, but was an excellent runner. However, the gradual changes in vegetation and climate and their limited mobility lead to their extinction.

STRUTHIOMIMUS

The Struthiomimus lived 100,000,000 years ago. This dinosaur was about six feet tall. Its name means 'Ostrich Imitator' because it looked like an ostrich without feathers, except for the long slim tail which was used for balance. The beak-like head had no teeth. Its food consisted of insects, fruit, small plants and dinosaur eggs. Strong hind legs supplied the speed which was its only defense against other ferocious beasts. Fossils have been found in Alberta, Canada.

ALLOSAURUS (or ANTRODEMUS)

A giant meat-eating dinosaur, this creature was 35 feet from the tip of his tail to his powerful jaws. He possessed strong, heavy hind legs on which he ran. Found as fossils in Late Jurassic to Early Cretaceous rocks of North America (Jurassic period preceded Cretaceous and ended 136,000,000 years ago).

BRONTOSAURUS

This huge vegetarian measured over 70 feet in length and weighed 60,000 pounds. As large as he was, the brain that controlled his awesome body was only the size of a walnut. Munching water plants in ponds and lakes the creature had only 24 weak peg-shaped teeth. He roamed the earth nearly 180 million years ago.

TYRANNOSAURUS REX

This fierce king of the meat-eaters was the last of the great carnivorous dinosaurs. Living during the Cretaceous period (135 million years ago) this tyrant was 45 feet from nose to tail with sharp curved teeth that extended 6 inches. This dinosaur could bite through the toughest hide and crunch the thickest bones.

TRACHODON

Named for his 2,000 rough teeth, this duck-billed creature spent most of his time walking in shallow water. His teeth were for grinding, not biting, and he was a gentle plant-eater. He lived over 135 million years ago.

TRICERATOPS

This creature was named for its "three-horned" face. He was 30 feet long and a great fighter. Roaming the earth 135 million years ago, Triceratops used his sword-like horns in fierce combat. This ferocious combatant was a plant eater.

STEGOSAURUS

Covered with a double row of heavy bone-plates all along its back, this plant-eating dinosaur used its vicious appearance as a protective device against his meat-eating predators. His hind legs were much longer than his front legs, causing him to move rather awkwardly. He lived during the Jurassic period over 180 million years ago.

Suggestions For A Dinosaur Land Scene

You may wish to reconstruct fascinating scenes of pre-historic monsters and the lands they inhabited. In this way, the pre-historic ages can be recalled and relived in modern times.

• Use a wood platform (drawing board, cutting board etc.) as a base for your dinosaur and mammal figures. (The effect of a deep crevice results if a narrow slit is cut through the board.)

• Shake imitation grass over fresh green paint to add color and texture to the board.

• Shape mountains, cliffs, caves and valleys with wire screening and a papier mache paste. (This can be made by mixing moist shredded newspaper with flour. Add the flour until a firm paste is formed.)

• Suitable paints for realistic finishing of your dinosaurs can be obtained in your local hobby shop. Either enamel or acrylic base colors may be used. Avoid laquers unless spray is applied; brush applied laquers with heavy concentrations of aromatic solvents may attack the plastic.

• Assemble thick groves and forests by attaching the lychen to taffy sticks, etc., and supporting this upright with modeling clay. Realistic vines (made of green string) interlaced between the trees adds to the scene's authenticity.

• Layout lakes and rivers using mylar, aluminum foil, glass plates, or aluminum pie plates, etc. Solid blue paint on the bottom surface with a number of upper surface streaks brings out the best effect using the glass plates. Strips of fine sandpaper will form the sandy banks along such waterways.

• The scattered debris, stumps, and logs of an ancient forest can be shown by using matchsticks, toothpicks or slits of balsa wood.

• To gain added realism use threads to suspend the flying monsters over the scene.

CAMERA OBSCURA KITS

The camera obscura is probably one of the oldest optical instruments in existance today.

Thomas Jefferson enjoyed a small one on his estate at "Monticello". Vistors can see this today. Picture size was small about 5" x 5". You can build a much larger size obscura with your kit and have a much brighter picture. Your Fresnel screen is a great improvement over the ground glass or opal glass of the old obscuras, giving you bright pictures clear to the edge of the screen. The best way to use your obscura is to point it out a window, focus the lens and view the outside scenes on the Fresnel screen. The darker the room, the more vivid the images appear. Focus the lens on a distant mountain scene, garden scenes, passing traffic, sunsets, sun, or moon. Swivel the obscura for a real panorama of natural color. With the equatorial base, you can view the sun, moon, eclipses, figure 3. When pointing the obscura at the sun, stop down the lens with a circular stop with about 1-1/4" diameter hole.

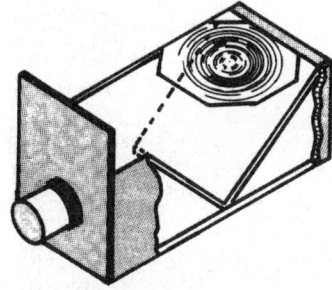

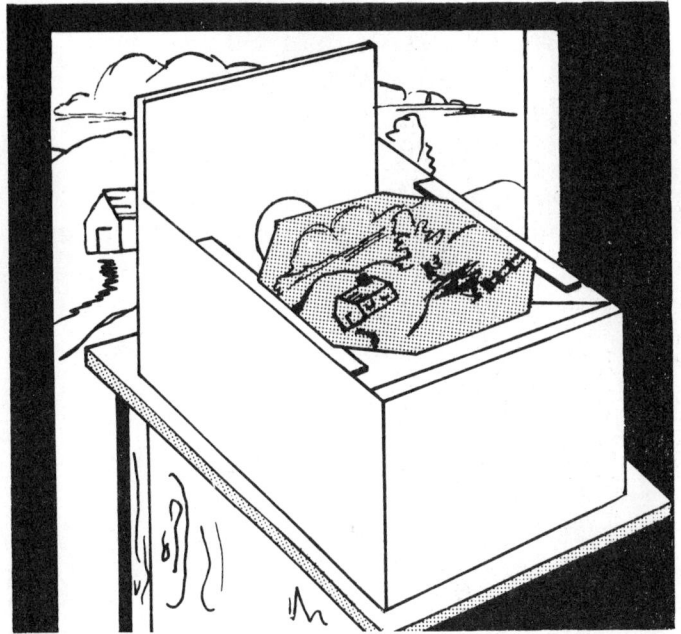

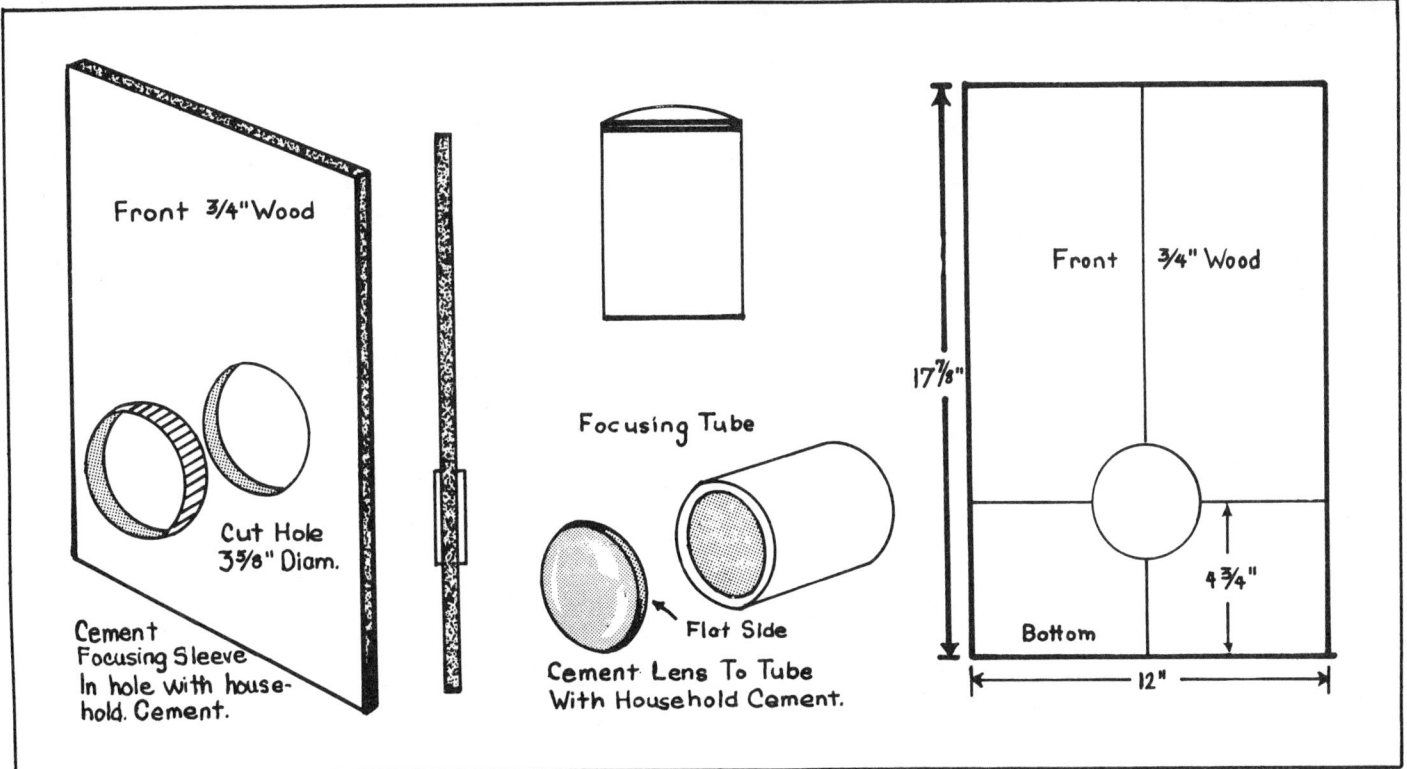

Front ¾"Wood

Cut Hole 3⅝" Diam.

Cement Focusing Sleeve In hole with household. Cement.

Focusing Tube

Flat Side

Cement Lens To Tube With Household Cement.

Front ¾" Wood

17⅞"

4¾"

Bottom

12"

Building the Obscura

Ordinary wood tools, hammer, saw, and drills is all that is necessary to build the model illustrated, but, heavy cardboard boxes can be converted also.

Before you start your obscura, purchase a mirror in the 5 & 10¢ store. Our mirror was framed and we removed the mirror from the frame. The mirror alone measured 11" x 13". Price for mirror was $1.50. If you cannot get the exact size, be sure to select one a little larger rather than a smaller one, then change the dimensions to fit your mirror. Largest dimension will be from top to bottom. Paint the inside of the box dead black; this cuts out glare from light colored surfaces and increases picture contrast. Use the Fresnel screen with the grooved side towards the lens. Your hardware store will cut you a piece of 12" x 12" double thick window glass to slide over your Fresnel screen; this will protect the screen from scratches, dust, etc. and provide a good surface for tracing or drawing.

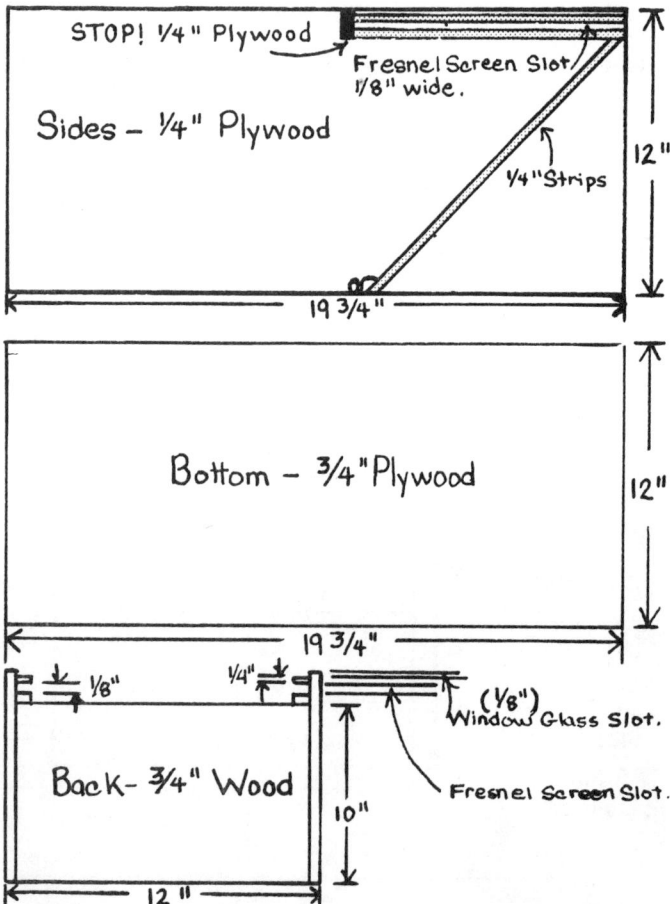

When cutting the Fresnel screen to a smaller size the middle must be used.

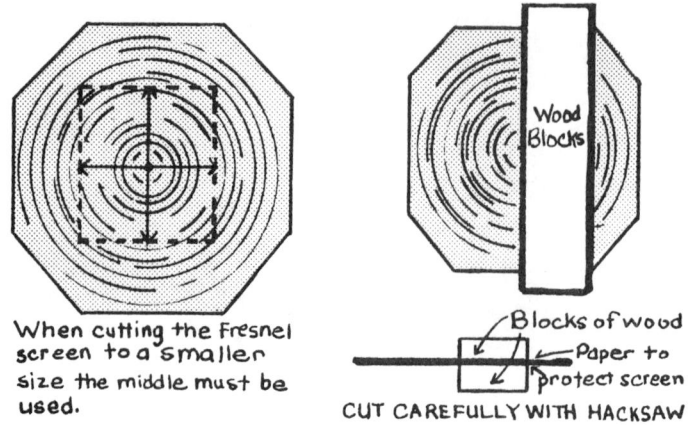

Blocks of wood
Paper to protect screen

CUT CAREFULLY WITH HACKSAW

Cutting the Fresnel Screen

If at anytime you want to cut the Fresnel screen to a smaller size, it is necessary to use the middle of the lens. For example, if you want a 5" x 5" size, measure 2-1/2" from both sides of center and top and bottom--see illustration.

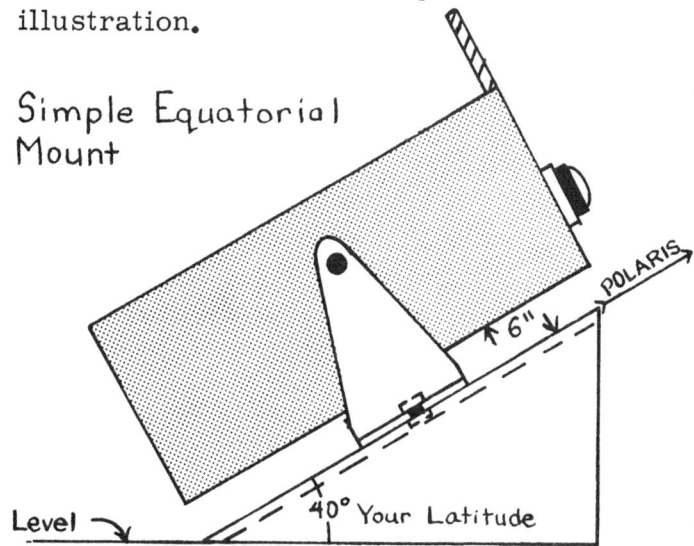

Simple Equatorial Mount

POLARIS

6"

Level

40° Your Latitude

Fork Mount - 3/4" Wood

Base - 3/4" Wood

Braces

Kit with Flexible Translucent Screen

All the dimensions for the Fresnel screen obscura are correct for this kit, but the flexible translucent screen will have to be framed. Make a light frame of wood strips and cement the edges of the translucent screen to the frame. The outer dimensions of the frame will be 12" x 12" to fit the obscura.

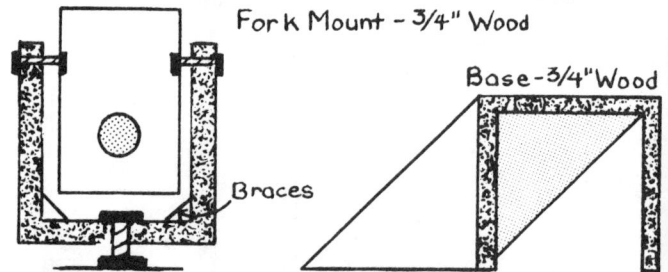

STOP! 1/4" Plywood

Fresnel Screen Slot, 1/8" wide.

Sides - 1/4" Plywood

1/4" Strips

12"

19 3/4"

Bottom - 3/4" Plywood

12"

19 3/4"

1/8"   1/4"

(1/8")
Window Glass Slot.

Back - 3/4" Wood

Fresnel Screen Slot.

10"

12"

LIQUID CRYSTAL

CAUTION

The Liquid Crystal solutions contain a chlorinated solvent and should be handled accordingly. Do not work in a closed or small area. Provide good ventilation. Exercise proper precautions.

Many plastic materials may be attacked by the solvent. Before applying the solution to any plastic surface, it is best to test a drop of the solution on a piece of scrap material or on an inconspicuous area. The black undercoat supplied is a water-soluble paint and if applied and dried without breaks will normally protect the base from the liquid crystal solvent.

Students or children should use these materials only under the supervision of an adult.

GENERAL Liquid crystal materials have the unique property of scattering light of various colors over a specific short temperature range, the color varying with temperature within the range. Since this process is reversible, and since the color change is very sensitive to small temperature changes, liquid crystals are useful for precise measurement of surface temperatures when they are applied as a thin coating. Conventional devices such as thermocouples and thermometers when used to measure the temperature of low mass materials often give erroneous results because their mass is relatively high. Liquid Crystals in coatings of about 25 micron thickness have a low mass. This feature coupled with a low specific heat provides a facility for measuring the temperature of low-mass materials without introducing large error due to heat absorption. The steady-state equilibrium of low heat systems are affected very little by the presence of the liquid crystal coating.

Hidden structural defects in materials can be detected as low or high temperature areas resulting from unusual heat conduction in the defect area. Operational hot spots in electronic systems can also be determined. Nonuniformity of radiant energy systems can

be detected by interposing in the energy beam a low-mass membrane coated with liquid crystals to measure the temperature at various positions. Electronic circuit, honeycomb panel, complex casting and biological tests are just a few of the areas in which liquid crystals have been used.

The iridescent colors exhibited by the liquid crystal materials are present over a very narrow temperature range, usually about 2 degrees Centigrade. Within this temperature range the materials exist in a state of molecular association that will scatter certain wavelengths of light. Upon cooling through this range, the sequence of colors will be blue, green, yellow, orange, red, then back to colorless. The blue color therefore indicates the higher temperature of the response range and the red color indicates the lower.

Since the colors observed are from a portion of incident light being scattered, they are best seen when observed against a black background. A practical procedure for many tests involves the application of a black coating as a prime to the surface prior to application of the liquid crystal coating.

PROCEDURE In using the liquid crystal coating, the normal procedure is to apply the liquid crystal solution by any convenient method such as brushing, flowing, dipping, or dropping solution onto the surface with an eye dropper. Best temperature indication is obtained if the coating is uniform, therefore some care in application is indicated. Under normal conditions, the solvent will evaporate in about 2 or 3 minutes leaving behind a coating of the clear, waxy liquid crystals. To provide accuracy of temperature measurement, the coating should be heated gently for a few minutes to drive off residual solvent. A low-mass coated part can be heated conveniently by holding close to an ordinary light bulb or other source of heat. Temperature indications can be made immediately thereafter.

Over a period of hours, it is possible for the liquid crystal coating to absorb chemical gases normally found in laboratory air. This will affect performance, and before re-use the coating should be heated gently to reactivate.

APPLICATION PROCEDURE There are three methods that are normally used for testing temperatures with the liquid crystal coating. In the first method, the coating is applied directly to the surface to be tested. The second involves the application of the black paint as a prime coat. In the third method the liquid crystal coating is applied to a sheet of thin black plastic film which is then held uncoated side in contact with the heated surface to be evaluated. With this method, the liquid crystals do not come in contact with the test surface.

1. direct application

In using the direct application method, the effect of the solvent upon the base should be considered as described above. If the surface to be tested is of dark color, the black prime coating is not necessary and the direct application is most convenient. If the base material is a light color, the indicating colors will be more difficult to observe. Usually some variation in the lighting of the part will facilitate observation.

When the liquid crystal coating is to be removed, a small amount of an organic solvent on a cloth will do the job. Lighter fluid is a convenient, but flammable solvent. If care is used, the liquid crystal material can be flowed off with solvent. The resulting solution can be re-used providing there has been no contamination.

2. black undercoat

Where the surface to be tested is a light color or subject to attack by the liquid crystal solution solvent, the black water base paint should be used as an undercoat or prime. Apply the black paint by any convenient method such as brushing, dipping, flowing, or spraying. For spraying, it may be necessary to thin the paint with a little water. About 10 to 15 minutes are normally required to air dry the black paint. Drying can be speeded up by the application of heat if desired. When the black coating is dry, the liquid crystal coating can be applied as described above under Direct Application. Removal of both coatings can be accomplished using first lighter fluid and then water.

3. indirect

The indirect method of use involves the application of liquid crystal coating to a sheet of thin black Mylar plastic which is then held against the surface to be tested. With this method there is less chance of surface contamination problems and the Mylar membrane can be easily re-used on other or succeeding parts. If the surface to be measured is not flat, usually narrow strips of the coated Mylar can be held to conform to surface curvature. When flat surfaces are involved, the wooden embroidery hoop is a convenient holder for the plastic. To mount the plastic, first adjust the thumb screw on the outer hoop to provide a snug fit with the inner hoop. Lay the smaller hoop on a flat surface. Lay a 5" x 5" sheet of the black Mylar glossy side down over the inner hoop so that plastic is stretched tight and free of wrinkles. Turn the assembly over, then the liquid crystal solution should be applied with an eye dropper to the inside (glossy side) of the plastic. Five or ten drops applied quickly while the hoop is flat usually will produce a uniform coating. After the coating has air dried a few minutes, the Mylar can be heated gently by placing it near a light bulb for a few seconds to drive off residual solvents.

TEMPERATURE SELECTION

Three liquid crystal solutions are supplied in this Kit.

These can be mixed to obtain the response temperature range desired.
Increasing the amount of the VL-401-R in the mixture RAISES the response temperature. Increasing the amount of the VL-401-L in the mixture LOWERS the response temperature. The VL-401-B broadens the response range from about 3 degrees Centigrade to as much as 10 to 15 degrees. The broadener also will shift the response range downward so its use will require an increased amount of the VL-401-R.

A mixing graph guide is supplied which will permit selection of any temperature range desired between about 18 to 71 degrees Centigrade. These upper and lower limits will vary slightly according to the lot numbers of the VL-401-L and VL-401-R solutions. Either of these solutions may be used by itself.

The mixing graph is a plot of percent of VL-401-R and percent of VL-401-L versus temperature in degrees Centigrade. Locate the temperature range desired on the temperature scale. Trace across this line to the point that the line intersects the curve. Trace down to the percentage scale and read percentage values. As a typical example, assume the temperature range of 30.5° to 32.5° is desired. On the graph these values correspond to 50% VL-401-R and 50% VL-401-L. Weight measurements or volume measurements may be used. Mixing 5 parts of VL-401-R and 5 parts of VL-401-L will result in a coating with a range of 30.5° to 32.5° C. When measuring temperatures with this coating, a red color indicates 30.5° C., a green color 31° C., and a blue color 32.5° C. Slight corrections or adjustments can be made. On the mixing chart in this Kit the values may vary slightly from the example. The response range of each lot of solutions will vary slightly, and the mixing graph supplied matches the solutions in this Kit.

When added to mixtures of the VL-401-R and VL-401-L solutions, the broadener VL-401-B will broaden the response temperature range and at the same time lower it. Therefore, its effect must be anticipated prior to mixing in order to compensate for the lowering.

In the use of the broadener, only general guidelines can be supplied, and some experimentation may be necessary to achieve the desired result. After addition of the broadener, adjustment of the response range can be made by adding the appropriate raising or lowering solution.

Take special care to assure that the bottles of solutions are kept tightly closed. A small evaporation of solvent will change the concentration of the solution in which case the mixing graph will not apply accurately. In the event that this does occur, corrections can be made by the addition of small quantities of the appropriate raising or lowering solutions.

The materials in this Kit are supplied for experimental purposes and no rights are granted under patents which may exist. The materials in this Kit are not believed to be a health hazard providing adequate precautions are taken in exposure to the chlorinated solvents. Toxicity of other components has not been fully investigated—— due caution should be exercised. F.D.A. approval has not been sought for use of these materials in direct contact with the skin.

The procedures and methods outlined here are meant only as a guide. Each testing situation is different and may require modifications for best results.

EXPERIMENTS

The following experiments are designed to demonstrate heat and thermal principles. For children and students, these experiments should be performed only under the supervision of an adult. OBSERVE THE VENTILATION PRECAUTIONS DESCRIBED IN THE INSTRUCTIONS.

While performing these tests, keep in mind that the liquid crystals (in their temperature range) change colors in the following sequence as the temperature is raised: red to orange to yellow to green to blue. The direction is easy to memorize since the colors are the opposite of our normal color-temperature association. While we usually think of red meaning hot, with liquid crystals it means cool. We usually associate blue with cool, with liquid crystals it means hot. Remember also that the change of colors is gradual, and therefore many in-between colors can be observed.

The experiments below are grouped according to the Liquid Crystal mixture that must be prepared. It is suggested that all of the experiments using the same Liquid Crystal mix be performed together to conserve materials and to avoid repeated preparation of the same mix. For example, when a "Red at Room Temperature" hoop is prepared, perform all experiments designed to use this preparation before going to the others.

The Liquid Crystals are semi-liquid, and dirt and dust from the air can stick to them and occasionally interfere with color observations. When the hoop is not being used, cover it with a piece of cardboard to keep it clean.

PREPARATION OF ROOM TEMPERATURE OPERATING LIQUID CRYSTAL MIX

Using any available thermometer, measure the room temperature. This should also be the temperature of the work surface on which you plan to work. Using a temperature conversion scale, convert the temperature reading obtained from degrees Fahrenheit to degrees Centigrade.

To prepare a mix for coatings which are "Red at Room Temperature", first locate the room temperature value on the temperature scale of the Mixing Graph. Follow this line across to the intersection with the curve marked "RED". From this intersection follow a line down to the mixture scale. Read the percentages of VL-401-R and VL-401-L solution required for the temperature used. (Use the curve marked "BLUE" to prepare the "Blue at Room Temperature" coating.)

Prepare a mixture of the VL-401-R and VL-401-L solution using the indicated percentages. This can conveniently be done by counting drops from an eye dropper. Since room temperature is normally in the 21° to 24° C(70° to 5° F) range, a room-temperature mix would require about 16 drops (80%) VL-401-L solution and about 4 drops VL-401-R solution. Small additions to the mixture can be made for minor adjustments up or down. The drop that falls from the

small end of a flat toothpick held against the tip of an eye dropper is approximately one-half the size of the normal drop.

Mount a piece of the black plastic in the hoop as outlined in the instructions. Be sure shiny side is toward inside of hoop.

Place this assembly flat on work table with shiny side of plastic up. Using an eye dropper, quickly drop 5 or 10 drops of the Liquid Crystal mix inside the hoop onto the center of the black plastic. If the solution does not flow out to give fairly large area of coverage, the hoop can be tipped slightly back and forth. With hoop flat allow the solution to dry for 2 or 3 minutes. Then warm it dry by holding the hoop close to a light bulb. The hoop is then ready for use.

PREPARATION OF 25 TO 35°C (77—95°F) BROAD RANGE LIQUID CRYSTAL MIX

The following formula will produce a mix for approximately 25° to 35°C coatings:
 9 parts VL-401-L Liquid Crystal Solution
 20 parts VL-401-R Liquid Crystal Solution
 5 parts VL-401-B Liquid Crystal Solution

Parts by weight or volume can be used. Counting drops from an eyedropper is convenient and economical.

Mount a piece of the black plastic in the hoop as outlined in the Instructions. Be sure shiny side of plastic is toward inside of hoop.

Place this assembly flat on work table with shiny side of plastic up. Using an eyedropper, quickly drop 5 or 10 drops of the Liquid Crystal Mix inside the hoop onto the center of the black plastic. If the solution does not flow out to give a fairly large area of coverage, the hoop can be tipped slightly back and forth. With hoop flat, allow the solution to dry for 2 or 3 minutes. Then warm it dry by holding the hoop close to a light bulb. The hoop is then ready for use.

THERMAL FINGERPRINT

(Use "Red at Room Temperature" Hoop)

This experiment demonstrates the high sensitivity of Liquid Crystals to temperature.

PROCEDURE:
1. Press a fingertip against a desk top, table top, book, or other nonmetallic surface for five (5) seconds.

2. Immediately after removing fingertip, place bottom of the coated black plastic upon the area.

3. The spot which had been pressed by fingertip will show as a higher temperature than surrounding area, as a result of heat left by the fingertip. Under normal test conditions, the color in the test area will change from the initial red, through the spectrum to blue or black indicating the higher temperature.

76

WARM AIR RISES

(Use both "Red at Room Temperature" and "Blue at Room Temperature" Hoops)

In this experiment it can be shown that warm air rises. When air is warmed, it expands and becomes less dense. Conversely, cool air contracts, becomes more dense and therefore falls. In a room that has still air, it can be shown that there will be several degrees temperature difference between floor and ceiling.

PROCEDURE:
1. Gradually lower the "Blue" hoop from table top height toward the floor.

2. Observe the gradual change to cooler indicating colors (green, yellow, orange, red).

3. Gradually elevate the "Red" hoop from table top height toward the ceiling.

4. Observe the gradual change to warmer indicating colors (orange, yellow, green, blue).

5. From the mixing chart knowing the mixtures used, estimate the temperature difference between the floor air and ceiling air.

6. In a similar manner, measure and estimate the temperature difference between various rooms, and locations within rooms.

HEAT GENERATED BY SURFACE FRICTION

(Use "Red at Room Temperature" Hoop)

PROCEDURE:
1. Rub a pencil eraser several quick strokes on the surface of a magazine, piece of cardboard, or other similar material.

2. Immediately, place the bottom side of the "Red at Room Temperature" hoop upon the rubbed surface.

3. Note that the friction of the rubbing has generated heat as indicated by the change of the Liquid Crystal color from red to blue color.

4. Determine how few strokes are necessary to produce enough heat to be detected.

HEAT GENERATED BY INTERNAL MOLECULAR FRICTION

(Use "Red at Room Temperature" Hoop)

Additional Materials Required:
Coat hanger or similar wire.
Large rubber band.

PROCEDURE: (A)
1. Obtain an old coat hanger or similar piece of wire.

2. Bend it back and forth sharply a few times.

3. Immediately place the wire against the bottom of the room-temperature hoop (as prepared above).

4. Note that where the bending took place in the wire that the temperature has risen as indicated by the Liquid Crystal color change from red through orange, green, to blue or black.

5. Repeat on separate section of wire. How few times can wire be bent and still generate a detectable temperature change?

Bending of the wire produces forced movement of the atoms of the metal against one another. This internal friction generates heat similar to the rubbing of two objects together.

PROCEDURE: (B)
1. Loop one end of the large rubber band over the "thumb screw" of the hoop.

2. Stretch it across the bottom of the hoop so that it is in contact with the black plastic.

3. While maintaining it in contact with the black plastic, quickly stretch it to about twice its length.

4. Immediately observe any color change of the liquid crystal coating on the top side.

5. Heat generated by the internal molecular friction when rubber band is stretched will show in Liquid Crystals by changing them to higher temperature colors (toward blue).

6. Allow the rubber band to contract quickly. Observe color change.

7. Is the process reversible?

HEAT OF SOLUTION

(Use "Blue at Room Temperature" Hoop)

When certain chemicals are dissolved in water, heat may be generated in the dissolving process. The heat generated will cause the temperature to rise. This is called the "Heat of Solution". There are certain chemicals which have a negative "Heat of Solution". Upon dissolving, these will absorb heat energy causing the solution to cool below original temperature.

Additional Materials Required:
One 4-oz. or other small drinking glass.
Baking Soda.
One teaspoon.

PROCEDURE:
1. Put 2 ounces of water in the small drinking glass. Allow this glass of water, a teaspoon, and the baking soda to come to room temperature by standing on work surface. The temperature of the water can be checked by touching the bottom of the glass to the bottom of "Blue at Room Temperature" hoop that has been prepared. When little or no color

change of the Liquid Crystals occurs, proceed to next step (#2).

2. Add the teaspoonful of baking soda to the water and stir rapidly for a few seconds.

3. When most of the baking soda has dissolved, touch the bottom of the glass to the bottom of the "Blue at Room Temperature" hoop.

4. Observe color change.

5. Does baking soda have a positive or negative "Heat of Solution"?

COOLING EFFECT OF EVAPORATING LIQUID

(Use "Blue at Room Temperature" Hoop)

Evaporating liquids absorb heat and therefore have a cooling effect upon surroundings. This absorbed heat energy is called "Latent Heat of Vaporization". The quantity of heat energy involved in this process is dependent upon the nature of the evaporating solvent and the quantity evaporated. The process is reversible, and the same quantity of heat energy is released when the vapor is condensed back to the liquid state.

PROCEDURE:
1. Allow one of the bottles of Liquid Crystal Solution and the "Blue at Room Temperature" hoop to remain close together for 15 minutes so they are at the same temperature.

2. Using a toothpick or eyedropper which has been wet with the Liquid Crystal Solution, apply a small amount of the solution to the back of the hoop.

3. Observe the immediate change of color at the wet area to cooler colors.

4. The solvent in the Liquid Crystal Solution is a fast evaporating organic solvent and the cooling effect of its evaporation is very fast. Water may be used as a substitute. The cooling effect of the evaporating water can be accelerated by fanning or blowing on the wet area to speed evaporation.

VARIATION IN TEMPERATURE OF FINGERS

(Use "25°to 35°C Hoop")

This experiment can show that different people frequently have fingers at varying temperatures, and that some people have both cool and warm fingers.

PROCEDURE:
1. Using the "25°to 35°C" hoop which was prepared above, place fingertips one at a time on the bottom of hoop. Observe color reached. A blue or black color is most frequently observed. Occasionally color will not elevate above yellow or green indicating cooler than normal finger temperature.

2. Check various other people.

3. Place fingertips on ice cube for a few seconds. Recheck temperature.

4. Determine length of time for temperature to return to normal.

CONVERSION OF LIGHT ENERGY TO HEAT ENERGY

(Use "25°to 35°C Hoop")

These experiments show that when light energy is absorbed by a black substance, that the light is transformed into heat energy which raises the temperature of the absorbing material. These experiments are best performed when room temperature is between 77° and 86° F (25° to 30°).

Additional Materials Required:
One - Sheet of White Paper (8-1/2" x 11")
One - Magnifying Glass or Lens.
One - Lamp with Regular 100 or 60 watt bulb.

Experiment A

1. Using the black paint and brush provided, paint an "X" or other letter in the center of the white sheet of paper. Allow the paint to dry.

2. Place the sheet of paper white side against the bottom of the "25°to 35°" hoop which was prepared above. The "X" should be away from hoop. Hold the assembly approximately 8 inches from the lighted 100 watt bulb so that the light falls on the "X" (a little closer for a 60 watt bulb).

   In about 5 seconds the pattern of the "X" will appear as a different color in the Liquid Crystal coating, indicating a higher temperature than the white areas of the paper.

3. The black painted "X", as an absorber of light converts the light to heat energy with the result that the temperature in the black area rises. The white paper as a non-absorber, reflects the light energy and remains cooler.

4. Remove the paper for the experiment below.

Experiment B

1. Hold the hoop about 3 feet from a lighted 100 watt bulb. At this distance the light striking the black plastic should not change the Liquid Crystals' color.

2. Hold the magnifying glass between the bulb and the hoop at a position which will focus an image of the bulb on the black plastic. Note that where the image is reproduced that the temperature immediately rises as evidence by immediate color change.

3. Move the magnifier so that image moves its position on black plastic.

4. Observe that where the light energy is received by the black plastic that the temperature immediately rises.

5. In this experiment the black plastic acts as the light absorber. As the quantity of light is increased (where the light is focused), the temperature rises higher.

HEAT CONDUCTION THROUGH METAL

(Use "25°to 35°C Hoop")

Additional Material Required:
Two similar 2' lengths of wire of different metals, such as coat hanger wire and bare copper wire of same diameter.

Container of hot water.

When one end of a material is heated and the other end is cooled, heat flows from the hot end to the cool end. The rate at which heat flows depends on the temperature difference between ends. The greater the difference, the greater the rate of heat flow. The rate of heat flow also depends upon the thermal conductivity of the material. Aluminum and copper possess good electrical conductivity, while the conductivity of iron and steel is less.

When one end of an uninsulated wire or bar of metal is heated and the other is cooled or at room temperature, the temperature will be progressively higher going from the cool to the warm ends.

PROCEDURE:

1. Stand one end of each wire in a container (such as one or two quart pan) of hot water. Allow top ends to lean against some vertical support.

2. Allow a few minutes for the wires to reach equilibrum.

3. Starting at the unheated end, gradually slide the "25° to 35°C" hoop down the bar until the complete range of colors (red through blue) is observed on each wire.

4. Note the distance from red to blue on each wire.

5. Note which wire shows the colors closest to the cool end.

6. Which wire is the best conductor of heat?

CRYSTALLIZING PAINT

CAUTION: Crystallizing Paints are not to be taken internally. They are extremely flammable and should not be used near open flame. For a complete list of precautions, see the label on the bottle.

General Instructions for Use: Crystallizing Paints can be applied to glass, wood, metal, ceramics, and most plastics. The paints can be applied by brush or can be poured from the bottle directly onto the surface to be coated. Crystallizing Paints will be dry to the touch after one hour, but should be allowed to dry completely for 24 hours. When completely dry, the paints are permanent under normal indoor conditions. The paint crystals can be scraped off or removed with hot, soapy water. Since the solvents in the paint may be harmful to some plastics, the paints should be tested on a non-critical section of the surface before use. Because the strong solvents in the paints will dissolve glue used in brushes, all brushes should be washed gently and completely with warm soapy water immediately after use. The use of expensive brushes is not recommended. (See our No. P-70,348 for a set of 144 inexpensive camel hair brushes.)

Uses: Crystallizing Paints have numerous artistic, decorative, and functional uses. Doors, shelves, and even glass aquarium walls (not plastic aquariums) can be decorated with layers of Crystallizing Paints (Figure 1). Brush on Crystallizing Paints for dramatic effects on tooled copper plaques. Abstract designs can be painted on vases, lamps, jewelry, bottles, etc. (Figure 2). Put holiday trimmings on Christmas balls and shiny wrapping paper. For privacy,

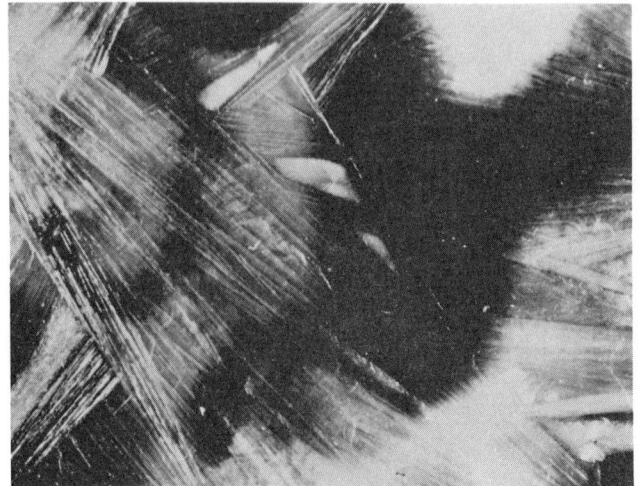

FIGURE 2

use an opaque layer of Crystallizing Paints on windows (Figure 3). Use layers of Crystallizing Paints on worn radios, cabinets, and other household objects to create a new surface (Figure 4).

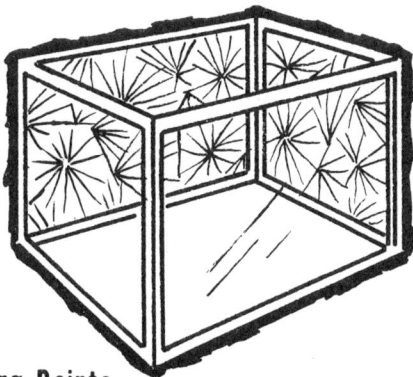

FIGURE 1

Crystallizing Paints
on the walls of aquariums

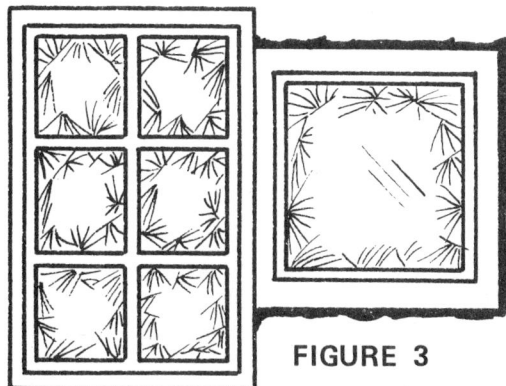

Crystallizing
Paints
on windows

FIGURE 3

FIGURE 4

Old surfaces can
be "revived" with
Crystallizing Paints

Our Crystallizing Paints are especially useful for creating psychedelic slides, color wheels, and other special effects accessories. Slides that have the qualities of professional, "organic" crystal slides can be created easily with this product. Required are 2" x 2" glass slides (available at most photo supply stores) and Crystallizing Paints. To prepare a slide, first clean the slide thoroughly, then paint or pour on the desired colors. As the slide dries, fascinating crystal patterns will form which, when projected by any slide projector, will rival in texture and patterns the most expensive professionally prepared slides. Some of the most interesting effects are a result of mixing two or more colors, and especially by placing two drops of different colors next to each other on the slide so that their borders touch. This will result in a "marbled" or "fringed" effect when two colors intermix. Eyedroppers are especially useful for placing different colors on top of, or next to, each other. Several other factors affect the type of pattern which finally results:

Thickness: In general, the thicker the layer of paint, the larger the crystals, and crystal patterns; but layers too thick dry very slowly and are not suitable for projection.

Temperature: If the slides are heated while they are drying, they will crystallize more slowly. The resulting patterns will not be as colorful, and the intermixing of two or more colors will be retarded.

Thinning (using solvents): Crystallizing Paints can be thinned with organic solvents such as methyl-ethyl-ketone or our No. 71,081 Thinner. The resulting slides are paler and more translucent.

Color Wheels: Spectacular color wheels for the Edmund Visual Effects Projector (Stock No. 71,057) can be prepared using Crystallizing Paints and blank discs for making color wheels (No. P-71,087).

Additional Techniques: The texture of the slides and color wheels can be varied. For example, putting two slides together after the paint has been applied and then slowly separating them results in a pattern with hundreds of tiny "arms". Dabbing the slide with a cloth or cigarette filter before it dries, results in a variety of unique patterns. Or, place a piece of screen or gauze on the slide until the paint is almost dry and then remove it. Additional hints for preparing all types of slides for projection can be found in Edmund's Unique Lighting Handbook, No. 9100.

PUMP AND FOUNTAINS

Moving water has fascinated man for centuries. The undulating action of ocean waves, a free running stream, and even the rain, have long been regarded as beautiful, soothing experiences. In the past, small fountain equipment has been nonexistent, and early models were extremely expensive. But now, you can re-create this natural beauty in your own home.

Fountains are not only pretty, they are healthful. Most homes are drier than desert air, especially in winter. This arid atmosphere causes mucous membranes to dry out, allowing germs that cause flu and colds to easily attack people susceptible to such ailments. Even our furniture is adversely affected by the dryness of our rooms. A small fountain placed in such areas not only helps to relieve these conditions by adding humidity to the air, but will also help to clean the air by removing some of the dust and smoke.

This pump is not restricted to fountain use only, but can be used in the construction of tabletop waterfalls by attaching a plastic tube over the "adapter insert" to carry the water to the top of the "fall". Capacity is two quarts per minute with a rise of 5", and one pint per minute at a rise of 10". It can also be used to make a small grist or saw mill for model train layouts. In science projects it can be used to make hydroelectric stations, human circulatory system models, water aeration and filtration, to name only a few. Although we do not offer instructions on these projects, information can be found in school science books and most encyclopedias.

NOTE: THIS IS NOT A SUBMERSIBLE PUMP. Do not place the pump in water. For information on use see paragraph entitled "Fountain Assembly". This pump is of unique design. The intake and exit of water is through the same opening. It has only one moving part, never needs oil, has a long life, and runs quietly. The electric power requirement is 110 volts, AC, 10 watts (ordinary house current). The pump circulates approximately 120 quarts per hour and is recommended for use with water only. However, liquid food coloring and perfume may be added to the water if desired. The danger of electric shock has been reduced by placing the contacts where they will not come in contact with the water and cannot be touched.

DO NOT OPERATE PUMP DRY. The pump can be used out-of-doors without danger from freezing, since as long as the pump is in operation, the small amount of heat generated by the pump will prevent freeze-ups. If the electricity is turned off in cold weather, drain the pump and fountain. Alcohol or anti-freeze may be added to the outdoor fountain in the winter to prevent freezing of the main body of water. However, we do not recommend this procedure since these chemicals present a hazard to birds and animals. Outdoor wire, also referred to as underground wire, should be used in this type of installation.

BOWL OR CONTAINER

In addition to your pump, you will need a bowl or container for the water supply. This can be of any shape (round, square, or free-form) and of any material (such as plastic, glass, cement, ceramic, wood, or rustproof metal) with a minimum diameter of 12" and a depth of 2-1/2" to 4". The center thickness of the container should

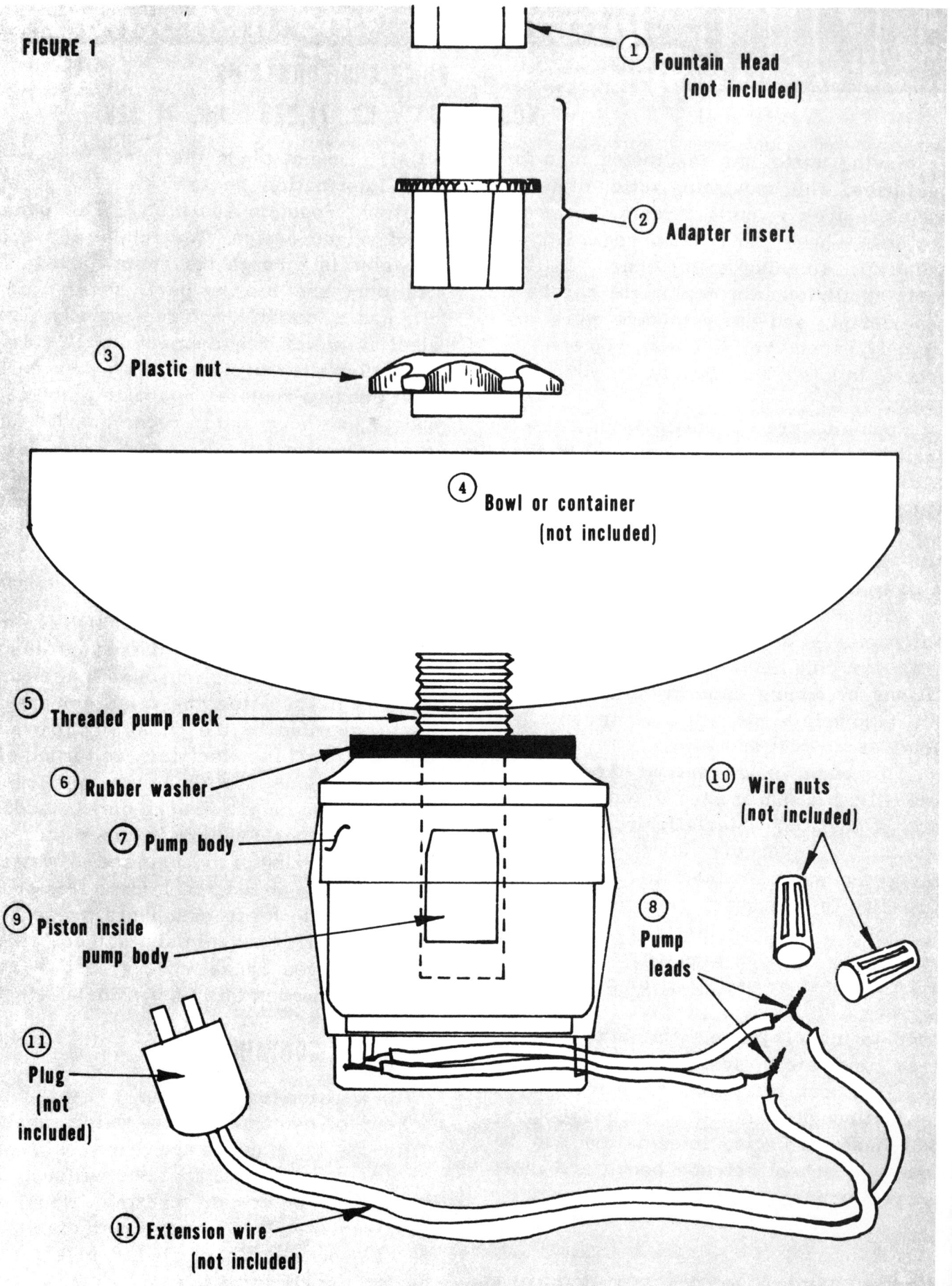

82

FIGURE 1

1. Fountain Head (not included)

2. Adapter insert

3. Plastic nut

4. Bowl or container (not included)

5. Threaded pump neck

6. Rubber washer

7. Pump body

9. Piston inside pump body

10. Wire nuts (not included)

8. Pump leads

11. Plug (not included)

11. Extension wire (not included)

not exceed 1/4" for normal installation; however, thicknesses up to 1/2" may be tolerated by inverting the plastic nut (Figure 1, No. 3). Drill a 7/8" diameter hole in the exact center of the container to accept the neck of your pump. For glass and ceramic bowl, this hole can be made with a ceramic drill bit obtained at most hardware stores, or by placing a 2" long, 7/8" diameter hardwood dowel stick or copper tube in the chuck of the drill press for use as a grinding rod, and slowly grinding through the bottom of the container, using a slurry of water and No. 80 alundum applied to the end of the rod as a cutting agent. No. 80 alundum is available in a 16-oz. shaker top can from Edmund Scientific Company under Stock No. 40,022. Do not attempt to force the cutting tool through the bottom of the container. Exerting undue force will only result in damage to the cutting tool and the container. For those who intend to make their own ceramic containers, it is suggested that they mold a 1" hole in a piece of test clay to determine its shrink rate during firing. The neck of the pump should pass through the hole with a minumum of clearance. In the case of wooden bowls, the hole may be made by using a wood auger bit, or by drawing a circle of the correct diameter in the center of the bowl and drilling a hole anywhere on the periphery of the drawn circle. The larger hole may then be cut out by using a coping or jig saw. If a metal container is to be used, draw a circle in the center of the bowl with a scriber or sharp nail. By drilling a series of small overlapping holes along this line the center material can be removed. The jagged inside diameter of this hole is then filed smooth with a metal file.

THE BASE

A hollow base will be required to house the body of the pump and act as a stand for the bowl. This base can be made from a matching or contrasting material and may be any shape and size desired, but a minimum height of 2" is required to properly house the pump body. An opening should be provided somewhere in the base to permit the electric cord to pass through. Attach the base to the underside of the container with an epoxy cement, being careful to center the two pieces so the container will sit level. If you are making your own ceramic container, the container and base may be made in one piece if desired.

FOUNTAIN HEADS

Each fountain head utilizes a plastic "adapter insert" (Figure 1, No. 2) which must be used. It is this part that permits the water to enter and exit through the same opening. Fountain heads are two basic types. One sprays water up into graceful arcs, while the other pumps the water to a given height from which it cascades back into the bowl. Fountain heads are available through our catalog or you can make your own from the vast variety of statuary on the market. The actual pumping distance should not exceed 10" in height. The nine-jet brass fountain head, Stock No. 71,226, can be adjusted to give the desired spray pattern by bending the jets. This should be done carefully, and by hand, rather than with tools which may crush the soft brass tubing.

FOUNTAIN ASSEMBLY (INDOORS)

Required parts are pump, bowl, base, tube of water-repellent sealer (bathtub sealer), insulated wire of desired length with a plug, and two wire-nuts. Attach your extension wire to the pump leads (Figure 1, No. 8). These can be secured by soldering or attached with wire-nuts. The connections should be insulated with plastic electrical tape. Remove the adapter insert (Figure 1, No. 2) by pulling it out with your fingers; no tools needed. Remove the plastic nut (Figure 1, No. 3) by turning to the left. Insert the threaded neck (Figure 1, No. 5) of pump into the

84

hole in the bottom of the bowl. NOTE: pump body (Figure 1, No. 7) is placed under the bowl. Run a thin bead of water-repellent sealer around the pump neck where it meets the inside of the bowl and allow to dry overnight. When the sealer is dry, replace plastic nut (Figure 1, No. 3) and tighten by hand. The rubber washer (Figure 1, No. 6) and sealer will prevent leakage. Replace adapter insert (Figure 1, No. 2) large end down. Place your fountain head in position by slipping the appropriate end into the adapter insert (See Figure 2). Fill the fountain with water to within 1" of the bowl top. The plastic adapter insert must be completely covered with water. However, in the case of deep containers, do not completely submerge your fountain head. Plug the electric cord from the fountain into a wall-socket, and your fountain will begin immediate operation. DO NOT RUN PUMP WITHOUT WATER.

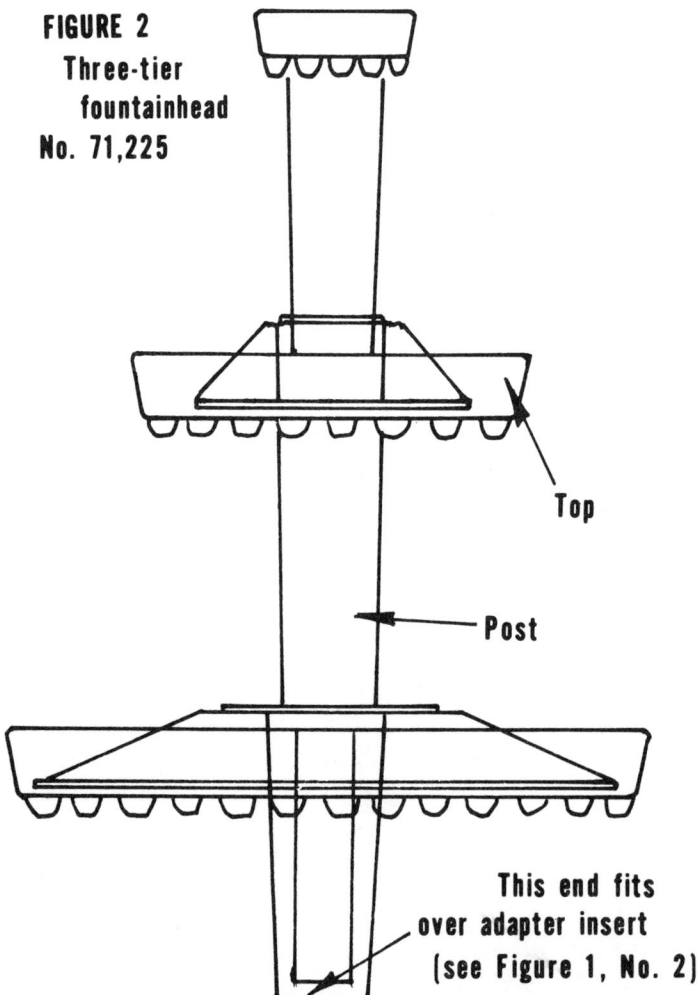

FIGURE 3

Paper clip (not included)

Pull up

Piston inside pump (see Figure 1, No. 9)

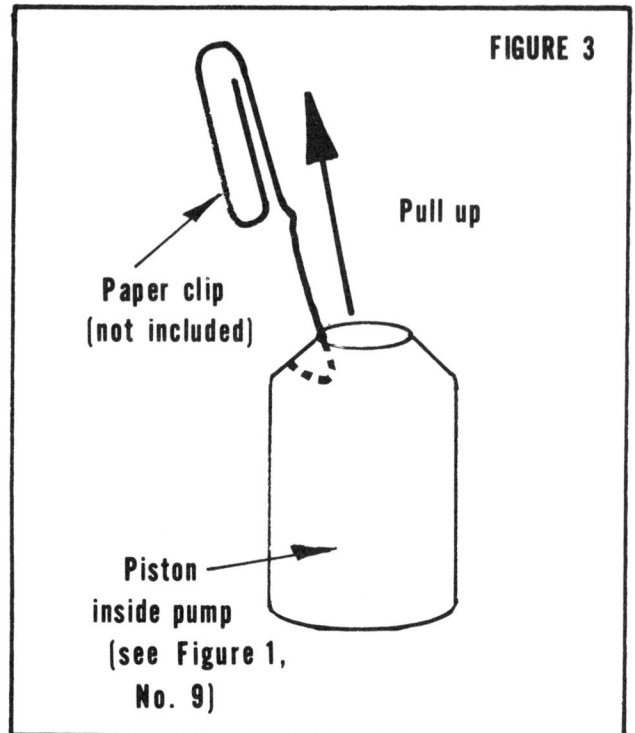

**FIGURE 2
Three-tier fountainhead
No. 71,225**

Top

Post

This end fits over adapter insert (see Figure 1, No. 2)

FOUNTAIN MAINTENANCE

Under average conditions, approximately one quart of water per day will evaporate from your fountain. It is very important that you maintain a full fountain. Since your fountain will remove some of the smoke and dust from the air, it is recommended that the fountain be emptied, cleaned, and fresh water replaced on a weekly basis. Do not submerge the entire unit in water when washing; the pump body (Figure 1, No. 7) is not waterproof. The addition of two tablespoons of vinegar to the water and operating the fountain for one hour will help dislodge the chemicals and minerals which may have collected in the bottom and around the waterline area of the container. If foreign matter should jam the piston (Figure 1, No. 9) inside the pump, the piston may be easily removed for cleaning by bending the end of a paper clip into a hook and inserting it down the throat of the motor into the small hole in top of the piston and pulling the piston out (Figure 3). After cleaning, the piston must be returned to its original position (small hole at top).

THE GREAT PYRAMID

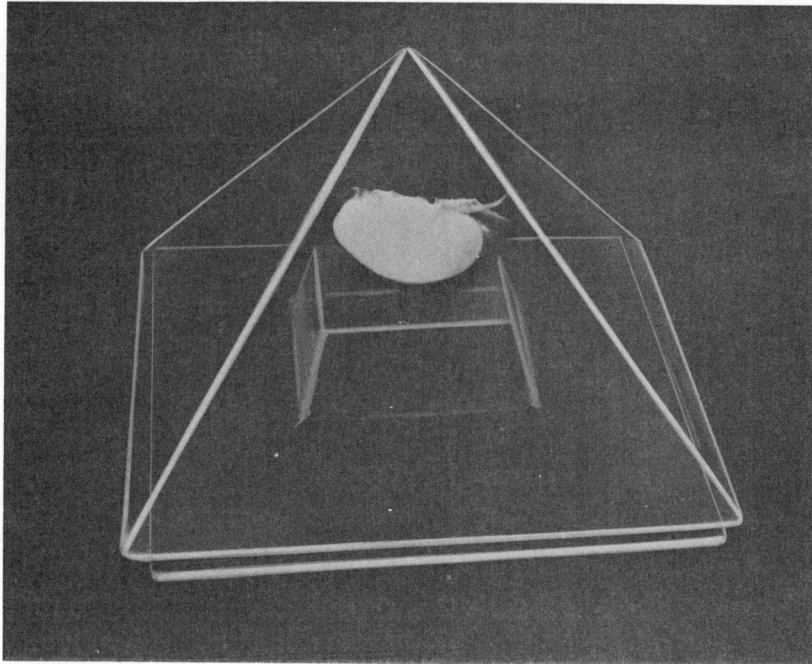

We have read many articles concerning the power of the pyramids. Things like the great mummy mystery and razor blade sharpening under pyramids led us to develop an interest in this subject. The Book, "Psychic Discoveries Behind the Iron Curtain" by Ostrander and Schroeder brought forth many interesting theories on this subject. While behind the Iron Curtain they discovered many families in Czechoslovakia were using pyramids in their homes. Upon questioning they received reports on the mysterious power of these forms. We feel many questions on the true power of these forms still remain unanswered. Many people have reported both positive and negative results with their experiments.

As we are all aware archaeological findings have shown amazing results of human mummified bodies. It also was very interesting that these bodies were for the most part located in chambers 1/3 of the height of the pyramid. Not only were the prepared bodies of the Pharoahs mummified but also many other living things. It seemed that animal carcasses did not decay but were, in fact, also dehydrated. Much of this strange phenomena was supposedly a result of the shape of the pyramid and the resonating energy from the apex of the pyramid. The Edmund Pyramid (No. 71,817) is built to the same geometric dimensions as the great pyramid including the exact angle of slope of 51 degrees.

The size of a pyramid is not important, but the geometric shape is critical. If we were to cut 4 isosceles triangles each measuring: Height 6", Base 9.4248", Sides 8.9676", Platform Height 1.9998", we would have a pyramid identical to the ancient ones used by the Egyptians. This also gives us the critical 51 degree slope needed. The platform must be 1/3 the height of the pyramid.

Setting Up for Experiments

Pick an area away from disturbing electrical interference such as radio or television. One face of the pyramid should face magnetic north, the same direction the Great Pyramid faced. To find magnetic north a compass would be helpful. When placing an object on the platform always keep the objects longest axis centered on the North-South axis.

Dehydration and Preservation

Generally the time needed to dehydrate depends on the moisture content and physical size of the specimen. Once begun, the subject should not be disturbed or damage may result. Once dehydration is completed a new specimen may be placed on the platform after removing the old one. Flowers, fish, and insects are excellent for experimentation.

Razor Blades

It is believed that the resonate cavity inside the pyramid vibrates the edges of a razor blade thus causing a sharpening of a dull blade. The blade should also be placed with the North-South axis along the longest axis of the object. First try 7-10 days of pyramid exposure before testing the blade. A blade of extreme dullness may take several months to sharpen. In excess of 50 shaves have been reported by this resharpening process.

Other Experiments

We suggest that other experiments be tried. Seed exposure to the pyramid may improve vegetable growing. Living objects (ants or insects), milk, cheese, and wine, may also show interesting results. Pin floating on water, coffee, tobacco freshening,....anything where aging is involved bears your investigation.

Note: A control makes your experiment more scientific (e.g. If you're testing meat rot retardation, put one hot dog in the pyramid, another in a plain cardboard box, and another completely exposed on a counter or shelf. Note the differences. On all your experiments use a control to see just what effect the pyramid had, if any.).

OPTICAL ILLUSIONS

HISTORICAL

Starting in the Mid-1800's the subject of optical illusions attracted a great deal of attention from many leading scholars of that period. Well known scientists including Zollner, Jastrow, Poggendorf, Wundt, Hering, and Helmholtz contributed to the subject of illusions and their scientific explanations.

Many explanations were contradictory and (strangely enough) the scientists nearly always failed to recognize illusions as being something more than laboratory curiosities. The fact that they were the outward expressions of human perception and effected judgement in many scientific areas was a factor rarely considered by these learned men.

With the coming of the twentieth century, interest in illusions had almost disappeared; they could be found only in collections of puzzles and children's books.

In the 1920's the field of transactual psychology was born. Giants like Adelbert Ames devoted their lifetimes to the study of visual perception. He, and others were convinced that the key to understanding human behavior was contained within the perceptual process. Ames work was little known outside the scholastic community until "The Morning Notes of Adelbert Ames, Jr." was published in 1960. Since then there has been a general revival of interest in the subject of illusions, awareness and perception. Many of the concepts of the classic illusions have been used and expanded upon by contemporary pop artists and illustrators.

It is hoped that this collection of illusions (some classic, some newer), will be of interest to the artist, the scientist and the student.

HATCHED LINE ILLUSIONS

This family of illusions is interesting because it is quite old and is the one which triggered the interest in optical illusions in the late 1800's.

The earliest of these, the Zollner Illusion was first published in 1860. (see figure A)

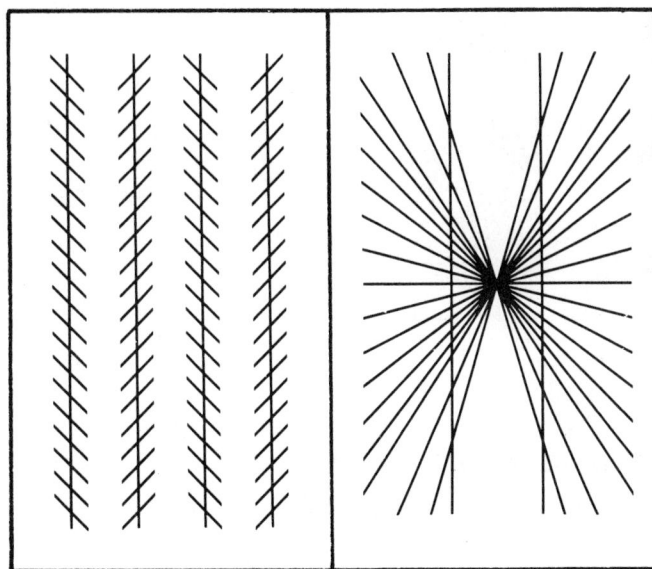

FIG. A   FIG. B

Although the long lines are parallel, the small cross hatching lines produce the very real illusion of making the vertical lines appear to alternately diverge and converge--they do not appear to be parallel.

Zollner discovered this curious illusion by accident. He observed it first on a piece of material purchased for making a dress.

In Wundt's variation, the vertical lines, although seemingly bowed inward, are straight and parallel.

In Hering's illusion, (see figure B) the vertical lines appear to bow outward, when in fact, they are also straight and parallel.

88

CROSSED-BAR ILLUSIONS

This family is based upon a pattern of illusions first developed over a century ago by the physicist, Poggendorff. The variation usually seen, has a tall vertical solid with two intersecting diagonal lines on the right and one on the left. The visual question is whether the left hand line is a continuation of the upper or the lower line on the right.

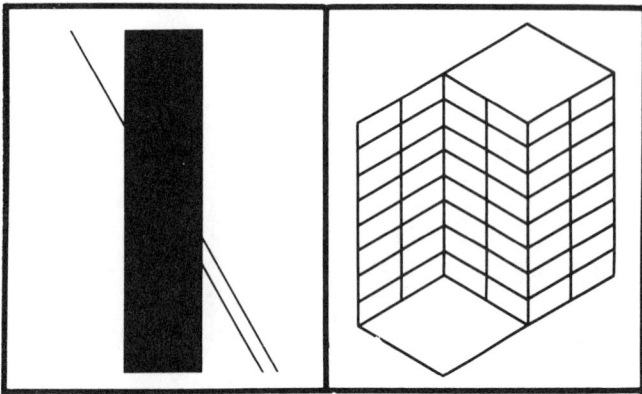

FIG. C   FIG. D

There are differing contradictory theories explaining this illusion, but sufficient to say, it operates strongly for most people.

PERCEPTION ILLUSIONS consists only of lines and dark masses, yet the minds of most people perceive it as a stack of four cubes.

This illusion depends upon the conditioning most of us received in learning to read. We look for dark printing on a white background and disregard the empty spaces surrounding the printed pattern. The dark masses are perceived as irregularly shaped globs with no perceptual significance. However, when we read the spaces surrounding the masses a word appears!

IRRADIATION ILLUSIONS

Many optical illusions depend on the way we perceive contrasts in brightness. A dark line or spot will appear darker as the brightness of its background is increased; conversely, a white spot will appear brighter as its background is darkened. This is called "irradiation". Irradiation also affects the apparent size of things. Bright areas will appear enlarged at the expense of adjacent dark areas.

Illustrations of this phenomenum appear frequently; the crescent of the new moon appears to be of larger radius than the faint outline of the feebly illuminated darker portion. Three irradiation illusions are included in this set. The first is the classic flags: the white center square appears to be larger than the black center square although they are both equal sized.

In the second it is extremely difficult to accept the fact that the distance between the black balls is exactly equal to the diameter of the balls--yet this is correct. Again the factor of the white area appearing to be larger than the black area is operating.

The combination of three illusions --the convergence illusions and the divergence illusion and irradiation. Irradiation makes the tips of the diamonds and the points of the stars appear lighter which steals away some of their perceptual length. The convergent tips of the diamond and the points of the star reduces their apparent length further. The divergence of the diamond and the star points (with respect to the intervening white space) makes the spacing appear greater.

These three illusion factors, all working in the same direction, makes the spacing between the diamonds and the star appear to be much greater than the length of the diamonds or the distance across points of the central star.

CONVERGENCE-DIVERGENCE ILLUSIONS

The form of the Muller-Lyder illusions consists of horizontal lines of the same length . . . one with converging arrowheads and the other with diverging arrowheads. The line with the converging arrowhead appears to be shorter.

This illusion, first described in 1889, is related to Zollner's convergence-divergence experiment of 30 years earlier. Very complex explanations have been developed to explain this illusion, but Zollner's claim that the leading of the eye inward by the converging lines as opposed to the leading of the eye outward by the diverging lines apparently is as good a theory as any.

The divergence illusions is another variation on the same principle.

The convergence-divergence illusion shows the same principle applied to interior areas.

The upper lines of each are the same lengths, but this does not appear to be so because of the influence of the vertical members of the polygons.

Wundt's area illusion is based on covergence-divergence principles. The two patterns are identical, yet the lower appears larger. It is the convergence towards the top arc of both figures and their positions one above the other which leads to this illusion.

OSCILLATING FIGURE ILLUSIONS

Certain geometrical illusions are not concerned with the false assessment of sizes and angles. Instead they depend upon the positive and negative perception aspects of the presented pattern.

Attention may be concentrated alternately on the dark and the light portions of the pattern. The mind oscillates between the two possible interpretations.

As the eye wanders we first perceive the pedestal, then we see two profiles.

Oscillation illusions are related to our perceptual experiences. Most everyone has been educated to look for colored patterns on a white background and we see the reverse pattern as a surprise when two possible interpretations are possible.

The oscillating figure illusion where one's attention wanders from the whole to the partial figure and perception oscillates between a telephone and a pair of small animals.

Another type is demonstrated in Thiery's figure and in Shroders Staircase illusion.

Because these designs have more than one possible perceptual interpretation, the mind considers the possibilities and the image. It seems to actually oscillate between the two possible interpretations in rapid succession and it is difficult to decide exactly what is being seen.

SIZE ILLUSIONS

There have been many optical illusions presented over the years that are dependent upon errors in size judgment that occur because of unusual arrangements of circles, lines, etc.

Five of these are included in this set. These are typical samples of size illusions in general.

TOP HAT ILLUSIONS

This illusion has been published many times. Although the height of the crown and the width of the brim are equal, the hat appears to be much higher than it is wide. It can be explained on the basis of masses.
The figure's size is estimated on the basis of the vertical rectangle which is obviously much higher than wide.

BISECTION ILLUSIONS

This illusion, which is equal in width and height, appears to be much higher than it is wide. It is generally explained on the basis of the viewer looking at the vertical line as a complete entity, but looking at the horizontal line as being two halves because of the bisection.

DIAGONAL ILLUSIONS

In this illusion the length of the line AX

equals the length of line AY. This inaccuracy in perception is due to the difference in the sizes of the parallelograms. Our mind tells us that the diagonal of the larger parallelogram must be larger than the diagonal of the smaller one. We disregard the factor of assymetry.

SIZE ILLUSIONS:

This illusion shows two equal sized circles in the apex of a triangle. The circle nearer the apex appears to be larger than the one farthest from the apex. This is an expression of a principle where a closely framed object appears to be larger than a similar object surrounded by open space.

This effect can be seen in nature. The moon appears to be larger when it is near the horizon than when it is high in the sky.

CURVATURE ILLUSION:

In this illusion we see three circular arcs--although it does not appear so, each of the arcs has the same radius of curvature. They all could be parts of the same circle; despite this categoric assertion, observers will be unshaken in their belief that the smaller arc is much "flatter" or has a longer radius of curvature.

Our assessment of radius length is generally based on the fraction of the circle that is displayed. In the semi-circle we have no difficulty locating the approximate center of the circle, but as the segment of arc gets smaller and smaller we will guess that the radius becomes progressively larger.

IMPOSSIBLE FIGURES

A good amount of interest in impossible figures has been shown in recent years. This is perhaps due to the increased sophistication of people as well as the general growth in graphics during the past decade. Since most impossible figures are based upon deliberate distortions of the commonly accepted rules of perspective, the increased knowledge of graphics has lend also to an increased interest in this form of optical illusions.

This impossible triangle is a relatively thin object that, because of perspective distortion, appears to dominate all three planes--length, width, and depth. Yet when analyzed, the figure cannot exist.
(see figure E)

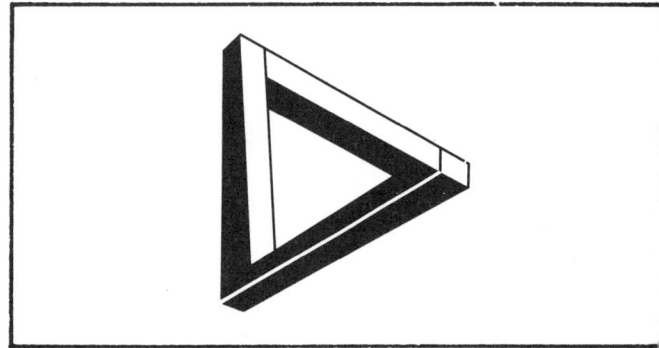

FIG. E

Chapter 4

MAGNETS

The early experimenters with magnets used natural lodestones, and found that they could be used in making navigational compasses that always pointed north. It wasn't long before man discovered that magnets could be made from other than natural minerals, and that, having been constructed, they could be used for countless other applications.

CERAMIC MAGNETS

Material:

For many years it has been known that barium ferrite, $BaFe_{12}O_{19}$, is a ferromagnetic material. Ceramic permanent magnets are a recent development and are made by a process known as sintering, which requires a metallic powder set in a die of the approximate shape desired. The powder is then subjected to high temperatures just below the powder's melting point. The added heat forms the powder into a nonporous, cohesive mass. There are two forms of ceramic magnets. The anisotropic (or oriented material) contains crystals which are aligned uniformly. The isotropic (or unoriented material) contains crystals of random orientation. The anisotropic form has an energy product equivalent to that of some other permanent magnet materials, but contains neither nickel nor cobalt, both of which are costly and difficult to obtain. High coercive force and resistance to demagnetization are two important advantages of this material.

Theory:

The magnetic properties of a permanent magnet result from the spinning of electrons within the atoms of the material. Electrons spin around their own axis as well as the atom's proton nucleus. Most materials have an equal number of electrons spinning in opposite directions, and so tend to cancel each other's effect. When more electrons are spinning in one direction than in the opposite direction, the material is magnetized.

Poles:

A ferrous bar that has been magnetized is said to have poles. Although in some magnets the poles are strongly localized in limited regions approximating points, in these magnets the poles are spread over a moderately large area. Magnetic poles have no physical reality, but are convenient concepts for picturing regions of distinct magnetic properties and other magnetostatic phenomena. On these ceramic magnets, the north pole, which is attracted toward the Earth's magnetic pole in the northern hemisphere, and the south pole, which is attracted toward the Earth's magnetic pole in the southern hemisphere, are located opposite each other on the surfaces with the largest area.

Holding power:

These magnets are anisotropic (or oriented), making their holding force quite strong in relation to their size. Although magnets already have a strong holding force (5 lbs.) this can be greatly increased by a relocation of the poles using steel plates (pole pieces or flux guides). The increase in strength results from moving the north and south poles closer to each other. Two plate-type pole pieces are included with each of your magnets. An increase in holding force can be gained by cementing steel plates to the north and south sides so that they protrude slightly along the 1-7/8" edge. About 45 lbs. or more of pull can be achieved by this method. See Figure 2.

Uses:

These magnets are useful in many varied applications. Their compact size and strength make them excellent for holding items to metal bulletin boards, desks, files, cabinets, or tool chests.

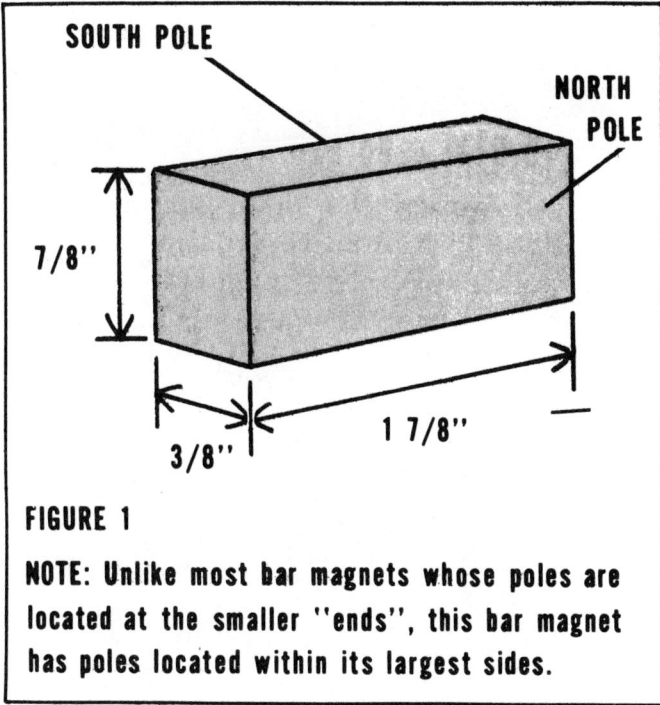

SOUTH POLE

NORTH POLE

7/8"

3/8"

1 7/8"

FIGURE 1

NOTE: Unlike most bar magnets whose poles are located at the smaller "ends", this bar magnet has poles located within its largest sides.

When arranged in a line the magnets form a magnetic rack suitable for holding tools, kitchen wares or medicine cabinet items. Name plates or temporary license plates are held securely as well as other metal to metal mountings. For convenience purposes, they can hold hard-to-handle lamps or can be attached to long rods for retrieving ferrous substances. You can tightly secure any door or house window without using conventional latches. These magnets also carry metal boxes or other metal parts very easily by attachment of a handle to the magnet and pole piece.

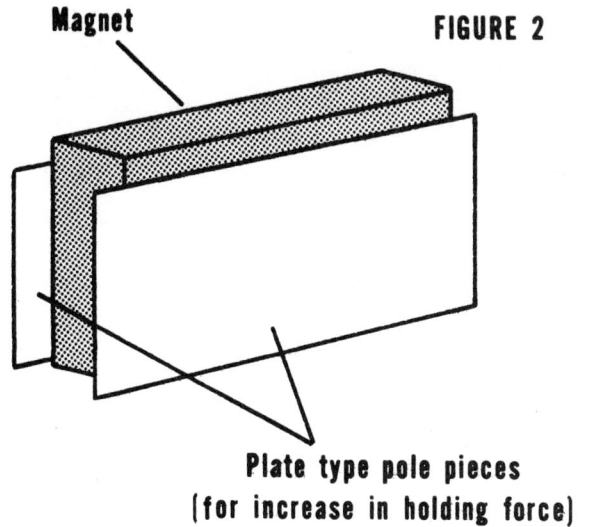

Magnet

FIGURE 2

**Plate type pole pieces
(for increase in holding force)**

MAGNETS

These magnets are designed for:

a. Lifting and carrying ferrous (iron or steel) objects from place to place or from hard-to-reach places such as wells, holes, shafts, sewers, and culverts.

b. Retrieving ferrous objects submerged in lakes, streams, bays, etc., or in tanks of water or other fluids.

c. Cleaning of ferrous turnings, chips, fragments, dust, swarf, etc., from industrial or home workshop areas.

The bottom face of your magnet is magnetic. The more of this face brought in contact with the ferrous object, the more effective the magnet will be.

The magnet's sturdy frame provides a convenient handle or tie-on. You can tie directly to the handle but we recommend passing a loop through both U-frame end supports for more even distribution of pull. Several magnets can be mounted on a bar, 2" diam. or smaller. This magnet bar if an ideal way to "sweep" the bottom of the lakes, streams, etc. When mounted on wheels, it makes a functional magnetic sweeper to pick up nails, hardware and other ferrous parts from plant floors, driveways, and parking lots.

Some tips to get longest life from your magnet:

1. Avoid dropping or hitting. The individual magnets can break if roughly

used. <u>Cracks</u> or <u>small</u> breaks in magnets will not usually reduce strength appreciably, though.

2. Keep the face clean and dry. Dry carefully after use in water.

3. After use in salt water or corrosive liquids, wash with fresh water and dry carefully.

4. Some rusting of the face will occur. Remove by light brushing with steel wool, wire brush, or abrasive paper.

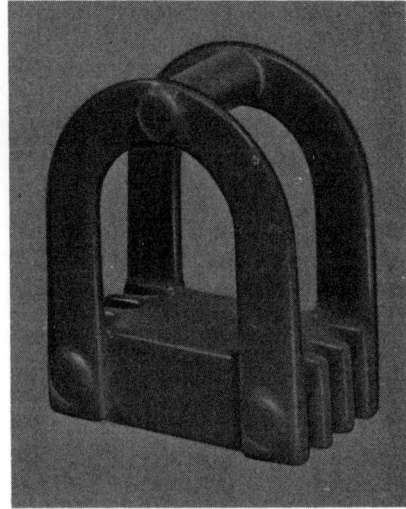

When storing the magnet, a light coating of oil on the magnetic surfaces will protect them against rust.

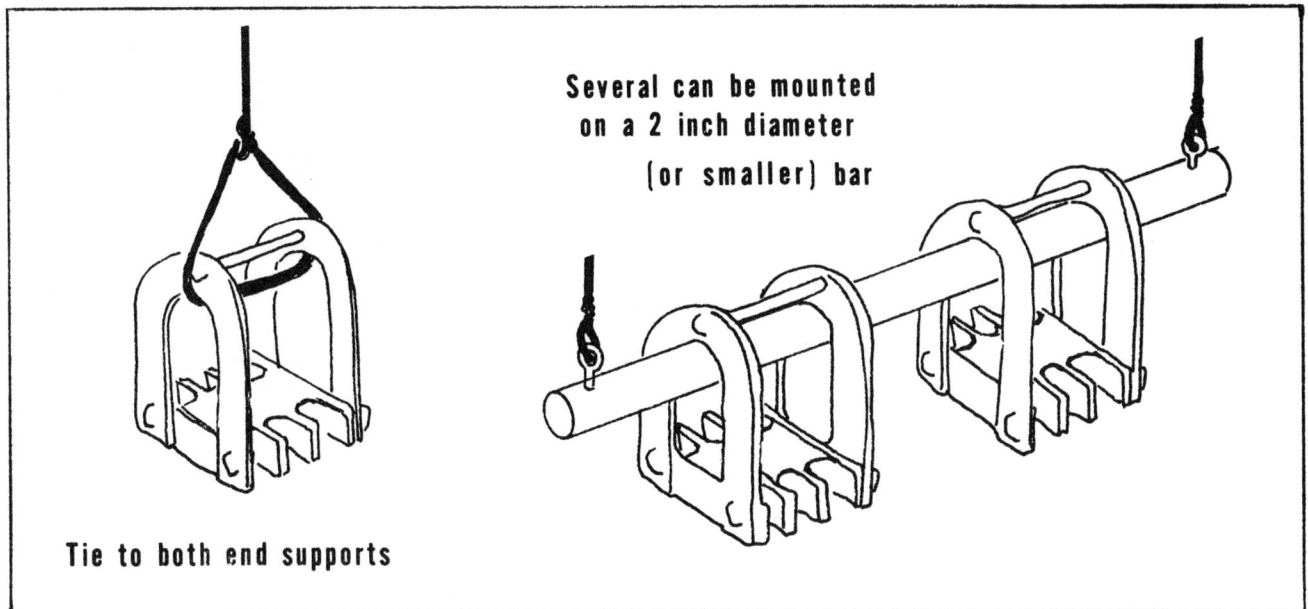

Several can be mounted on a 2 inch diameter (or smaller) bar

Tie to both end supports

Stock Nos 71,135 and 71,150 are protected by a tough, seamless, heavy duty, resilient coating of plastic that is heat fused to all surfaces except the bottom face. This coating allows use of the magnet in corrosive environments including most acids, alkalis, salts, plating solutions, and some organic solvents. The coating will never crack, chip or harden with age and has very good abrasion resistance. The magnetic surfaces are not coated since this would reduce the holding power.

Stock No. 71,134 Magnet is uncoated and we do not recommend its use in salt water or other corrosive environments.

CAUTION: KEEP FINGERS FROM BETWEEN MAGNET AND FERROUS OBJECTS (INCLUDING OTHER MAGNETS)! YOU CAN GET IN QUITE A PINCH!

MAGNETIC FLOOR SWEEPER

NOTE: To facilitate shipping, no handle is included with your sweeper. Purchase standard mop or push broom handle at hardware store.

The lifting potential of the Magnetic Sweeper is supplied by powerful ceramic magnets which are permanently magnetized and will not lose their strength unless subjected to extremely high magnetic fields. The use of a "keeper" is unnecessary, and the unit may be left standing on steel (or near motors, transformers, etc.) indefinitely without harm.

The ceramic magnets are made of Barium Ferrite which has a strong magnetic field (ferro-magnetic). Sintered ceramic permanent magnets of this type have been manufactured in the United States under various trade names since 1954. These magnets are anisotropic (the tiny magnetic fields within the magnet itself are oriented in a specific direction by a special manufacturing process). This is what makes them so strong.

ASSEMBLY

Hold the body of the sweeper in one hand and screw the wooden handle (you've purchased) in with the other hand. The handle should be tightened securely into magnet base assembly.

LOADING

For removing steel or other ferrous metals from floors, parking lots, etc, the operator simply moves the Magnetic Sweeper with a push-pull carpet sweeper motion across the area from which the pieces are to be retrieved. The magnet base assembly will become loaded along its entire length. The sweeper does not

have to come in direct contact with the pieces being removed because they will jump a distance of 1" to the magnet base assembly.

UNLOADING

Hold the loaded magnet base assembly in one hand, 6" or more away from suitable trash container. The palm of one hand should rest at the center of the magnet base assembly with the handle between second and third fingers. The magnet base

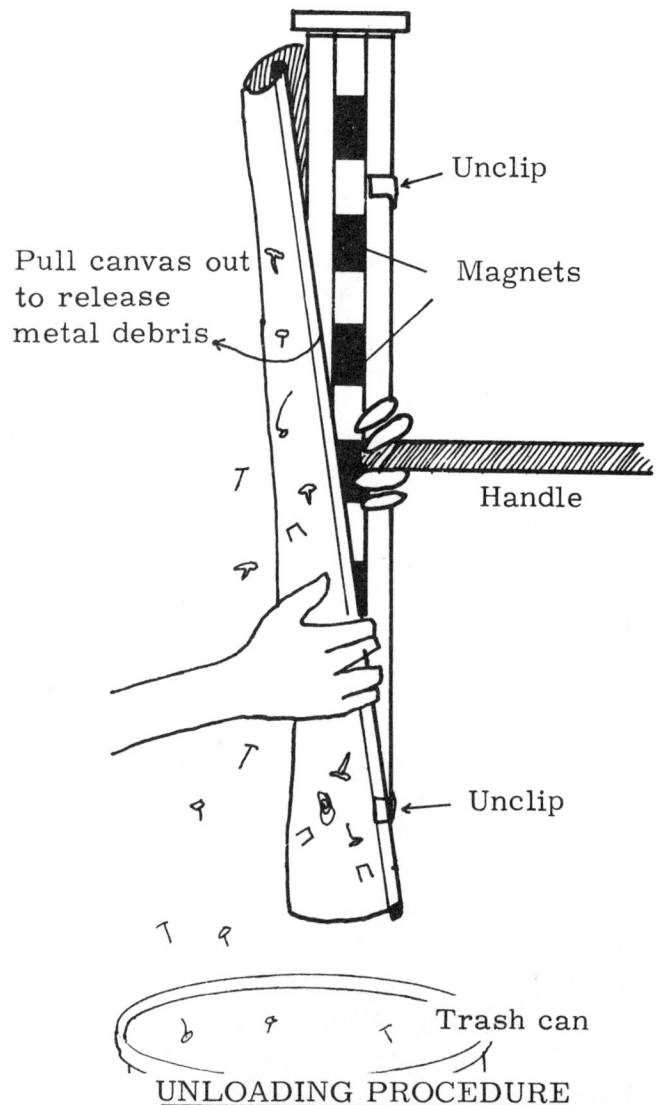

Unclip

Magnets

Pull canvas out to release metal debris

Handle

Unclip

Trash can

UNLOADING PROCEDURE

assembly should be in a vertical position during unloading. With the other hand, grasp the canvas covered rod and pull it from under the spring clips. Continue to pull rod and all the metal pieces will drop into the container. Now, return the canvas covered rod to its original position under the spring clips. You are now ready for another sweeping.

CARE

There are no parts in the assembly to get out of order - little or nothing to wear out.

APPLICATIONS

Many uses will be found for the Magnetic Sweeper such as attaching to plant trucks, retrieving dropped hardware in assembly areas, removing tramp iron, nails, tacks, nuts, bolts, shavings, etc. from parking lots, driveways, aisles, etc. The design is simple and compact and a little thought on the part of the operator will allow the unit to be readily adapted to many applications. There are many magnets supplied in the Edmund Catalog.

ADJUSTABLE GAP MAGNETS

Adjusting The Gap Width:

Your adjustable gap magnet is shipped with the pole pieces in contact with each other, so that they will act as a "keeper". Since this prevents the magnet from demagnetizing itself, the pole pieces should always be returned to this position if the magnet is to be stored for any length of time.

To set the poles to the desired gap, first loosen the four thumb screws holding the pole clamps in place. Push the flat end of one pole piece from the side of the magnet until one pole piece is past the leg of the magnet (it will take approximately 50 pounds to move the poles, so pulling on the other pole piece at the same time is advisable). When the pole piece is free from the magnet leg-not just out of the pole clamp, but actually away from the leg - it can be pulled away from the magnet. The remaining pole piece can be set to the desired position and locked in place by tightening the thumb screws. This pole should be positioned so the gap is centered in the magnet. The gap width is most easily set by placing a wood or nonferrous metal block of the desired size on the positioned pole piece and then sliding the other pole piece into position. Do not remove the block until all screws are tightened. CAUTION: Never place fingers between the poles when the thumb screws are loose; the attraction of the unlike poles is great enough to bring them together with considerable force.

A FEW TYPICAL USES OF THE ADJUSTABLE GAP MAGNET

A. Magnetizer

Small magnets or tools may be magnetized by placing them between the poles of the gap magnet; this will not weaken the magnet. If a number of same size items are to be magnetized, the pole pieces can be locked in place and the magnets passed between the poles. If a variety of sizes are to be magnetized, one pole may be left loose. Always place a piece of heavy paper or thin, nonferrous metal between the item to be magnetized and the gap magnet poles. If not, the item will be held with such force that the pole pieces will have to be removed to remove the item. Magnets should be re-magnetized with the same polarity as they were originally magnetized. A simple magnetic compass (check the Edmund Catalog for a complete listing) will show whether a pole is north or south by indicating north or south respectively when held near the pole. Placing the south pole of the magnet to be remagnetized against the north pole of the gap magnet (and vice versa) will properly remagnetize it with the same polarity. If an item has not been previously magnetized, magnetize it so both poles are located along the side which touches the material to be held.

The time that the item to be magnetized remains in the gap of the magnet won't effect the degree of magnetization; however passing the magnet through the gap several times will often increase the

magnetization. If large objects are to be magnetized the pole pieces may be used with the large flat ends facing each other; however, the flux density in the gap will be decreased.

B. Source Of Magnetic Field

The graph shown on page 3 shows the typical magnetic flux as measured at the center of the gap for various gap widths. These measurements were taken with

the conical ends of the pole pieces facing each other; values when flat ends are facing will be somewhat less.

C. Induced Electromotive Force Demonstrator

Connect a small loop of wire to a galvanometer, and move it through the gap magnet so that the plane of the loop is perpendicular to the axis of the poles. The galvanometer will deflect to indicate that an electromotive force is induced within the wire in accordance with Faraday's Law of Induction. The direction of the galvanometer deflection will show that the resulting current is in agreement with

Lenz's Law.

Rotation of the loop within the gap of the magnet will demonstrate the principle of operation of the A C generator. If the galvanometer terminals are reversed every half revolution as would normally be done by a commutator, the principal of operation of the D C generator can be demonstrated.

D. Demonstrate Force On A Current Carrying Conductor

Suspend a light flexible wire in the gap of the magnet so that it is free to move and pass a D C current through the wire. The wire will move in a direction perpendicular to the plane formed by the wire and the axis of the magnet poles. A 1-1/2 volt dry cell will usually supply enough current if the wire is not too heavy. For large or repeated deflections of the wire, the Edmund 1.2 volt nickel cadmium rechargeable

battery is recommended since it is capable of delivering over 60 amperes of current for short periods of time. Do not leave the battery connected to the wire for more than a few seconds or the wire will overheat.

Varying the magnet gap width will show that the force is dependent on the magnetic flux density. A quantitative study may be made using current balance techniques to measure the force.

E. Demonstrate Eddy Currents

Demonstrate eddy currents produced by induced EMF within a conductor by suspending a 2" wide strip of copper by one end so that it is free to swing. Start the strip swinging by tilting the bottom to a given height and then releasing it. Note how long it takes for the strip to come to rest. Repeat the procedure with the strip swinging between the poles of the gap magnet. The swinging strip will stop in a much shorter time. Eddy currents induced

within the strip cause a resultant force in the direction opposite to the direction of motion of the strip. The dependence of the breaking action on the strength of the magnetic field can be investigated by varying the width of the gap.

Repeat the experiment with a strip that has several slots along its length to illustrate the effectiveness of laminated transformer cores in reducing eddy currents.

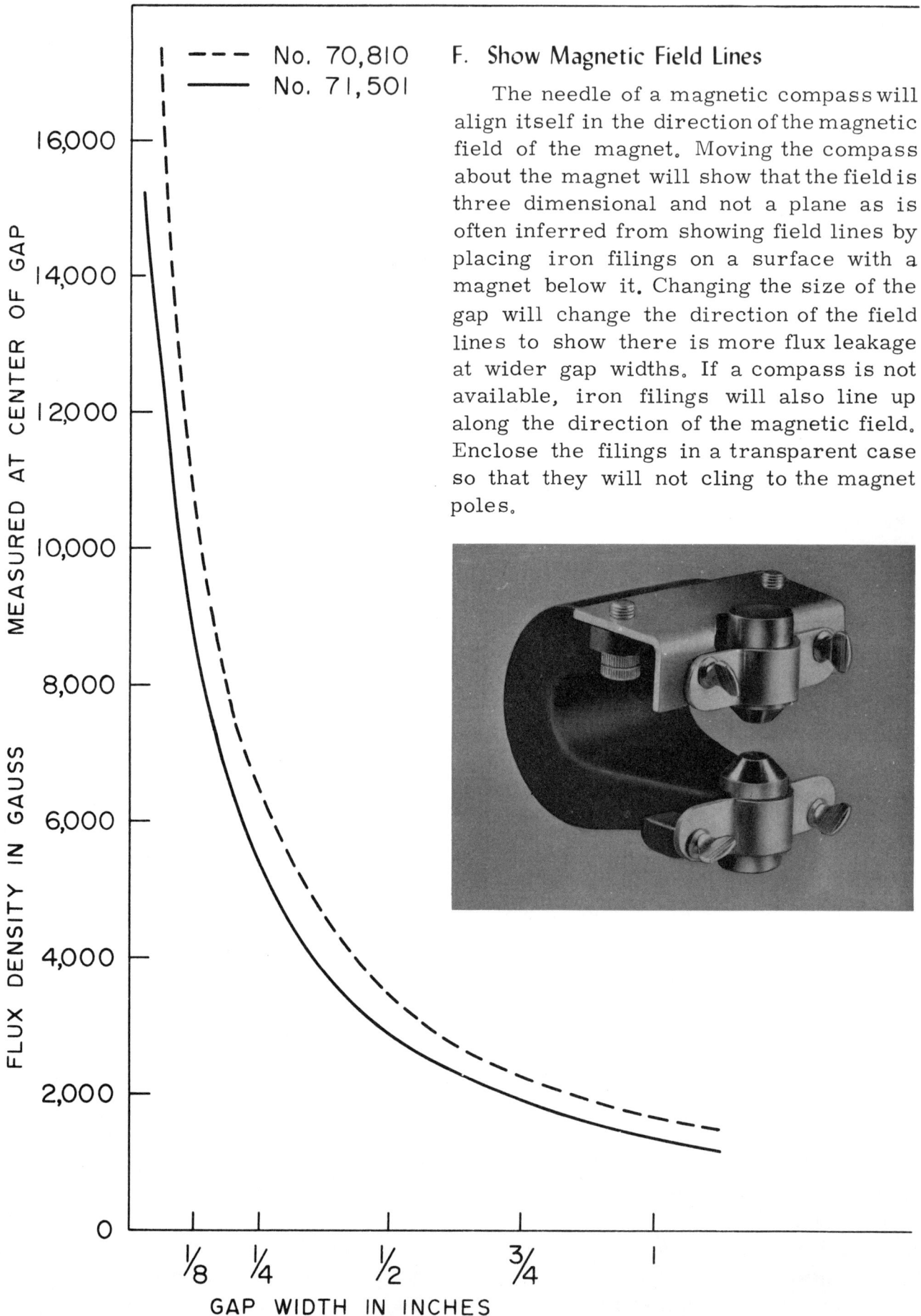

Chart legend:
- - - - No. 70,810
───── No. 71,501

(Graph: FLUX DENSITY IN GAUSS — MEASURED AT CENTER OF GAP (vertical axis, 0 to 16,000) versus GAP WIDTH IN INCHES (horizontal axis, 1/8, 1/4, 1/2, 3/4, 1))

F. Show Magnetic Field Lines

The needle of a magnetic compass will align itself in the direction of the magnetic field of the magnet. Moving the compass about the magnet will show that the field is three dimensional and not a plane as is often inferred from showing field lines by placing iron filings on a surface with a magnet below it. Changing the size of the gap will change the direction of the field lines to show there is more flux leakage at wider gap widths. If a compass is not available, iron filings will also line up along the direction of the magnetic field. Enclose the filings in a transparent case so that they will not cling to the magnet poles.

GIANT ELECTROMAGNET

This magnet requires two (2) 1½ volt* Flashlight Cell, Burgess No. 2 or Eveready No. 935. When the coil is energized, a current of approximately 0.7 ampere flows. The unusual lifting or holding power of this magnet is due to the extremely close contact between the iron parts. These iron parts are carefully machined to within a fraction of one thousandth of an inch. They should be protected against nicking or other damage.

Very little additional holding force is obtained using higher coil currents. The normal holding force for a typical magnet is as follows:

At 0.7 ampere (2 Volts) Greater than 550 lbs.
    1.0 ampere (3 Volts) 650 lbs. Coil will overheat in 30 mins.
    1.3 ampere (4 Volts) Greater than 720 lbs. Coil will overheat in 5 mins.

*A normal, fresh 1½ volt cell delivers a lower voltage under load, in this case about 1 volt. With use, the voltage declines further.

MAINTENANCE INSTRUCTIONS

The magnet surface and yoke should be well protected against damage due to nicks, gouges or corrosion. It is recommended that the surfaces be wiped clean and then lightly greased before storage. The grease should be removed prior to operation.

The magnet coils should not be operated at a power input exceeding 10 watts except for short intervals and as noted in instructions.

I EXPERIMENTS WITH DIRECT CURRENT

Theory — Lifting Power (holding force)

The lifting power of a magnet depends upon:

1. The area of contact between iron core and yoke;
2. The flux density at the point of contact.

The force may be expressed as follows:

(eq 1-1)

$$F = \frac{B^2 A}{8\pi}$$

where B is the flux density in maxwells per square centimeter, A is the area of contact in square centimeters. F is the lifting force in dynes.

The flux density (B) depends upon the number of turns of wire in the coil, the current, the length of the magnetic circuit, and the permeability of the magnetic circuit materials. Assuming that the cross sectional area of the magnetic circuit is uniform, which is nearly so,

(eq 1-2)

$$B = \frac{4\pi NI}{10\left[\dfrac{L_1}{\mu_1} + \dfrac{L_2}{\mu_2}\right]}$$

where N is the number of turns of copper wire in the magnet coil (approx. 350)

I is the current in amperes- approx. 0.7amp. at 2.0volts

L_1 is the length of iron circuit- 3cm.

μ_1 is the permeability of iron; around 500 or more. (it varies with flux density.)

L_2 is the distance between core and yoke (inside and outside contact points).

μ_2 is the permeability of air (unity for nonmagnetic materials).

The magnet surfaces are ground smooth to make L_2 as small as possible. A value of .0005 centimeter would be reasonable.

FIGURE 1 ELECTROMAGNET ASSEMBLY

1. 3/8" eyebolt
2. size D flashlight batteries
3. alligator clip (detach clip when magnet is not in use)
4. battery clip
5. lock nut
6. electromagnet core
7. coil
8. coil lead wire hole
9. magnet yoke
10. 3/8" eyebolt

Assemble the magnet as shown in Figs. 1 and 2. The eye bolt in the magnet core is attached by chain or cable to a suitable support. The magnet yoke should be pressed firmly against the core. Loop a piece of heavy cable or chain between the two eye bolts to prevent free fall of the yoke when released. Attach weights to the lower eye bolt. A load of 500 lbs. or more will be required to break the magnet apart. The yoke should not be allowed to strike the floor as the machined surface might be damaged.

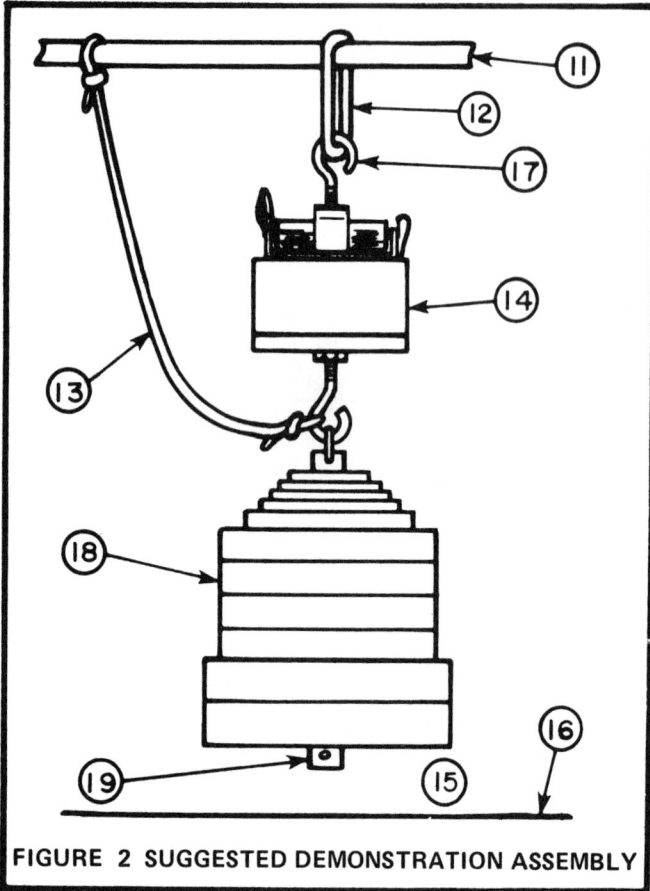

FIGURE 2 SUGGESTED DEMONSTRATION ASSEMBLY

11. bar or other support capable of holding several hundred pounds
12. support rope, chain or heavy wire
13. retaining cord to prevent damage to yoke from falling
14. magnet and yoke assembly (figure 1)
15. 3" or 4" space between tray and floor. This interval should be small so that load is not placed on yoke retaining cord when magnet and yoke part
16. floor
17. eyebolt
18. weights
19. stop-bolt

II Experiment No. 1—Magnetic Flux and Magnetomotive Force

Magnetic lines of force obey the simple flow equation:

(eq 2-1)

$$flow = \frac{driving\ force}{resistance}$$

an equation which applies to electricity, heat, people, money and numerous other things.

Magnetic flow is usually referred to as **flux**, and is generally designated by the symbol ϕ. We speak of a flux of so many lines of force or so many maxwells.

The driving force is usually called the **magnetomotive force**, and is generally designated by the symbol f. It is directly related to the number of electrons revolving around the iron core per second. In a coil of wire, the magnetomotive force of the coil is given by the expression:

(eq 2-2)

$$f = \frac{4\pi}{10}(NI)$$

where f is the magnetomotive force in gilberts
N is the number of turns in the coil
I is the current flow in amperes thru the wire

The resistance to magnetic flux is termed **reluctance**. Reluctance is proportional to the length (L) of the magnetic circuit thru which the flux must flow. It is inversely proportional to the cross sectional area (A) of the magnetic flux conductor (iron core), and inversely proportional to the magnetic permeability of the magnetic circuit material (μ).

If the magnetic circuit includes more than one material (air for instance plus iron) one resistance term must be calculated for each of them. The same applies if areas differ. Total flux, ϕ, maxwells, should not be confused with flux density, B, maxwells per square centimeter.

Allowing then, for more than one reluctance term —

(eq 2-3)

$$\phi = \frac{\frac{4\pi NI}{10}}{\frac{L_1}{\mu_1 A_1} + \frac{L_2}{\mu_2 A_2}} \quad etc.$$

Where $\frac{L_1}{\mu_1 A_1}$ is the reluctance of the iron portion of the circuit

and $\frac{L_2}{\mu_2 A_2}$ is the reluctance of the non-magnetic portion of the circuit

$A_1 = A_2$ for this particular magnet but this is not usually so in commercial magnets.

In this experiment, we wish to verify the relationship between flux, ϕ and coil current, I. We will assume that all other things remain constant, an assumption not strictly correct since the permeability of iron varies somewhat with the flux density.

Set up the electromagnet as in Lifting Power Theory.

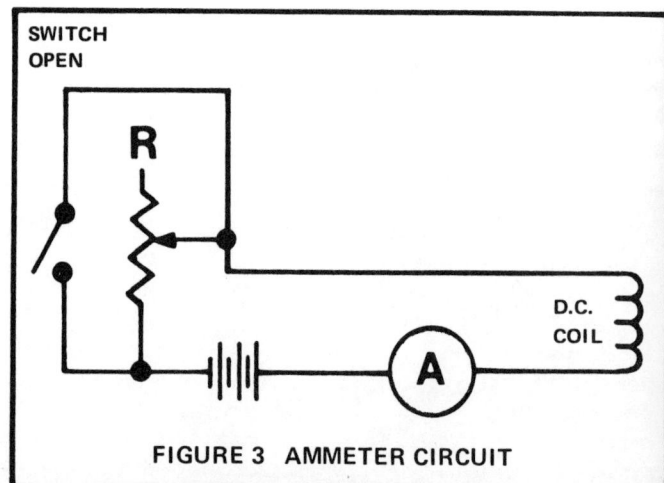

FIGURE 3 AMMETER CIRCUIT

An adjustable resistance of 0 to 10 ohms or more and an ammeter, 0 to 1 ampere, are connected in series with the magnet coil (Figure 3) to allow measurement of the coil current. Press the magnet yoke against the core and apply a current of ½ ampere or more to the magnet coil. Attach weights totaling about 100 lbs. to the magnet yoke. Slowly reduce the coil current until the load breaks away. Record the exact coil current at the moment of break.

(Record the total weight including fixture, magnet yoke and weights.) Physical dimensions of the magnet core and yoke will be helpful.

Questions for each run:

(1) What is the lifting force in **dynes** (not pounds or grams)? 1 lb. = 4.448×10^5 dynes.
(2) What is the **total** contact area between core yoke? An accurate rule (machinist's rule or vernier caliper) should be used.
(3) From the lifting force and area. calculate B (eq. 1-1).
(4) Calculate B again from the values given for N, I , and μ. See Lifting Power Theory (eq. 1-2).
(5) Compare results and explain discrepancies between answers to questions 3 and 4.

Prepare a graph showing the lifting power of the magnet (F) against magnetomotive force ($_f$). Prepare another graph showing flux density (B) (Question 3) against magnetomotive force ($_f$). Note any evidence of magnetic saturation.

III   Experiment No. 2 — Air Gap

Obtain a few pieces of smooth paper all of similar thickness. Suspend the magnet again as in Fig. 2. But place a sheet of paper between magnet core and yoke. Apply current to the magnet coil and note the smaller lifting power of the magnet coil and note the smaller lifting power of the magnet. Repeat this experiment with greater thickness of paper.

(eq 3-1)

$$\phi = \frac{\dfrac{4\pi NI}{10}}{\dfrac{L_1}{\mu_1 A_1} + \dfrac{L_2}{\mu_2 A_2}}$$

Any increase in either L_1 or L_2 will decrease ϕ and, thus, lift. Since μ is the permeability of air (all non-magnetic materials have a value of μ = 1) an increase in air gap lowers ϕ much more than a change in core length. Also, as L_2 increases, more magnetic flux flows directly across the pole faces of the core and less flows to the yoke.

Since lifting power depends upon ϕ **squared** (eq. 1-1) a small air gap reduces lift greatly.

IV   Experiment No. 3 — Retentivity

Arrange the magnet again as in Fig. 2 and apply a weight of less than 25 lbs. It will be observed that if the current is started briefly and then interrupted, the magnet will continue to support the small load. Once the load is pulled away, however, replacing the yoke will not result in its holding again. The iron core is said to retain a magnetic field. The retained magnetomotive force of the iron is quite small and is easily destroyed by opening the magnetic circuit or by applying a

very small current in the reverse direction. Large lifting magnets are frequently fitted with reversing switches to demagnetize them quickly.

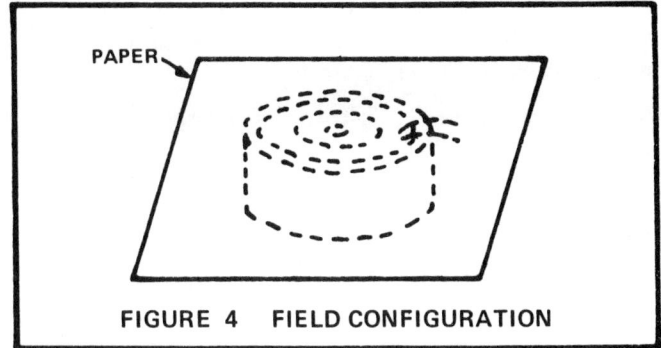

FIGURE 4   FIELD CONFIGURATION

V   Experiment No. 4 — Field Configuration (Fig. 4)

Remove eye bolt from the magnet core and lay the core on a flat surface, open side up. Lay the coil in the magnet core and lay a piece of paper or sheet metal other than iron over the magnet face. Set the switch to on and proceed to sprinkle iron filings on the paper or metal sheet. The filings will accumulate at points where the magnetic field is most intense. Bringing a magnetic object near the magnet will concentrate the magnetic field in that area and the iron filings will migrate accordingly, particularly so if the magnet is vibrated slightly.

SUGGESTIONS FOR FURTHER STUDY

Not all that is magnetic is iron or even cobalt or nickel. Certain alloys of manganese and aluminum, together with copper or silver (Heusler Alloys) are also magnetic. Liquid oxygen or liquid air is quite magnetic. Chromium, manganese and several rare earth elements are fairly magnetic, though less so than iron.

The electrical resistance of metals increases in dense magnetic fields. This phenomenon is fairly pronounced for bismuth, and magnetic intensities are often measured by this change in electrical resistance. A fairly sensitive wheat-stone bridge is required to detect this change.

A large number of materials are magnetic at low temperatures. Each magnetic material has a certain temperature (Curie point) above which it loses its magnetism. Iron loses its magnetism at a red heat, the Heusler alloys at temperatures not far above 100° C. The iron alloy used in cigarette lighter flints has a Curie point near 100° C.

DEFINITIONS

In a study of magnetism, the meaning of the various terms used may not be readily apparent to the beginner. The following is a list of terms used in this manual and their generally accepted definitions, units and symbols.

Current (I) (ampere) is the rate of flow of electricity.

Electromotive force (E) (volt) is the force or pressure causing current to flow in an electrical circuit.

104

Resistance (R) (ohm) is the property of a circuit opposing the flow of current.

Magnetic flux (φ) (maxwell) is the magnetic flow or lines of magnetic force through a magnetic circuit. The maxwell is one line of force.

Flux density (B)   (gauss) is the flux per unit area. The gauss is one maxwell per square centimeter.

Magnetomotive force (F) (gilbert) is the force which causes flux in a magnetic circuit. The gilbert is equal to $\frac{4\pi}{10}$ ampere-turns.

Reluctance (R) is the magnetic resistance to flux. The unit reluctance limits the flux to 1 maxwell with a mmf of one gilbert.

Permeability (μ) is the magnetic conductivity of a material. The permeability of air and many other substances is unity (in CGS units).

Chapter 5

SOLAR HEAT

Imagine being able to heat your home simply by using the rays of the sun. Solar energy can also be used to do many other tasks, from providing electric power, to cooking frankfurters!

I. How A Solar Water Heater Works

A solar water heater collects the sun's energy in a material that absorbs light. The light energy changes to heat energy and the absorbing material transfers the heat energy to water. Finally the water is stored to keep it from cooling. To keep the heat from escaping into the air, the absorbing material is covered with glass or plastic, a material opaque to energy in the form of heat. Light waves will travel through the glass, but the heat waves emitted by the absorbing surface will not; thereby heating the water. Insulation on both the sides and back of the glass cover and absorber also keep heat from escaping. (Fig. 1)

The three basic types of solar water heaters presented in this book represent a cross section of average water heating needs. They are:

1. Domestic solar water heaters at standard American house pressure that supply hot water at $40°$ to $60°$ above air temperature. These units are used as a sole means of heating water, or are used as an auxiliary unit that preheats the water for your standard water heater to save energy and expense. (Fig. 2)

2. Auxiliary solar water heaters at house pressure that supply water $10°$ to $40°$ above air temperature. These can be used for summer water heating in the warmer locations of the nation. (Fig. 3)

3. Low grade solar water heaters that can be used for pools, baths, or heat storage that are operated at atmospheric pressure. (Fig. 4)

There are two main varieties of solar water heaters operated at house pressure: thermosiphon or pump operated flat absorbers feeding a separate storage tank (Fig. 2); and collector/storage type solar water heaters that both absorb the sunlight and store the heated water in one unit without a separate storage tank. (Fig. 3) This book stresses information on these two, because the bulk of domestic water heating needs can be satisfied with them. A mention is made of other uses of solar energy for heating pools and baths to save energy on these luxuries.

My hope is that by reading this book you will understand what type of unit is best suited for your needs, and how you would generally construct it. For specific construction plans, many of the small details will have to be worked out by yourself. The "Sample Heater Plans" section will help you do this. A sample plan for each of the three major types of solar water heaters is included.

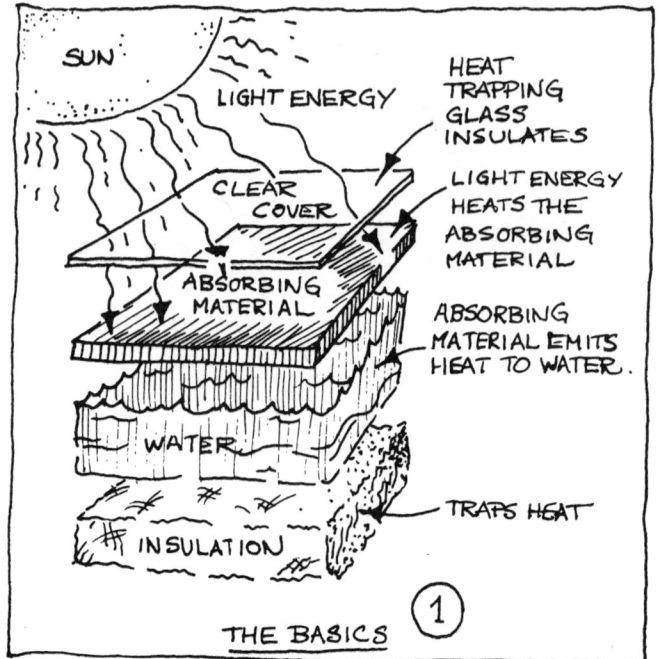

THE BASICS ①

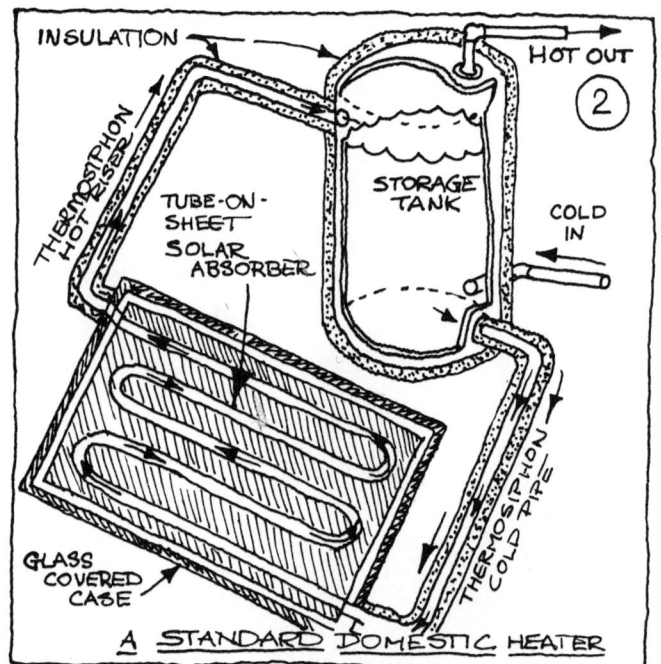

A STANDARD DOMESTIC HEATER

THE ABSORBER

Absorbers vary in shape and efficiency. The most efficient absorb as much sunlight as possible, transfer the light energy through the width of the absorber material, then emit the energy to water in the form of heat. These three processes are called absorption, conduction, and radiation or emission. Copper, aluminum, and steel perform these functions well and are frequently used to construct absorbers. More exotic materials

PLASTIC OR GLASS COVER
WATER TANK PAINTED BLK. (ABSORBER)
③
STORAGE
INSULATED PIPE
SOLAR HOT IN
REFLECTOR
TAP HOT OUT
ABSORBER BOX
COLD FEED
HOT COLD
REGULAR WATER HEATER
- SAVES ENERGY
  - SAVES MONEY
  - NO LACK OF HOT WATER
  - AT HOUSE PRESSURE

AN AUXILIARY DOMESTIC HEATER

CLEAR PLASTIC COVER VENT/OVERFLOW
2" ABOVE BED
WATERBED IN FULL SUN ABOVE TUB
SOLAR WARM FEED INSULATE IF OVER 20'
INSULATION
COLD FEED
OLD BATHTUB
LET WATER SIT IN BED ALL DAY.
BATHE IN EVENING
④

A LOW GRADE SOLAR HEATER

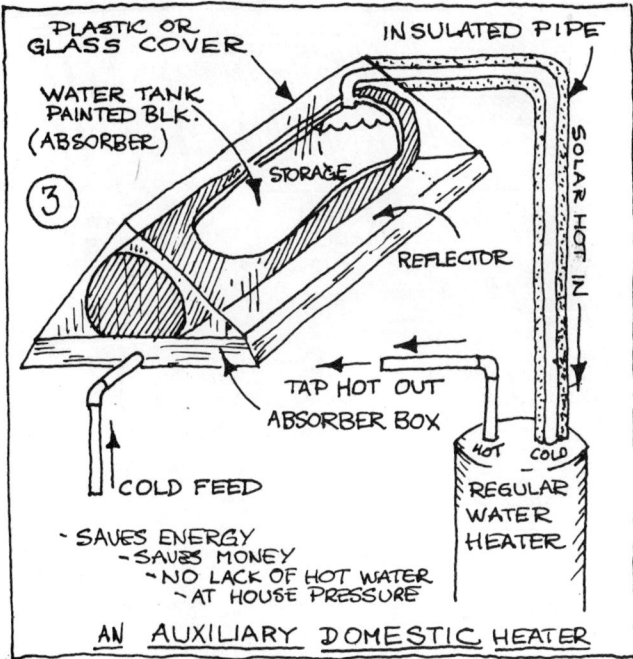

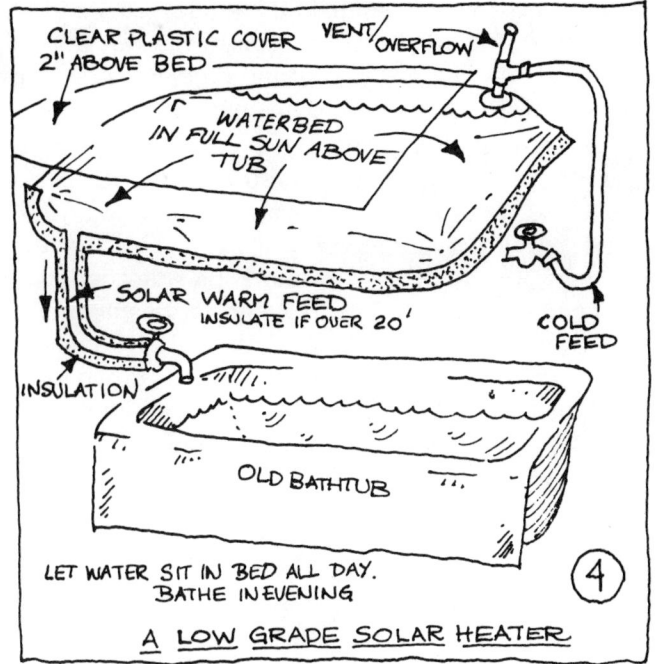

such as asphalt or concrete have been successfully used as absorber materials. Fig. 5 compares some of the more commonly employed absorber materials and their ability to transfer heat.

ABSORBING MATERIALS - SOLAR ABSORBERS.

	CONDUCTS (BTU/HR/FT. °F)	EMITS	EXPANDS (IN./IN°F ·10⁶)
COPPER	225	90%	9.5
ALUMINUM	134	20%	12.7
GAL. STEEL	28	94%	6.4
STAINLESS STEEL	10	—	9.5
PYREX	0.99	—	1.9
FILM PLASTIC	LOW	—	HIGH
PLASTIC PIPE.	LOW	—	HIGH

LIGHT IS CHANGED TO HEAT BY MOLECULAR ACTION IN THE ABSORBING MATERIAL.

(MANY MATERIALS ARE NOT LISTED.)
⑤

LIGHT HITS MATERIAL
MATERIAL SURFACE ABSORBS
MATERIAL CONDUCTS HEAT
REF.
HEAT EMITS TO WATER
(ABSORBING) MATERIAL

Flat Plate Absorbers (Fig. 6)

Water can be cascaded over, held within, or moved around the absorbing material. In most flat plate absorbers the water is under pressure and within pipes or tubes that are brazed, glued, or wired to the flat piece of metal. This bonding is very important because a poor bond will not transfer the heat to the tube material. Brazed or soldered bonds are much better than glued or wired bonds. When tubing is soldered to or part of a flat plate, the water going through the tubing will absorb much more heat than if the tubing was by itself. (Fig. 7)

The spacing of the tubes is as important as the choice of absorbing material and the method of bonding. This spacing varies with different metals and with the size of the tube. Fig. 8 shows what size of tubing and how far apart the tubing should be on a good absorber made of the metals listed.

There are a variety of flat plate absorbers that are not as efficient as the metal ones above, but will work depending on your needs. One is plastic pipe wired to aluminum roofing. Another could be two sheets of corrugated steel soldered together. (Low pressure only.) A design dating to 1936 uses galvanized steel pipe bedded in asphalt.

The arrangement of the piping on the flat absorbing material will control the amount of heat absorbed, how much pressure is lost, and how hot the water in the absorber will be allowed to get. Fig. 6 illustrates various pipe layouts.

A sinuous or serpentine zigzagging of the pipe is cheaper and easier to construct than pipes in parallel, but does not have as good flow characteristics as the pipes in parallel. The serpentine arrangement will cause friction in the pipe, thus dropping the water pressure. The water temperature can rise through one pass of the absorber higher than in an absorber with vertical pipes. Some Australian experiments have shown that the serpentine absorber may

108

sometimes reach such high temperatures that deposits of impurities that are in the water will form on the inner wall of the pipe, slowing the flow of water through the absorber.

Thermosiphon action is a weak force, and if the pipe diameter is too small or if the distance back and forth in one of the pipes is too long, the water will not circulate properly, causing the storage water to heat too slowly and the absorber to become too hot. The serpentine arrangement should be short enough in length and large enough in diameter so as not to restrict the flow of water to the point of inefficiency. In most cases of thermosiphon circulation, a 1/2 inch pipe should be no longer than 60 feet, and a 3/4 inch pipe no longer than 100 feet.

Pipes in parallel cause less overheating and less pressure drop when the absorber is operating by thermosiphon action. The one drawback is that this arrangement is more expensive and more work than bending a pipe back and forth. In pipes of parallel design the water has less of a distance to travel to make a complete run through the system; the cold water is fed in through headers at the bottom of the absorber, and the hot water out headers at the top. These headers must be larger in diameter than the pipes in contact with the absorber material.

The thickness of the pipe wall is important. The thicker the pipe wall the longer it takes for the heat to transfer through the material to the water. Galvanized pipe, plastic hot water pipe, and copper pipe are acceptable. If you use plastic pipe be sure that it can withstand high temperatures, otherwise it could fail, depending on the design. Many absorbers use copper pipe brazed to steel or copper. If you are going to bend the pipe, use type "L" or type "K". It is usually bought in 60 foot coils and bends easily.

These piping systems are used in commercial hot water heaters, at house pressure, that take advantage of the natural circulation. If pumps are used to circulate the water, a spiral arrangement can be used.

Cylindrical Absorbers (Fig. 9)

Besides flat plate absorbers there are many water heaters that are made up of cylinders in sequence. At least three Japanese water heater manufacturers use 6 inch pipe made of plastic, stainless steel, or glass as the absorbing surface. Usually these are gravity fed systems that people use to fill their communal baths in the evening, and are not really suitable for the American homeowner because of their slow

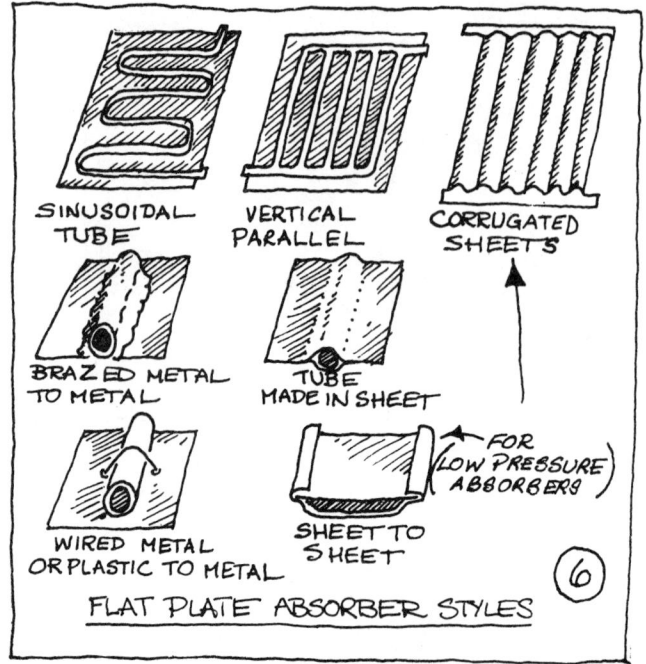
FLAT PLATE ABSORBER STYLES

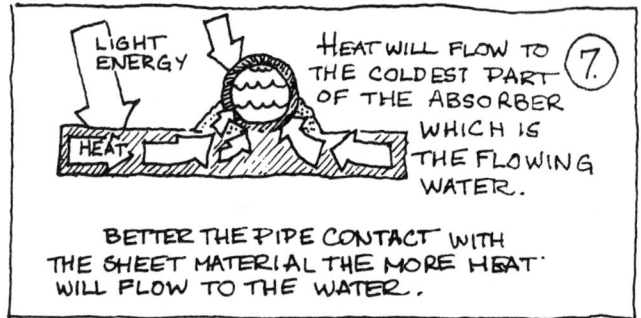

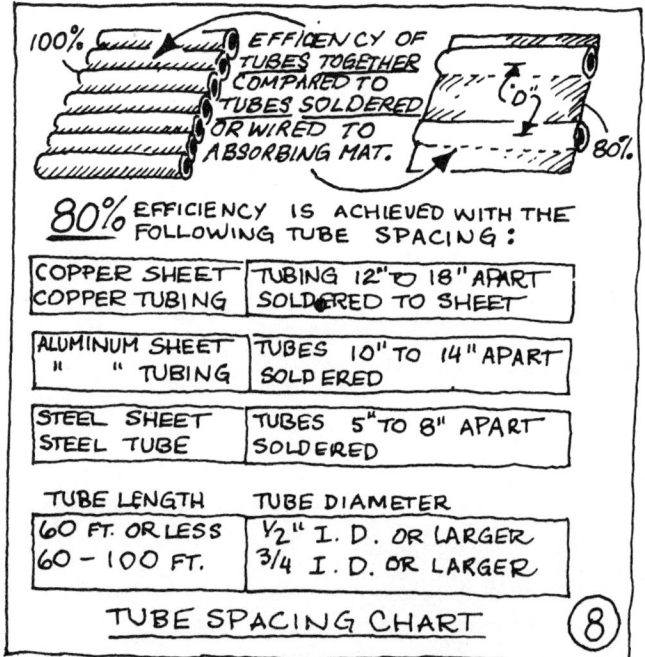
TUBE SPACING CHART

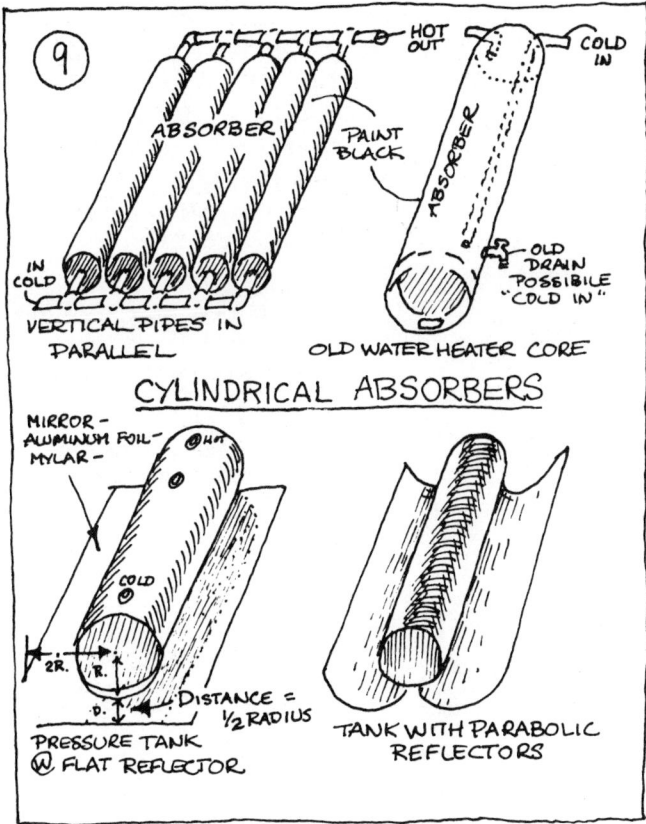

CYLINDRICAL ABSORBERS

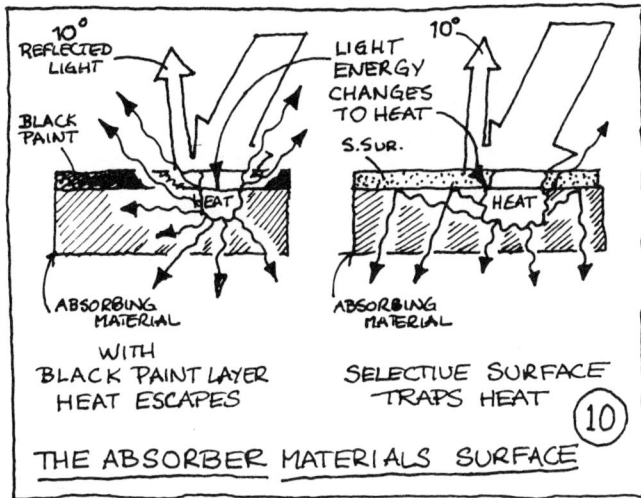

THE ABSORBER MATERIALS SURFACE

night. The units with separate insulated storage will give hot water early in the morning, while the cylindrical units usually will not.

To increase the absorbing surface of the cylindrical absorbers, designers have put reflectors behind them so that the whole surface is being hit by light. These reflectors are of two types, flat and parabolic. The flat reflectors need no focusing and can be set up in one position behind the cylinder. The parabolic reflectors are curved in such a way that light hitting the reflector is focused at a point much like a magnifying glass in the sun is focused to start a fire. This focusing heats the water very quickly, but the reflector must be constantly aimed at the sun. This type reflector is almost useless when there is cloud cover, whereas the flat design will reflect solar energy even when it is fairly cloudy.

The materials most frequently used for reflectors are aluminum, silvered plastic, and mirrors. For its price and reflectivity, aluminum foil glued to a surface seems a good alternative. Mirrors are expensive, and silvered plastic, like all plastics, decays in sunlight. The reflectivity of aluminum, silvered Mylar®, and glass mirrors is over 80% of the light energy hitting them. Reflectors will improve any type of absorber, but in many cases are unnecessary.

THE ABSORBER MATERIALS' SURFACE (Fig. 10)

All surfaces reflect some light. The absorber with the least amount of light reflecting off of its surface is going to absorb more of the light energy and transfer it, as heat, to the water. We see reflected light as color. Whatever we are looking at absorbs all the colors of the light spectrum except for the one it appears to be. That color reflects off of the object and enters our eyes where our brain classifies it as red, blue, green, and so on. The one exception to this is the noncolor black. It really is not a color, for we see black when no light is being reflected into our eyes. This is why solar water heater absorbers are painted black. They are absorbing as much sunlight as possible.

A certain amount of light is reflected off any surface and gives it its glossy appearance. The less gloss, the less light is lost to reflection. Thus, flat black paint is used to coat absorber surfaces. This coating should be as thin as possible, otherwise there is a small energy loss in the transmission of heat through the paint.

Besides the flat black paint covering for the absorber surface, there is a whole new field of

warm-up time and poor heat holding at night. They are, nonetheless, successful in Japan.

Cylindrical absorbers 6 inches to 24 inches in diameter have often been used for low grade solar heating because of their economy. Old water heater cores, pressure tanks, large diameter plastic pipes, well casings, and aluminum irrigation pipe have been used in this type of solar water heater. The absorber and the water storage are one. The drawback of this type of heater is that it cannot hold heat through the

110

what are called "selective surface coatings."
These are very thin layers of electroplated
materials that let in light energy but trap heat,
much on the same principle as the glass absorber
coverings. The coatings on the metal are opaque
to heat trying to escape from the absorber base
material, but transparent to the light energy
passing through to the material below.

In the section on "Solar Alchemy" there are
formulas for these various coatings that will
improve the efficiency of the absorber up to 20%.
Any commercial manufacturer of solar water
heaters should investigate these coatings. For
home use, unless you are an absolute perfection-
ist or simply interested in their use, sprayed
on flat black paint will give you plenty of hot
water as long as the absorber area is adequate.

THE ABSORBER COVER

As the absorber material gets hotter than
its surroundings, it starts giving off or radiating
heat—with the option of radiating in two directions, back into the air or through into the water.
Efficient solar water heaters utilize designs that
optimize the transfer of this heat to the water.
Good flow characteristics and circulation in
your absorber pipes is important in maintaining
a high temperature difference between the hot
material of the absorber surface, and the cooler
circulating water within the absorber, thus in-
ducing a heat transfer to the cooler water. To
further insure the heat transfer and prevent your
absorber from heating the atmosphere, a transparent material covers the absorber and acts as
a greenhouse, trapping the heat emitted from the
absorbing material. (Fig. 11) It is this combination of hot air, hot absorbing material, and cooler water that makes glazing the absorber so
important. Without glazing, the water would get
warm, but be unusable for domestic water
heating where temperatures of over 120° F. are
needed.

The most common cover material is ordinary
window glass. It must be clear, not tinted. It is
used because it transmits as much as 90% of the
incoming sunlight, while it is not transmissive
to the heat rising off of the absorber.

Individual panes under 6 square feet can be
glazed with "single strength" glass. Panes of up
to 30 square feet can be glazed with "double
strength" or"crystal glass."

The transmittance of window glass varies
with the angle at which the solar light waves hit
it. (Fig. 12) If the glass is perpendicular to the

rays of the sun it will transmit 88% of the light.
But, if the light is hitting the glass from the
side at an angle of over 60° from perpendicular,
much of the solar radiation is reflected by the
surface of the glass. There are anti-reflection
coatings that can be put on the glass, but the expense of using this process doesn't improve the
efficiency enough.

Many solar absorbers are double-glazed.
They have two glass covers; one on top of the
other. This holds the heat over the absorber
better than just one cover. Less heat is lost to
the night air. Three glass and four glass covers
have been tried, but energy is lost due to the
added reflection of the third and fourth cover,
while the additional heat they hold is minor. The
minimum distance between covers is 1/2 inch.

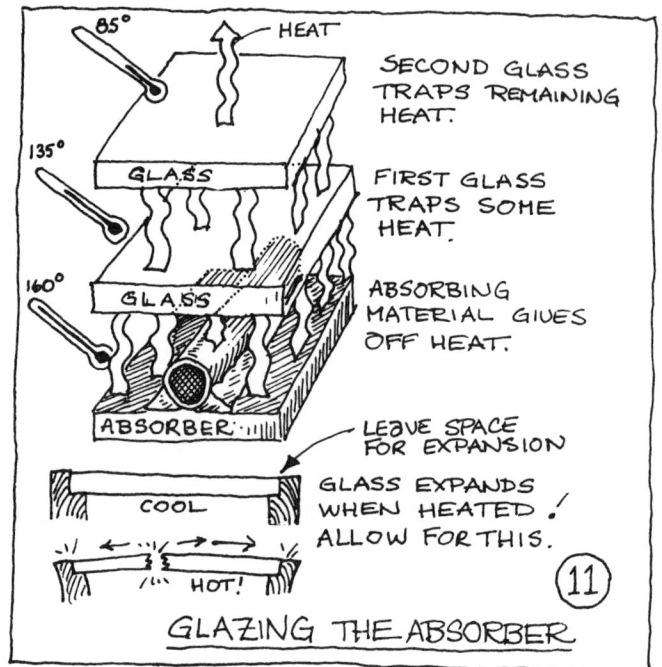

GLAZING THE ABSORBER

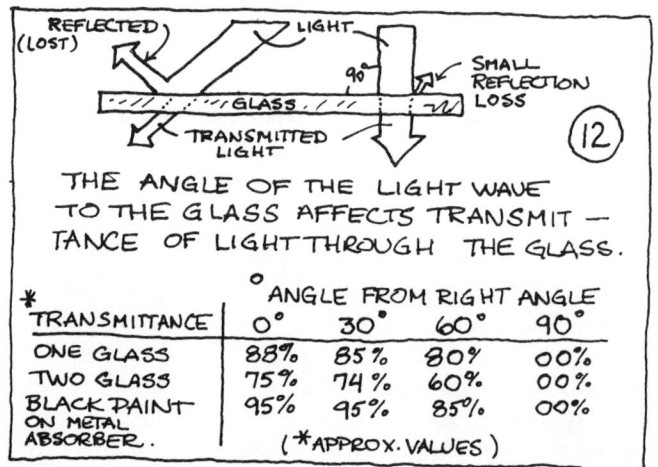

THE ANGLE OF THE LIGHT WAVE
TO THE GLASS AFFECTS TRANSMIT-
TANCE OF LIGHT THROUGH THE GLASS.

*TRANSMITTANCE	° ANGLE FROM RIGHT ANGLE			
	0°	30°	60°	90°
ONE GLASS	88%	85%	80%	00%
TWO GLASS	75%	74%	60%	00%
BLACK PAINT ON METAL ABSORBER	95%	95%	85%	00%
	(*APPROX. VALUES)			

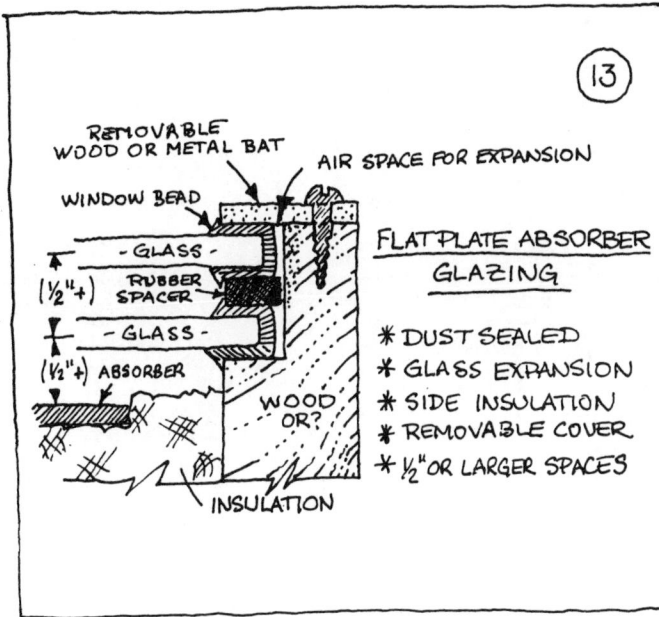

(13)

REMOVABLE WOOD OR METAL BAT

WINDOW BEAD

AIR SPACE FOR EXPANSION

- GLASS -

(½"+)

RUBBER SPACER

- GLASS -

(½"+) ABSORBER

WOOD OR?

INSULATION

FLAT PLATE ABSORBER GLAZING

* DUST SEALED
* GLASS EXPANSION
* SIDE INSULATION
* REMOVABLE COVER
* ½" OR LARGER SPACES

(Fig. 13) One problem with double glazed absorbers is that they can get too hot, and, if a shadow falls across the glass of a hot absorber, it may break the glass. This can happen only under extreme conditions, but precautions should be taken in the design stage of the heater.

Glass is prone to breaking under heavy snow loads, hail, and vandalism. It is also expensive; from $1.00 to $2.00 a square foot. Nonetheless, due to the small size of solar water heater absorber areas, glass is most often used. It is ageless, will not collect dust by static electricity, and water runs off of it readily. This last point is called good wettability.

Plastic films as absorber covers have certain limitations that make them less desirable than glass. They have poor wettability, high temperatures reduce their strength, wind can stretch them, and light over a period of time will break them down to a brittle and opaque substance little resembling what you started with. There is the additional problem that plastic can build up static electricity, collecting dust on its surface.

However, plastics can be, and are, used, and there are a variety of plastics available. "F.E.P. Teflon" has a lifetime in direct sun of twenty years, "Tedlar" has a life of 9 years, "Mylar W" a life of 4 years, and "polyvinyl chloride" a life of 1/2 year, and "polyethylene" a life of 1/4 year. Tests were made in the Florida sun under ordinary conditions that would be encountered if the plastics were used as absorber covers.

Corrugated, glass fiber reinforced plastics made for greenhouse use are manufactured to last years in the direct sun, and make adequate absorber covers. Do not confuse these greenhouse panels with the corrugated fiberglas panels that are sold in most hardware stores or lumber yards, as they are not the same. These do not have the same transmissibility, and are not protected against breaking down in sunlight. Since these greenhouse panels have a high reflectivity, double-glazing the absorber with it only lowers the absorber efficiency. Also, algae growth on these panels is a problem. These panels work well for Type II and III low grade solar water heaters. (See water use chart.)

Sheet plexiglass will weather well, but like roll plastics, it collects dust due to static electricity. It scratches more easily than glass, and will not trap the heat rising from the absorber as well.

In sealing the absorber cover to the absorber box, let the glass or plastic have room to expand, and make the seal as dust tight as possible. (Fig. 13) Rubber gaskets are most commonly used, although weather stripping found in most hardware stores could also be used. Plexiglass and other plastic sheet coverings expand much more than glass, and must float over the absorber in rubber welting or silicone beading. A four foot long piece of sheet plastic will expand and contract more than an inch in length at the temperatures created in solar water heater absorbers.

Clean the cover extremely well before you seal it into the absorber box. The cover top will clean itself in the rain or you can hose it off. The underside of the cover cannot be cleaned unless it is disassembled. Ordinary condensation will occur on the underside of the cover which is distilled water and perfectly clean. It will not affect the efficiency of the absorber if there is no dust in the absorber case. Experiments have shown that these drops of condensed water act like little lenses that change the direction of the light waves but do not block them. Any dust mixed with the water will, however, build up a sediment that will block the light. The underside of the cover can be cleaned every year or two if necessary. Thus, ideally, you want a semipermanent dust tight seal.

THE ABSORBER BOX AND INSULATION

The absorber box can be made out of any material you wish to use. Wood, metal, and fiberglas have been used with success. Any box that you make will be subject to the outdoors, so treat it like anything that will be outdoors for a long time. Steel should be coated so it doesn't rust, and wood should be painted with exterior paint unless you use cedar or redwood, or some other wood that is impervious to weather.

The box must be constructed to support itself and the water in the absorber. In many designs the absorber will have to be tilted toward the sun and propped up. This is discussed further in "Your Climate and Solar Water Heating" and in the section "Placing and Bracing" your heater. Water weighs nearly seven pounds per gallon, and, if your collector and storage are one unit, the box will have to bear a lot of weight. For flat plate collectors with piping the weight isn't very serious; you can save money here by building the absorber box out of simple low-cost, lightweight materials.

To further trap the heat that the absorber material is radiating, it is necessary to insulate it on the back and sides. (Fig. 14) Not only should the absorber be well insulated, but all pipes going to a storage tank, all storage tanks remote from the absorber, and all lines going to your regular water heater should be insulated. This is necessary to keep the efficiency of the heater as high as possible, because of the low grade nature of the energy you are using. A car engine seldom operates above 10% efficiency, while good solar water heaters operate at efficiencies above 40%.

Insulation is measured by what is called the "R" factor, or thermal resistance. Thermal resistance is the opposite of thermal conduction. If you pick up some common fiberglas insulation

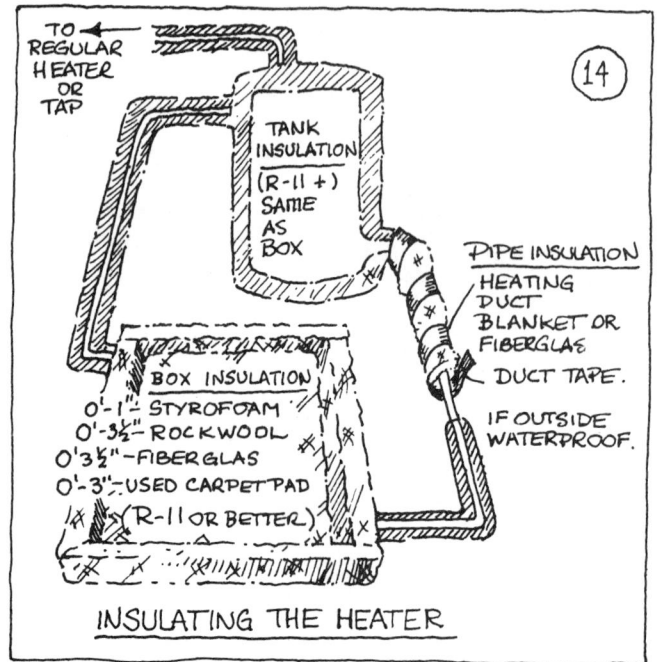

INSULATING THE HEATER

it will have stamped on it R-8, R-11, etc. An insulation with an R factor higher than R-11 is what you want to insulate your absorber, storage tank, and lines.

Insulate the absorber box with at least a two inch space filled with insulation. Make sure that there is no contact between the absorber and the exterior box.

Well-insulated storage tanks remote from the absorber will keep the water hot all night. Pump operated and thermosiphon heaters with separate storage are popular for this reason.

CIRCULATING THE WATER AND DRAWING IT OFF

Water in solar water heaters is circulated naturally by thermosiphon action, also called natural circulation, or is forced by pump. Good circulation or flow is necessary to bring more water in contact with the hot absorbing material and to keep that water cooler than the surrounding material that is radiating heat. Most solar water heaters take advantage of natural circulation. (Fig. 15)

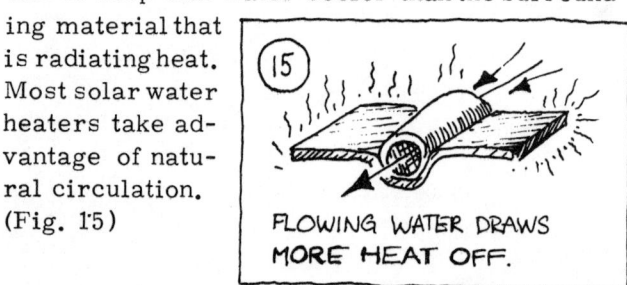

FLOWING WATER DRAWS MORE HEAT OFF.

Collector/Storage Heaters (Fig. 16)

In a water heater composed of a cylinder that is both its storage and absorber, the water circulates itself. As the water is heated by the sun it becomes lighter and rises to the top of the tank, being replaced by denser colder water that also becomes hot and rises, etc. Currents are set in motion by this heating process and are taken advantage of by feeding the cold water into the bottom of the tank and drawing the hot water off of the top. House pressure systems feed directly into the absorber/storage tank.

The way in which the hot and cold water mix is very important, and many home built solar water heaters fail here because they are placed in a position that allows too much cold/hot water

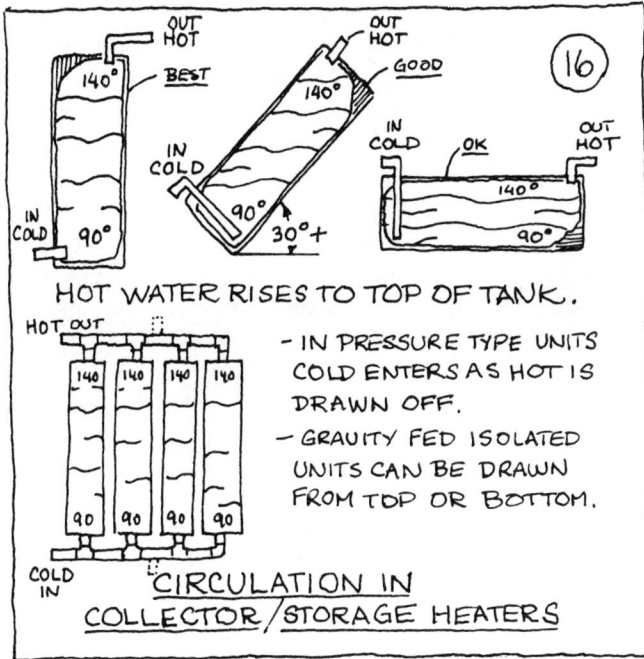

HOT WATER RISES TO TOP OF TANK.

- IN PRESSURE TYPE UNITS COLD ENTERS AS HOT IS DRAWN OFF.
- GRAVITY FED ISOLATED UNITS CAN BE DRAWN FROM TOP OR BOTTOM.

CIRCULATION IN COLLECTOR/STORAGE HEATERS

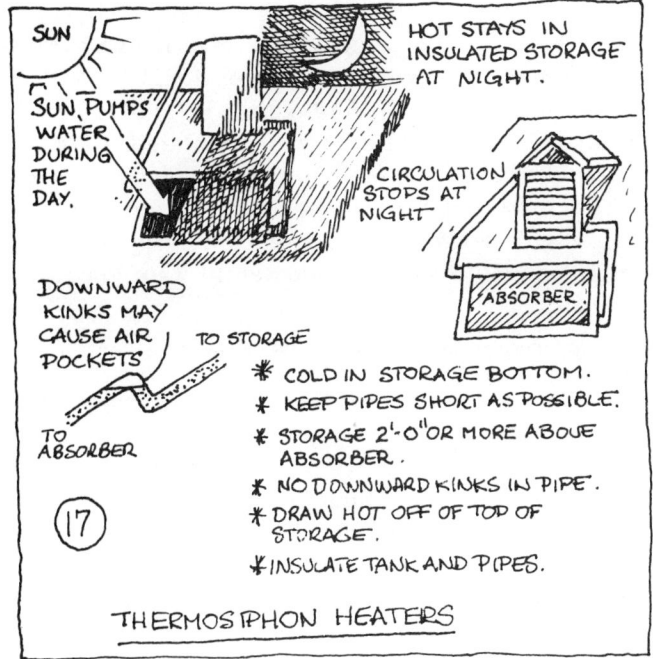

* COLD IN STORAGE BOTTOM.
* KEEP PIPES SHORT AS POSSIBLE.
* STORAGE 2'-0" OR MORE ABOVE ABSORBER.
* NO DOWNWARD KINKS IN PIPE.
* DRAW HOT OFF OF TOP OF STORAGE.
* INSULATE TANK AND PIPES.

THERMOSIPHON HEATERS

mixing. Any cylindrical unit under pressure will necessarily have the cold feeding in the bottom and the hot out the top. To avoid cooling your heated water that has risen with cold, the tank can be placed at an angle of over 30°. A near horizontal position creates turbulence in the water that inhibits water stratification, but can be used if necessary as shown in (Fig. 16).

Solar water heaters that are remote from a cold water source can be drawn from either the top or the bottom. The water in the top will be hottest, but overall, the water in the whole heater will be hotter than one fed constantly with cold. Some Japanese bath heaters are constructed along this simple design.

Thermosiphon Heaters (Fig. 2 and 17)

In domestic water heating units the heated water storage is frequently separate from the absorber. If this storage tank is insulated and located at least two feet above the absorber, and the pipes arranged cold to cold and hot to hot as in (Fig. 2), natural circulation occurs. As the water in the absorber is heated and rises to the storage tank, a continuous flow will develop between the absorber and tank. During the night the hot water, because it is lighter, stays in the insulated storage tank. During the early morning hot water is available in this kind of system, a major reason for its popularity. This type of

heater is commonly referred to as a thermosiphon solar water heater.

Thermosiphon solar water heaters will not operate if the storage tank is even with or below the absorber. In this case reverse circulation occurs at night, cooling the water. The colder water sinks to the lowest part of the system; this should never be the storage tank in a natural circulation heater.

When there is enough room in the attic of a house, it is possible to install a thermosiphon solar water heater by hiding the solar storage tank in the attic itself. Care must be taken however, in the way the thermosiphon return pipes are installed. Both the hot and cold thermosiphon pipes should be as short as possible to prevent friction, between the pipe and water, which could slow the weak thermosiphon flow. If there are any quick downward kinks in these two pipes, an air pocket may form in the top of the kink and slow or stop thermosiphon flow. (Fig. 17) The pipes should always rise as straight as possible to the tank without interruption. This is a small, but important quirk, found only in naturally circulated solar water heaters. Pump type circulation doesn't have this problem.

The tanks of thermosiphon heaters will function best if they are in a vertical position. The water will stratify in this position better than in a tank on its side. More hot water can be drawn as cold is fed into the tank.

With the tank in the rafters of the house, precautions should be taken to protect the house if the storage tank springs a leak. A drainage pan beneath the tank with a hose leading to the outside will provide this protection.

The transfer pipes going to and from the storage tank should be well insulated. As mentioned above, the shorter these pipes are, the less flow and heat losses will occur. 3/4 inch pipe with heating duct insulation wrapped around it is adequate for most domestic water heaters.

Pump Operated Solar Water Heaters (Fig. 18)

Where it is impractical to use thermosiphon heaters with the storage tank at least two feet above the absorber, water can be pumped through the absorber to a tank below. In a pressurized system where the absorber piping exceeds 100 feet in length, thermosiphon circulation is difficult to induce, water warmup time is delayed, and in some cases the absorber may overheat. Under these circumstances a pumped system will work much better. Some people may not want a storage tank on their roof, or be unable to build a tank appropriately situated above the absorber.

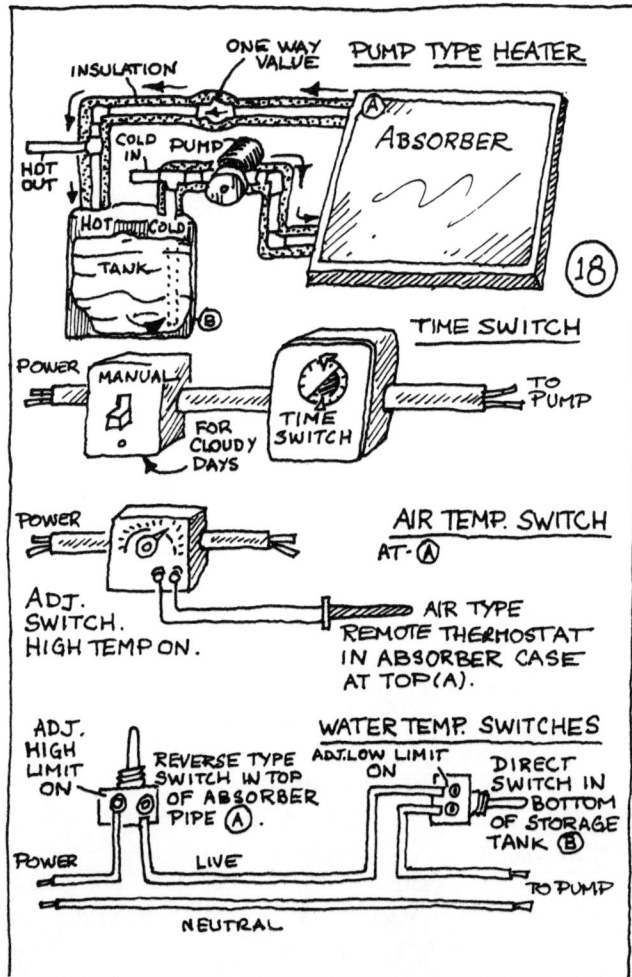

This is further reason to use a pumped system. Quick installation and long distance handling may make pumped absorbers more practical. Pumped systems are often desirable because the solar heated water can be circulated through a gas or electric water heater. This takes the heating load off the electric or gas heater, cutting expenses without inconvenience. The extra solar heater storage tank is then unnecessary.

A very weak pump can be used. The pump should be able to withstand the head pressure of raising the water to the roof top where absorbers are usually located. The pump need only circulate the water being stored one time every few minutes. Flow rates as low as 20 gallons per hour are more than adequate. When purchasing a pump be sure that it is designed to operate under pressure, if the solar water heating system is at house pressure. Solar water heaters using water at atmospheric pressure can be pumped with a wide variety of pumps available for pools, basements, or campers.

When using pumps to circulate the water, the distance from the storage tank to the absorber isn't important, but insulating the pipes to and from the absorber is necessary.

For a pressure solar water heating system using a pump, the pump can be located near the storage tank for easier servicing. It then pumps water up from the colder bottom of the storage tank to the bottom of the absorber, and back to the hotter top of the storage tank. At night when the absorber is off, to prevent reverse circulation, a one-way valve is installed so that the hot water in the storage tank cannot rise into the absorber. If this one-way valve isn't used, reverse circulation will occur and the solar water heater will become a nighttime water cooler. The valve is installed on the hot water return to the tank, opening in the direction of the tank. Household hot water is drawn off the hot circulation pipe near the storage tank. Cold is fed into the tank bottom, either separately or by the cold circulation pipe before the pump. (Tank, cold feed, pump, then absorber in that order.)

Switching the Pump On and Off (Fig. 18)

The pump should operate only when it is sunny and the water in the storage tank is cold.

The least sensitive way to operate the absorber pump is with a time switch. Time switches should be set for daytime, giving the absorber time to warm up some in the early morning. A manual switch is needed for cloudy days. This system does not take into consideration the absorber or storage tank temperatures.

An air temperature switch (located on top of the absorber box) operating the pump is more sensitive than the above. It will operate when the absorber reaches a certain temperature, low or high. Fluctuations in temperature of the circulating water will not create a lot of on-off cycles when the system starts operating in the morning. This situation could arise with a single high temperature-on, water temperature switch. The switch itself should be adjustable to accommodate climate and heating situations.

A reverse and direct water temperature switch connected in series will provide the most sensitive pump operation. The reverse switch in the hot exit of the absorber pipe will connect when the water in the top of the absorber reaches a fixed temperature. The direct switch in the bottom of the storage tank will connect when the water is a certain number of degrees below that of the high limit switch. The pump will not operate when the tank temperature is above the absorber temperature. Energy is never wasted by pumping already heated water through the absorber. Heaters with this pump switch design have been made and are in use, but I question the ability of absorbers to withstand the high temperatures of uncirculated water when the pump switch is off.

A typical high pressure absorber would be used on an apartment house. Where a number of families are involved, a single large absorber would be impractical. It is easier to install small modular units connected in parallel. Caution must be taken to slant the absorbers as shown, and install an air bleeding device in the highest section of the absorber matrix. This is because water will bubble as it is heated and give off its impacted air. If this bleeding wasn't done, an air pocket would form in the top of the storage tank and eventually work its way to the top and inconvenience the user. (Fig. 19)

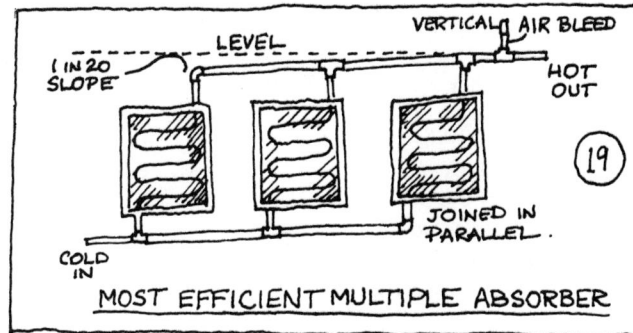

MOST EFFICIENT MULTIPLE ABSORBER

CONCENTRATOR SOLAR PANELS

Concentrator panels are a revolutionary new type of silicon solar panel which has photo voltaic capabilities unheard of until recent years. These panels are manufactured of specially designed concentrator type solar cells in series, with a blocking diode, on a uniquely designed, water-cooled copper jacket. Normal silicon solar cells break down with the heat produced by more than two or three suns. The concentrator cells, however, are continuously cooled by water flowing underneath them. The cells themselves are affixed to the water-cooled jacket with a special heat-conductive epoxy. When the cell heats, it passes this heat through the conductive epoxy into the water-cooled chamber in the back of the panel. This allows the heat to be dissipated uniformly, so the panel does not burn itself out.

The results of recent scientific discoveries have allowed us to manufacture a concentrator panel which will produce, in a linear fashion, a voltage and current output directly related to the amount of sunlight to which the panel is exposed. These particular cells are the most efficient of their kind. They have been tested to produce ten times more power than their rating at one sun, when the panels are exposed to an equivalent of ten suns of light.

Further testing of these panels indicates that they could possibly deliver up to twenty suns' worth of electricity, if 20 suns were concentrated on them and they were properly cooled. **It is imperative that the water flow underneath the cells be maintained to keep the temperature level of the panel at a minimum.** This water flow has the advantage of not only producing: (1) more electricity per dollar invested in panels, but also (2) gives the by-product of reasonably warm water. Tests indicate that the water temperature varies depending on the amount of sun and the volume of the water reservoir. Our tests indicate the water temperature was in the area of 140 to 150°, with one-gallon of reservoir water during our test at 10 suns. The flow of water can be maintained passively by thermal syphon, or actively, with the use of a small electric pump.

In order to get concentrated light on the panel it is necessary to focus the sunlight in some fashion so that a maximum amount of light hits the entire area of the panel. This may be accomplished in a number of ways, two of which follow.

(1) A focusing concentrator configuration such as the **Winston Crab Eye** (Fig. A), that will usually work without much of a sun-tracking problem.

(2) Another way to track the sun is to use a **telescope clock drive** (Fig. D). This arrangement has to be reset each day. When using both the clock drive and a water pump it is necessary to parallel the output of the solar panel with a standby battery pack. The reason being that if a heavy cloud covering should suddenly cut the sun's intensity, the tracking device and pump would shut down and take the panel out of its synchronous sun-following pattern. Also, as a result, if the pump were not active the water beneath the panel would immediately come to a boil and the panel would possibly consume itself from residual heat.

We presently offer Concentrator Panel, **No. 72,195,** a 2 x 19 x 3/4" solar concentrator panel nominally rated at .125 amp, 12.5 volt. This rating is under a one full sun condition. When intensified to a 10-sun concentration it will provide well over one full ampere at 12.5V. Should it be concentrated to a 20-sun condition, it would provide 2 full amperes (See Fig. B).

We also offer **No. 61,103,** a 6 x 2 x 3/4" solar concentrator panel. This will produce .125 amp @1.5V, nominally under a 1-sun condition. Similar to the above, under a 10-sun concentration this will also produce 1 amp @1.5V. If this panel were concentrated to a 20-sun condition, it would provide 2 amps @1.5V.

To immediately put your concentrator to work we suggest the following Edmund Scientific Co. products:

(1) No. 80,087, which consists of a 48 x 42" highly aluminized mylar cemented to durable sheets of white card stock. This highly reflective material can be placed in a parabolic curve suitable to gather the sun's light over either of these panels (Fig. C). You will have to construct a suitable frame to hold the aluminized mylar in the proper parabolic curve (Fig. E). The frame itself can be attached to any Edmund clock drive. We suggest No. 85,112, a medium duty power clock drive and pedestal on the equatorial telescope mount. This clock drive, in addition to the aluminized mylar, will serve to image the sun in a concentrated mode on either of the panels discussed above (Fig. D).

MAINTENANCE

The solar panel is maintenance free. As it is converting light to electricity, it is natural that its light-collecting surface should be kept clean. Thin layers of dust, dirt or ice will not considerably decrease its efficiency. Rain usually removes dirt and restores the original surface. It is possible that unusual contaminants may require cleaning; in such cases, soap and water are sufficient to remove dirt.

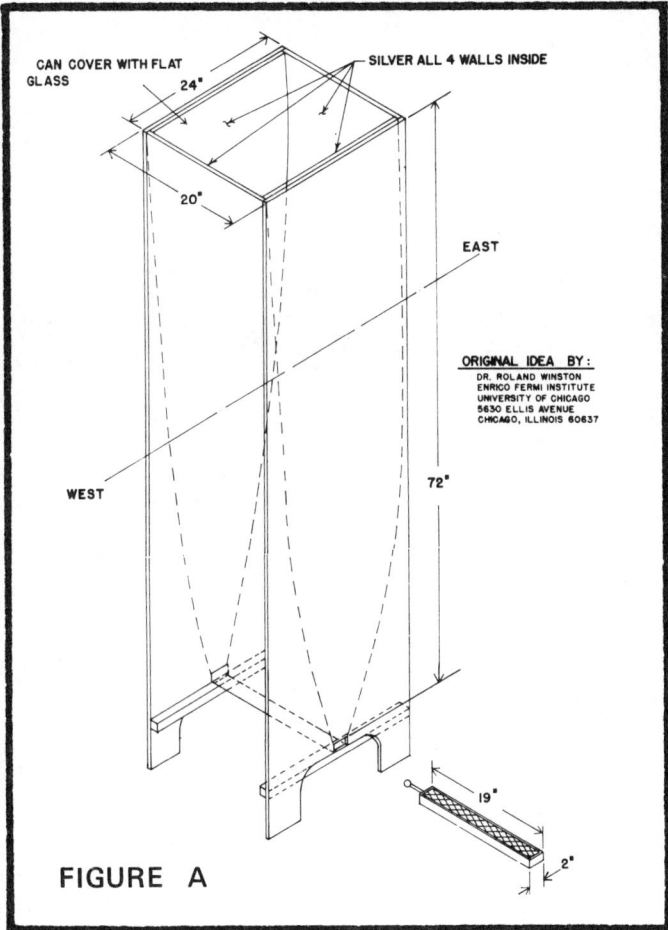

FIGURE A

CAN COVER WITH FLAT GLASS
SILVER ALL 4 WALLS INSIDE
24"
20"
EAST
WEST
72"
19"
2"

ORIGINAL IDEA BY:
DR. ROLAND WINSTON
ENRICO FERMI INSTITUTE
UNIVERSITY OF CHICAGO
5630 ELLIS AVENUE
CHICAGO, ILLINOIS 60637

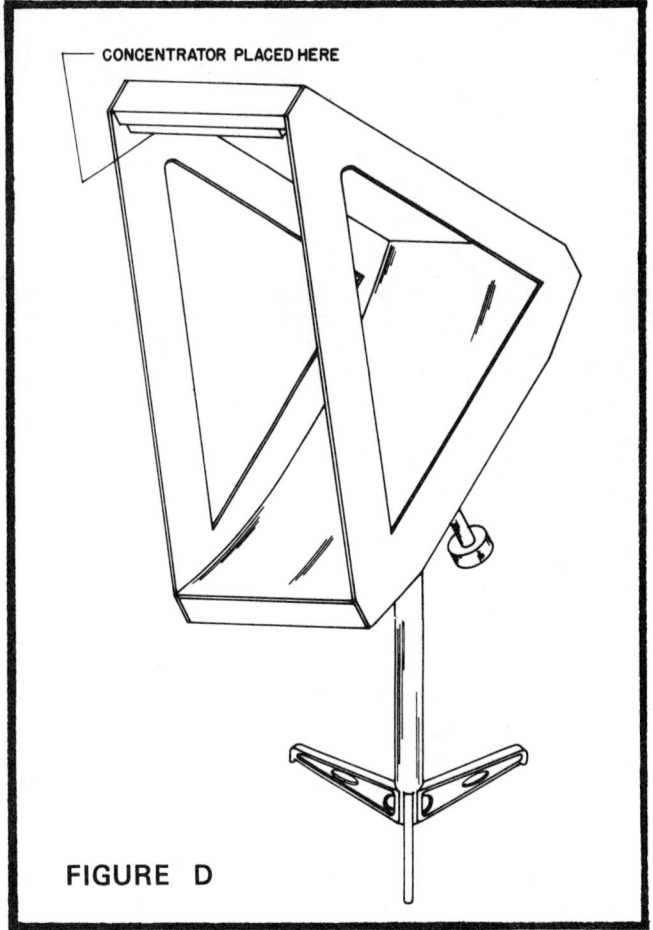

CONCENTRATOR PLACED HERE

FIGURE D

FIGURE B

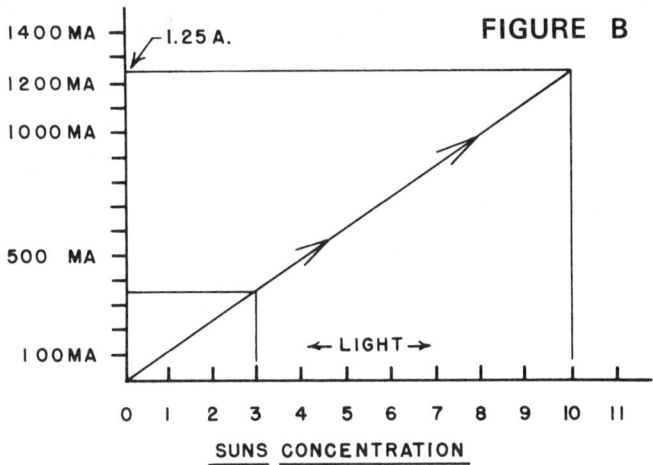

1400 MA
1.25 A.
1200 MA
1000 MA
500 MA
100 MA

←— LIGHT —→

0 1 2 3 4 5 6 7 8 9 10 11

SUNS CONCENTRATION

FIGURE E

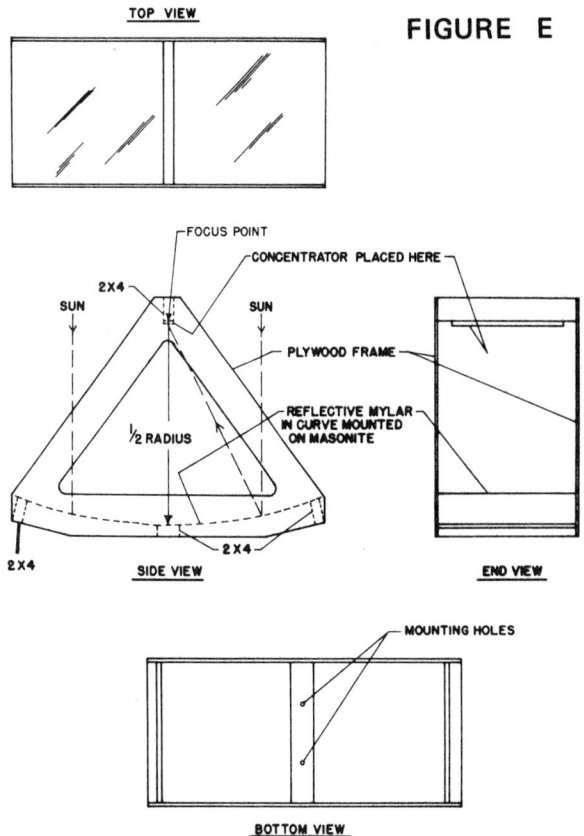

TOP VIEW

FOCUS POINT
CONCENTRATOR PLACED HERE
2X4
SUN   SUN
PLYWOOD FRAME
½ RADIUS
REFLECTIVE MYLAR IN CURVE MOUNTED ON MASONITE
2X4   2X4
SIDE VIEW   END VIEW

MOUNTING HOLES

BOTTOM VIEW

FIGURE C

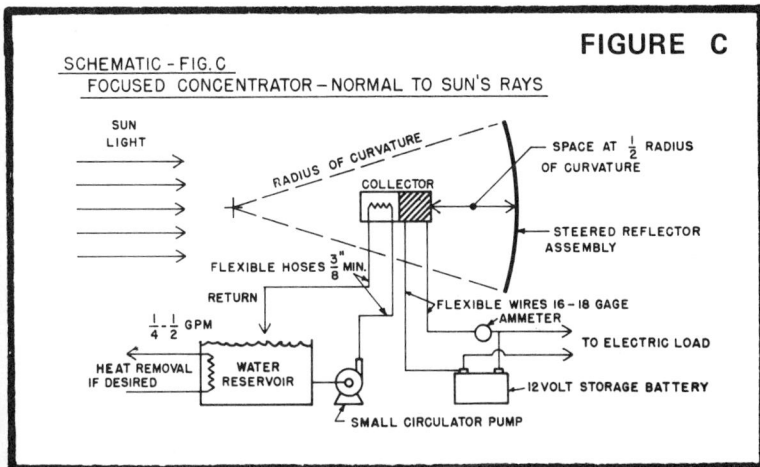

SCHEMATIC - FIG. C
FOCUSED CONCENTRATOR - NORMAL TO SUN'S RAYS

SUN LIGHT
RADIUS OF CURVATURE
COLLECTOR
SPACE AT ½ RADIUS OF CURVATURE
STEERED REFLECTOR ASSEMBLY
FLEXIBLE HOSES ⅜" MIN.
RETURN
¼ - ½ GPM
FLEXIBLE WIRES 16 - 18 GAGE
AMMETER
TO ELECTRIC LOAD
HEAT REMOVAL IF DESIRED
WATER RESERVOIR
12 VOLT STORAGE BATTERY
SMALL CIRCULATOR PUMP

SOLAR PANELS

General

The solar energy conversion device which you have just purchased represents the greatest value to date in the solar cell field. These highly efficient devices are constructed from silicon, like the solar cells that power our satellites and manned vehicles in space. A new process has made it possible to produce these cells on a commercial basis, allowing more power for less dollars.

Solar energy is a non-polluting, ecologically safe source of power. At any instant, the sun delivers 1000 watts per square meter to the earth's surface. Most of this energy is absorbed as heat by the earth, sea and air. The solar cells now make it possible for you to tap the unlimited energies of the sun, and to produce power without pollution.

These solar cells and panels are offered in many configurations, each suited to a wide range of applications.

Each cell in these panels is tested at 2,800°K color temp., at intensities equivalent to sunlight at 25°C ±3°C. Each works from -65 to 125°C and has a transparent protective coating. All operate without a plastic lens (formerly needed to increase efficiency) for just about any solar energy application. Cells conservatively rated at 100mW/cm^2 light intensity at .45v, 25°C. All are silicon n/p type.

Solar Panels

Edmund Solar Panels are currently in active use at the South Pole and all over the world. They operate under the most demanding situations to deliver the maximum energy attainable from the sun. When used with a suitable battery, the panel/battery combination can deliver electrical power during both day and night.

Each panel consists of varying arrangements of silicon solar cells, in series, with a blocking diode. These cells convert light directly to electricity. The panels provide DC power to operate various equipment directly, or can be attached to a rechargeable battery supply to charge battery for intermittent high current use. They supply power in any location where a reasonable amount of sunlight is available. Each panels is only 0.25" thick and hermetically sealed and weatherproofed for outdoor installation. Panels conservatively rated at 100mW/cm^2 light @25°C. They are supplied with polarized leads.

No. 72,194: 7V, 1.2 Amp, 8 Watt Solar Panel

This panel charges any 6-volt battery. It measures ¼ x 10¼ x 20", and is made from full 3-inch cells. The unit has polarized Teflon-coated leads and contains a series blocking diode to eliminate battery discharge during non-light conditions.

No. 80,249: 14.5V, 1.3 Amp Solar Panel

This panel charges any 12-volt battery. It measures ¼ x 20 x 20" and is made of full 3" cells. It delivers 20 watts at full sun and has a series blocking diode and Teflon-coated leads.

No. 80,250: Mounting Bracket

A rugged, heavy duty (withstands winds to 150 knots), 20 x 20" Universal Mounting Bracket for positioning unit toward the sun. Made from white enamel painted aluminum. Use on telephone poles or a 2" pipe. Use with 20 x 20", 20-watt panel (No. 80,249) or any panel of similar dimensions.

Here are a few advantages of these amazing new solar cells:

1. They are many times more efficient per cost than any offered before.
2. They are extremely flat and do not require a plastic lens for efficiency.
3. The most powerful solar cell available on today's market.
4. Developed through space technology and testing.
5. Can be placed in series for more voltage or parallel for more current.
6. Provide sufficient power to be useful in many varied electronic circuits.
7. Provides less bulk per output than previous models.
8. Has no moving parts to wear out.
9. Has virtually unlimited life.

Materials

Materials in all solar panels are weather-resistant. In general, epoxy fiberglas and silicone materials are utilized, exhibiting long life under terrestrial environmental conditions. They are able to withstand mechanical or thermal shock. In special cases other materials and additional surface layers may be added to achieve high impact resistance or to avoid icing.

Installation

All solar panels may be left permanently exposed to the sun or artificial light source, as the amount of charge delivered is directly related to the amount of light it receives. The preferred installation is also acceptable (if it provides the most exposure to the sun). More than one panel may be interconnected in series or parallel to provide the necessary power requirements.

Operating Temperature

The solar panels operate in a wide temperature range without change in specifications. The panels are able to operate between -70 to +150°F. Efficiency increases at lower temperatures and decreases at higher temperatures.

Maintenance

The solar panel is maintenance free. As it is converting light to electricity, it is natural that its light-collecting surface should be kept clean. Thin layers of dust, dirt or ice will not considerably decrease its efficiency. Rain usually removes dirt and restores the original surface. It is possible that unusual contaminants may require cleaning; in such cases, soap and water is sufficient to remove dirt.

Applications

The solar cells and panels can be used in a variety of applications. They can provide enough power to operate a desk top mini-computer. They can also be used to supply the operating power for remote telemetry stations. The U.S. Forestry Service uses similar panels at stations which are snowbound much of the year. As long as there is sunshine, the panel will effectively produce electricity at a very low cost. The solar panel can keep a trickle charge on a boat's·battery during the daytime. This is very useful on a sailboat where there is usually no generator available to charge the battery. The built-in diode prevents the battery from discharging at night. The solar panel makes it possible to leave your battery on the boat during the winter.The constant charge provided by the panel will prevent the battery from freezing. To use the solar panel as a battery charger, simply connect the + lead of the panel to the + terminal of the battery and the - lead of the panel to the - lead of the battery.

Some other Applications:
1. Signal buoys at sea
2. Direct operation of small motors
3. Irrigation pumps
4. Alarm Systems

HOW PANEL WORKS

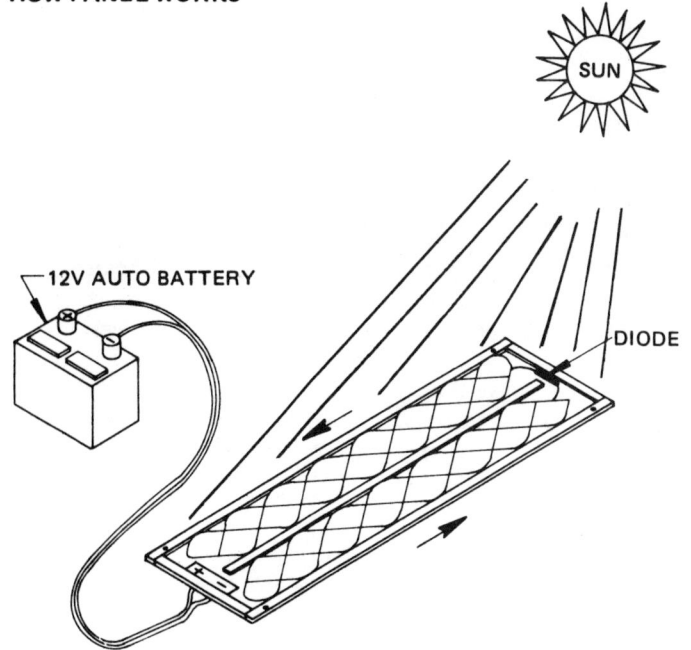

SOLAR CELLS AND PANELS

General

The solar energy conversion device which you have just purchased represents the greatest value to date in the solar cell field. These highly efficient devices are constructed from silicon, like the solar cells that power our satellites and manned vehicles in space. A new process has made it possible to produce these cells on a commercial basis, allowing more power for less dollars.

Solar energy is a non-polluting, ecologically safe source of power. At any instant, the sun delivers 1340 watts per square meter to the earth's surface. Most of this energy is absorbed as heat by the earth, sea and air. The solar cells now make it possible for you to tap the unlimited energies of the sun, and to produce power without pollution.

These solar cells and panels are offered in many configurations, each suited to a wide range of applications.

Here are a few advantages of these amazing new solar cells:

1. They are 5 to 10 times more efficient per cost than any offered before.
2. They are extremely flat and do not require a plastic lens for efficiency.
3. The most powerful solar cell available on today's market.
4. Developed through space technology and testing.
5. Can be placed in series for more voltage or parallel for more current.
6. Provide sufficient power to be useful in many varied electronic circuits.
7. Provides less bulk per output than previous models.
8. Has no moving parts to wear out.
9. Has virtually unlimited life.

Materials:

Materials in all solar panels are weather-resistant. In general, epoxy fiberglas and silicone materials are utilized, exhibiting long life under terrestrial environmental conditions. They are able to withstand mechanical or thermal shock. In special cases other materials and additional surface layers may be added to achieve high impact resistance or to avoid icing.

Installation

All solar cells & panels may be left permanently exposed to the sun or artificial light source, as the amount of charge delivered is directly related to the amount of light it receives. The preferred installation is at a 45°angle oriented toward the south, but horizontal or vertical installation is also acceptable (if it provides the most exposure to the sun). More than one panel may be interconnected in series or parallel to provide the necessary power requirements.

Operating Temperature

The solar panels operate in a wide temperature range without change in specifications. The panels are able to operate between -70° to +150°F. Efficiency increases at lower temperatures and decreases at higher temperatures.

HOW PANEL WORKS

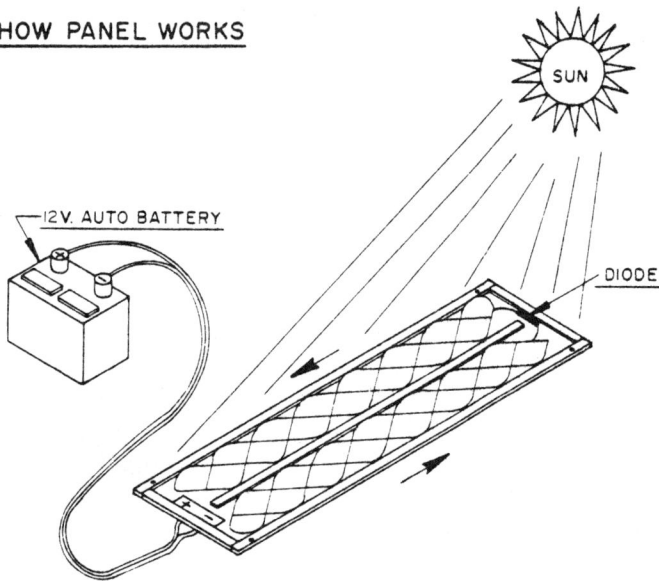

Maintenance

The solar panel is maintenance free. As it is converting light to electricity, it is natural that its light-collecting surface should be kept clean. Thin layers of dust, dirt or ice will not considerably decrease its efficiency. Rain usually removes dirt and restores the original surface. It is possible that unusual contaminants may require cleaning; in such cases, soap and water is sufficient to remove dirt.

Applications

The solar cells and panels can be used in a variety of applications. No. 72,097 and 72,068 can provide enough power to operate a desk top mini-computer. They can also be used to supply the operating power for remote telemetry stations. The U.S. Forestry Service uses similar panels at stations which are snowbound much of the year. As long as there is sunshine, the panel will effectively produce electricity at a very low cost. No. 72,123 was especially designed for use on small boats. The solar panel can keep a trickle charge on the boat's battery during the daytime. This is very useful on a sailboat where there is usually no generator available to charge the battery. The built-in diode prevents the battery from discharging at night. The solar panel makes it possible to leave your battery on the boat during the winter. The constant charge provided by the panel will prevent the battery from freezing. And the panel works just as well on cloudy or overcast days. To use the solar panel as a battery charger, simply connect the + lead of the panel to the + terminal of the battery and the - lead of the panel to the - lead of the battery.

Some other Applications:
1. Signal Buoys at sea
2. Direct operation of small motors
3. Irrigation pumps
4. Alarm Systems

REFERENCES
1. Halliday & Resnick, "Physics", Parts
   I & II, John Wiley & Sons, New York.
   Supplementary p. 46 (1966)

Chapter 6

ASTRONOMY

The movement of the stars and planets can keep you absorbed for hours. Science has probed the heavens to an extent never before imagined possible, and the astronauts have carried astronomical instruments to an area beyond the filtering screen of the heavens to where more-clear and lucid views could be had. Now you too, can probe the skies, and learn the true wonders of nature that science is able to reveal.

HOW TO USE YOUR 3-INCH REFLECTOR

PERFORMANCE *Data*	
LIGHT POWER	YOU CAN SEE STARS TO 10½ MAGNITUDE
RESOLVING POWER	DOUBLE STAR — 3 SECONDS OF ARC
MAGNIFYING POWER	30X ...UP TO 90X POSSIBLE WITH BARLOW

EYEPIECE

EYETUBE HOLDER

EYEPIECE TUBE (FOCUSING TUBE)

FINDER 3X 7° FIELD

SUPPORT

SUPPORT

MAIN TUBE

BASE BRACKET

FINDER MOUNT

KEEPER

WING NUT

PREFITTING LEG BOLTS

FORK

TRIPOD HEAD

SOUTH LEG

THUMB TACK TO IDENTIFY SOUTH LEG (NOT SUPPLIED)

TELESCOPE SET UP FOR USE
... IS POINTING SOUTH ON MERIDIAN NEAR CELESTIAL EQUATOR

YOUR Edmund 3-inch Reflecting Telescope is made with precision optical elements and the complete telescope is tested and collimated to make sure you get a workable instrument. You can see the rings around Saturn, pick out the Straight Wall on the moon and resolve many of the famous M-objects including diffuse nebulae and open clusters of stars. In light grasp, the 3-inch reflector will show stars to 10½ magnitude, putting over 400,000 stars within reach of the big eye of your telescope. Extra power up to 90X can be obtained with the Barlow lens. High power is used mainly for moon and planetary detail and splitting very close double stars.

ASSEMBLY

In order to make shipping easier the tripod legs and the finder telescope are not attached. In fitting the legs, it is best to seat the heads of the carriage bolts as a bench job (see drawing). The bolts are then knocked out with a mallet and the final assembly to tripod head is easily made without a lot of heavy hammering in an awkward position. The legs should

be spread 26 to 30 inches apart. Turn the assembled tripod so that the leg opposite the slanting top of tripod head is toward the south, as shown in drawing. This is the proper position of the tripod for stargazing. Mount the telescope on the cradle by means of the bolts and wing nuts provided.

The finder telescope is assembled with its own optics and is ready to use except that you must fit it to the base bracket. To mount the finder, the wire supports are spread slightly and slipped over the end of the finder tube, after which the supports are fitted between the base bracket and keepers, as shown in drawing. It is worthwhile to look through and test the finder before you mount it. The scope is 3-power and shows a wide 7-degree field which you'll appreciate when it comes to finding sky objects. The alignment of the finder to center on the same target as the main telescope should not be done until you are satisfied with the alignment (collimation) of the main telescope itself. If you are in a hurry to get a "first look," you can of course use the telescope without the finder.

Collimation

THE SECRET of collimating a reflector is to look at just one thing at a time. First, check the position of the diagonal--it should be squarely under the eyepiece tube. There is no adjustment for this but since it is checked at the factory, no adjustment should be necessary. Second, direct your attention to the reflection of main mirror seen in the diagonal. It should appear as at B in the drawing. If off to one side (A), adjust by twisting the diagonal base slightly; grip the metal, not the mirror. A fault indicates an error in angle. There is no adjustment for this; if your scope shows a bad fault it will be necessary to bend the diagonal base to correct the error.

Third, direct your critical attention to the small reflection of the diagonal. This should be centered, as at E. One nice feature about the 3-inch reflector is that its small size permits you to see exactly what happens when you turn the main mirror adjusting nuts. This being the case, no adjusting rules are needed although it is helpful to remember that the reflection moves away from the nut you tighten.

Note again that the first part of collimation is to center the main mirror reflection in the diagonal--this is entirely a diagonal adjustment. The second part is to center the small reflection--this is entirely a main mirror adjustment. At all times, try to keep your eye centered in regards to the eyepiece tube. You can check your eye position by noting the amount of wall seen around the inside of the eyepiece tube. A sighting ring may be used if desired.

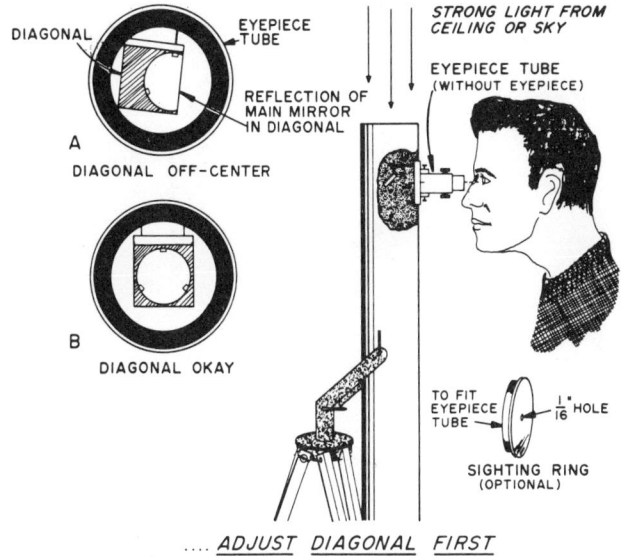

DIAGONAL / EYEPIECE TUBE / REFLECTION OF MAIN MIRROR IN DIAGONAL

A — DIAGONAL OFF-CENTER

B — DIAGONAL OKAY

STRONG LIGHT FROM CEILING OR SKY

EYEPIECE TUBE (WITHOUT EYEPIECE)

TO FIT EYEPIECE TUBE — 1/16" HOLE

SIGHTING RING (OPTIONAL)

.... *ADJUST DIAGONAL FIRST*

.... *THEN ALIGN MAIN MIRROR*

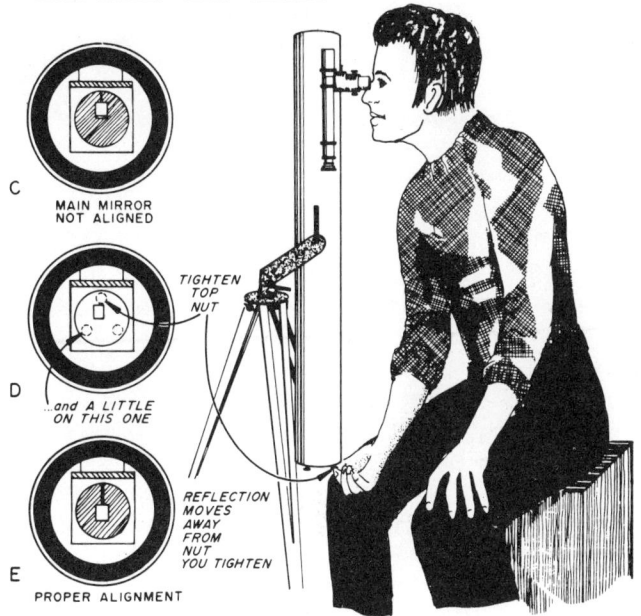

C — MAIN MIRROR NOT ALIGNED

D — TIGHTEN TOP NUT ...and A LITTLE ON THIS ONE

E — PROPER ALIGNMENT

REFLECTION MOVES AWAY FROM NUT YOU TIGHTEN

HOW A REFLECTING TELESCOPE WORKS

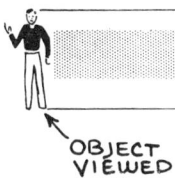

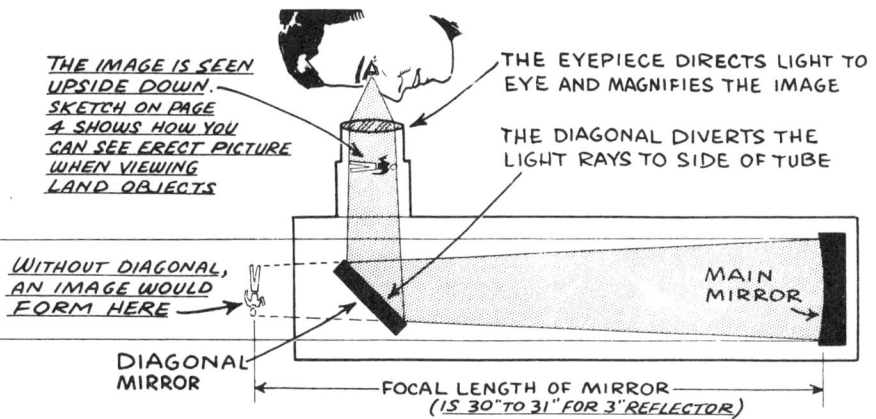

THE IMAGE IS SEEN UPSIDE DOWN. SKETCH ON PAGE 4 SHOWS HOW YOU CAN SEE ERECT PICTURE WHEN VIEWING LAND OBJECTS

THE EYEPIECE DIRECTS LIGHT TO EYE AND MAGNIFIES THE IMAGE

THE DIAGONAL DIVERTS THE LIGHT RAYS TO SIDE OF TUBE

WITHOUT DIAGONAL, AN IMAGE WOULD FORM HERE

OBJECT VIEWED

DIAGONAL MIRROR

MAIN MIRROR

FOCAL LENGTH OF MIRROR (IS 30" TO 31" FOR 3" REFLECTOR)

BIG DIPPER ABOVE POLE WITH MIZAR ON MERIDIAN (JUNE, 8-9 o'clock)

MIZAR AND ALCOR IN 16' FIELD (Telescope View)

SHORT FORK EQUATORIAL MOUNT

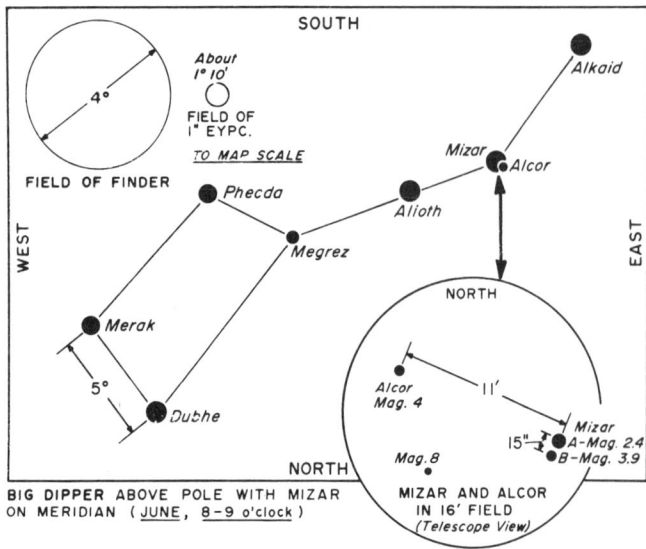

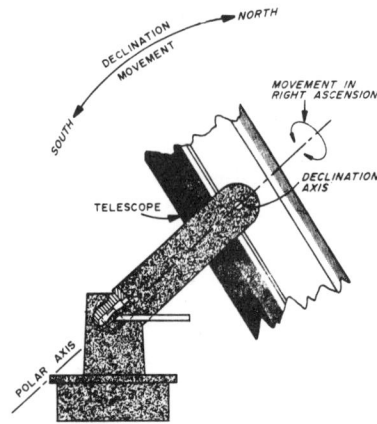

Observing HINTS

IF PRACTICAL, start your stargazing with objects in the southern sky. The moon and all of the planets are located in this general area, as well as many interesting star clusters, double stars and nebs, all visible with your 3-inch reflector. You will find the equatorial mount very easy to manipulate for south sky objects because the action is a simple up and down movement in declination, and an east-west movement in right ascension. Tension on the polar axis is applied by means of the triangular pressure plate and thumb screw, using only minimum tension. More tension is required on the declination axis to keep the scope from falling down of its own weight.

You can stand on either side of the telescope. The average person looks with his right eye, and in such case a position on the east side of telescope is the most comfortable. The finder is also on the east side so that you don't have to change your position to use it.

For north sky objects, the telescope is swung around to point north. All equatorial mounts have a complex movement for north sky objects, and you may find the action confusing. Also, with this particular mount, a crescent of the northern sky near the zenith is inaccessible. For these reasons, you may find it much handier to observe the north sky by turning the telescope and mount around, that is, putting the south leg to the north. When this is done you lose the equatorial action, but you get a simple up-down, east-west movement the same as south sky--and all of the north sky is accessible.

FIELD OF VIEW

Much time is wasted trying to find sky objects with the small field of the 1 inch eyepiece. The diagram above may explain why. Notice that with the big 7-degree field of the finder, you can see a goodly area of sky, whereas the 1 inch eyepiece covers just a tiny circle of sky. So—have your finder properly adjusted--and use it! Even with the big field of the finder, beginners have difficulty in pointing the scope at a sky object. You may find it helpful to rough-sight the object along the top of the telescope tube; then pick it up in the finder and finally in the telescope eyepiece.

FOCUSING

Focusing is done by moving the eyepiece tube in or out with a slight twisting movement. Practice on daytime objects until you get the "feel" of it. On star objects, exact focus is obtained when the star image is made as small as possible. Focusing is made more difficult by the fact that a light-duty mount tends to vibrate more than a larger, heavier one. The trick is to steady the tube with your hand and make the focusing movement as smoothly as possible. Any vibration will make the star image a large, dancing blob of light. After you think you have the best focus, take your hands off the tube and do not touch the eyepiece with your face. Give the telescope a few seconds to settle down and you should then see your star image clearly and distinctly. Once exact focus is obtained, you need not repeat the operation unless you think it is possible to obtain a better focus.

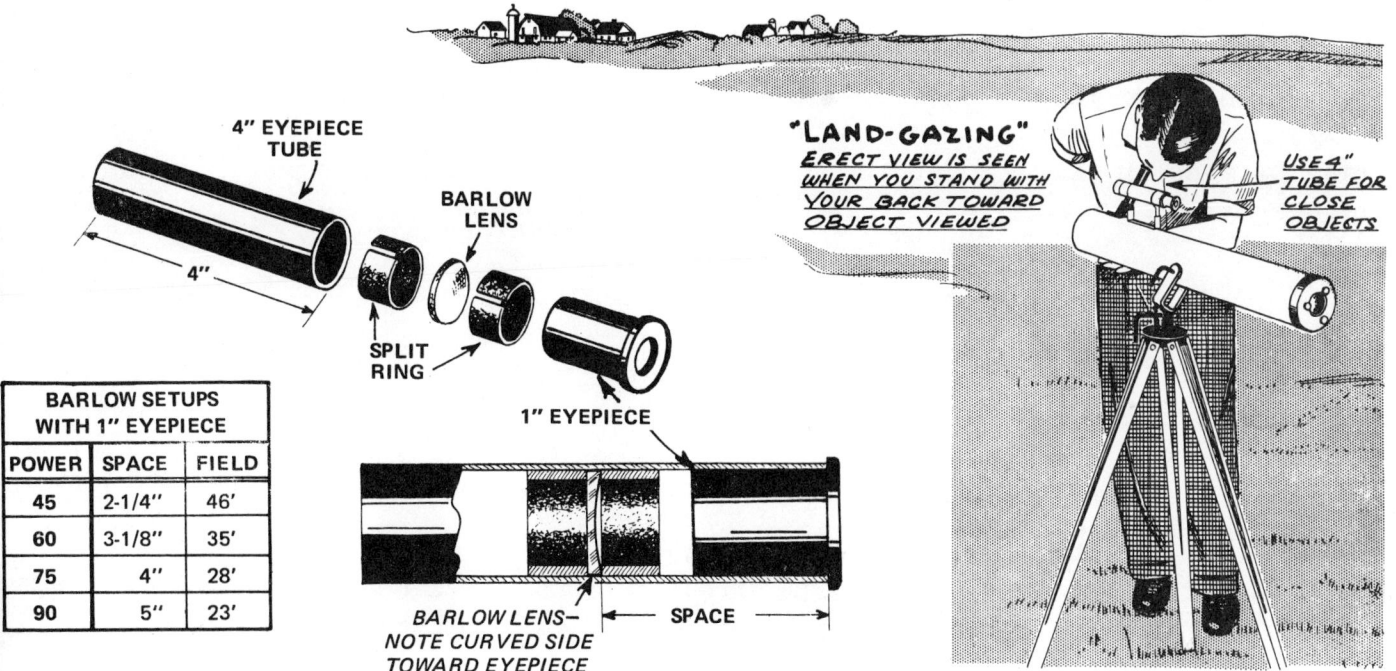

4" EYEPIECE TUBE

BARLOW LENS

SPLIT RING

1" EYEPIECE

BARLOW LENS—NOTE CURVED SIDE TOWARD EYEPIECE

SPACE

"LAND-GAZING"
ERECT VIEW IS SEEN WHEN YOU STAND WITH YOUR BACK TOWARD OBJECT VIEWED

USE 4" TUBE FOR CLOSE OBJECTS

BARLOW SETUPS WITH 1" EYEPIECE		
POWER	SPACE	FIELD
45	2-1/4"	46'
60	3-1/8"	35'
75	4"	28'
90	5"	23'

THE BARLOW LENS PROVIDES A SIMPLE YET PRACTICAL WAY TO OBTAIN EXTRA MAGNIFICATION WITH YOUR 1" EYEPIECE

MAGNIFICATION

Very little actual magnification will be noted in viewing stars because they are so far away as to appear as mere pinpoints of light even when viewed at the highest power of the world's largest telescopes. The thing that makes a star look big is simply how much light the objective (mirror) can pick up. Also, a bright star puts out more light than a faint one and appears to be bigger in the telescope. The bright giants of the sky such as Vega, Antares, Rigel, Sirius, etc., are unmistakable in any telescope and these brilliant beacons serve as guideposts to lead you to fainter, even invisible, sky objects.

The effect of magnification can be seen instantly on any extended sky object, such as the moon, planets and double stars. A 3-inch telescope will split double stars down to 3 seconds of arc separation, but for a starter you should not try anything closer than about 8 seconds of arc. The Trapezium at the end of the dark bay in M 42, Orion, is a fine multiple star (four stars) with a minimum separation of 8 seconds. The best "first double" is Mizar in the Big Dipper, with a comfortable separation of 15 seconds of arc. The diagram on previous page shows how Mizar looks in the telescope. Note that while the 1° 10' field of the eyepiece seems small compared to the dipper, it is quite large compared to individual sky objects. The diagram shows only 1/5 of the visible field, yet in this area you can see Mizar A and B and also the rider

(Alcor) 11 minutes away. Some idea of the immensity of outer space can be gained from the fact that it would take 4 million planets the size of our earth to span the tiny distance between Mizar A and Mizar B.

BARLOW LENS

The drawing above shows how the Barlow lens is combined with the 1 inch eyepiece to obtain high magnification. The greater the distance between Barlow lens and eyepiece, the higher the magnification. Select the power you want and then locate the Barlow lens at the proper "space" from the end of the tube. It will be necessary to tape the 2½" long eyepiece tube to the end of the 4" barlow tube when using the barlow at 60, 75 or 90 power. Fit the eyepiece in place and focus in the usual manner, the only difference being that the Barlow requires more "out" travel of the focusing tube than the eyepiece used alone.

LAND-GAZING

Day views at 60-power are wonderfully clear, bright and highly magnified--you will enjoy using your telescope in this fashion. Use the 4 inch eyepiece tube for this since its longer length allows you to focus near objects--you can get down to about 40 yards. The object viewed can be seen fully erect if you stand with your back to object and then look into the eyepiece, as shown in drawing above.

MOTORIZED CLOCK DRIVE

The motorized clock drive for astronomical telescopes is designed to be attached easily to any equatorial mount. With slight changes that can be made in any machine shop, it can be adapted to fit many home-made equatorials and those of other manufacturers.

ADAPTATIONS NECESSARY FOR INSTALLATION ON EQUATORIALS

If the holes in the Eccentric Pin Support and/or the gear shaft holder are too large for your mount, then you should have bushings made of the proper thickness to make up the difference.

If the holes are too small, then you should have the polar axis and polar axis housing machined down to the appropriate diameters.

	Clock Drive Diameter	Clock Drive Diameter
Hole in Pin Support	1-1/2"	1"
Hole in Gear Shaft	1"	5/8"

ATTACHING THE CLOCK DRIVE TO THE EQUATORIALS

The polar axis is held in its housing by a metal collar with a set screw. Remove and discard this collar.

Slide the pin support onto the polar axis housing. Do not tighten it into place yet.

Position the gear shaft holder on the polar axis shaft with approximately .003" clearance between it and the end of the axis housing. Tighten the two set screws which can be located through clearance holes in the outer aluminum casting. Be sure the two cylinders at the top are snugly against the eccentric pin and clamped tightly in place.

USING THE CLOCK DRIVE

The clock drive motor operates on 110 volt, 60 cycle A.C. A 3-prong grounded plug is included for safe outdoor use (especially in wet areas). When using extension cords and inverters or other devices that attach to the line cord, do not attempt to defeat the purpose of the ground. For use where such current is not available, it can be driven from an automobile storage battery and an inverter.

If you use your telescope close to an electric outlet, you can use a light duty extension cord. But remember that the greater the distance from your power supply the heavier your extension cord should be in order to prevent a drop in voltage which could prevent your drive from functioning properly.

BALANCING THE TELESCOPE

With a clock drive attached, your telescope will track celestial objects best if the telescope is properly balanced and oriented.

To adjust the balance of your telescope, loosen the polar axis lock knob and the two thumb screws on the end of the gear shaft so that the instrument moves freely on the polar axis. Move the counterweight or counterweights back and forth until you find the setting that permits the telescope to remain in any position in which it is placed without tightening the lock knob or the gear thumb screws. This can be done only by trial and error. It may take considerable time, but it will be worth it. If you attempt to use a clock drive with an unbalanced telescope, you will not be able to track objects properly and the gears and motor of the drive may be unnecessarily worn by the strain that lack of balance imposes on them.

When the instrument is in balance, tighten the two thumb screws just enough to give slight resistance when you turn the instrument by hand on the polar axis. Do not overtighten. With the proper amount of tension, the special clutching arrangement will permit the clock drive to turn the instrument as it should, yet at any time you can shift the telescope by hand to observe a different celestial object without having to disengage the clutch.

Do not retighten the polar axis lock knob. This should be left loose. It may, if desired, be removed entirely to eliminate the possibility of its being tightened accidentally. If you remove the lock knob, however, it is wise to replace it with a machine screw of the same thread cut short enough so that it will not touch the shaft when screwed all the way in. This will keep dirt from entering the bearing through the lock knob hole.

USING THE TELESCOPE WITH CLOCK DRIVE

Once your telescope is well balanced and properly oriented, you can enjoy the advantages of automatic clock drive. When moving the telescope on its polar axis by hand, do so slowly and without sudden jerky motions. When the object is centered in the field, lock the declination axis and that's all there is to it. The clock drive will automatically compensate for most of the apparent motions resulting from the rotation of the earth on its axis.

MANUAL TRACKING COMPENSATING LEVER

This is the rotatable pin operating between the two short cylinders screwed down on the housing. It serves as a universal joint and also as a fine adjustment for tracking. A short (4" - 5") length of tubing can be fitted over the pin to make a sensitive and smooth adjustment action.

When you are tracking a heavenly body for long periods of time with the clock only, the object may gradually leave the field of view in the eyepiece.

If this happens move the slow motion lever to bring the object back into the field of view. At all times this lever is available to move easily from star to star within a limited area without having to bodily move the telescope.

Occasionally lubricate all of the bearings of the drive with light, non-gumming machine oil. The motor is permanently lubricated. If through excessive condensation or as a result of a sudden shower the clock drive gets wet, dry it off carefully and wipe the worm with light oil to prevent rusting.

128

CLOCK DRIVE

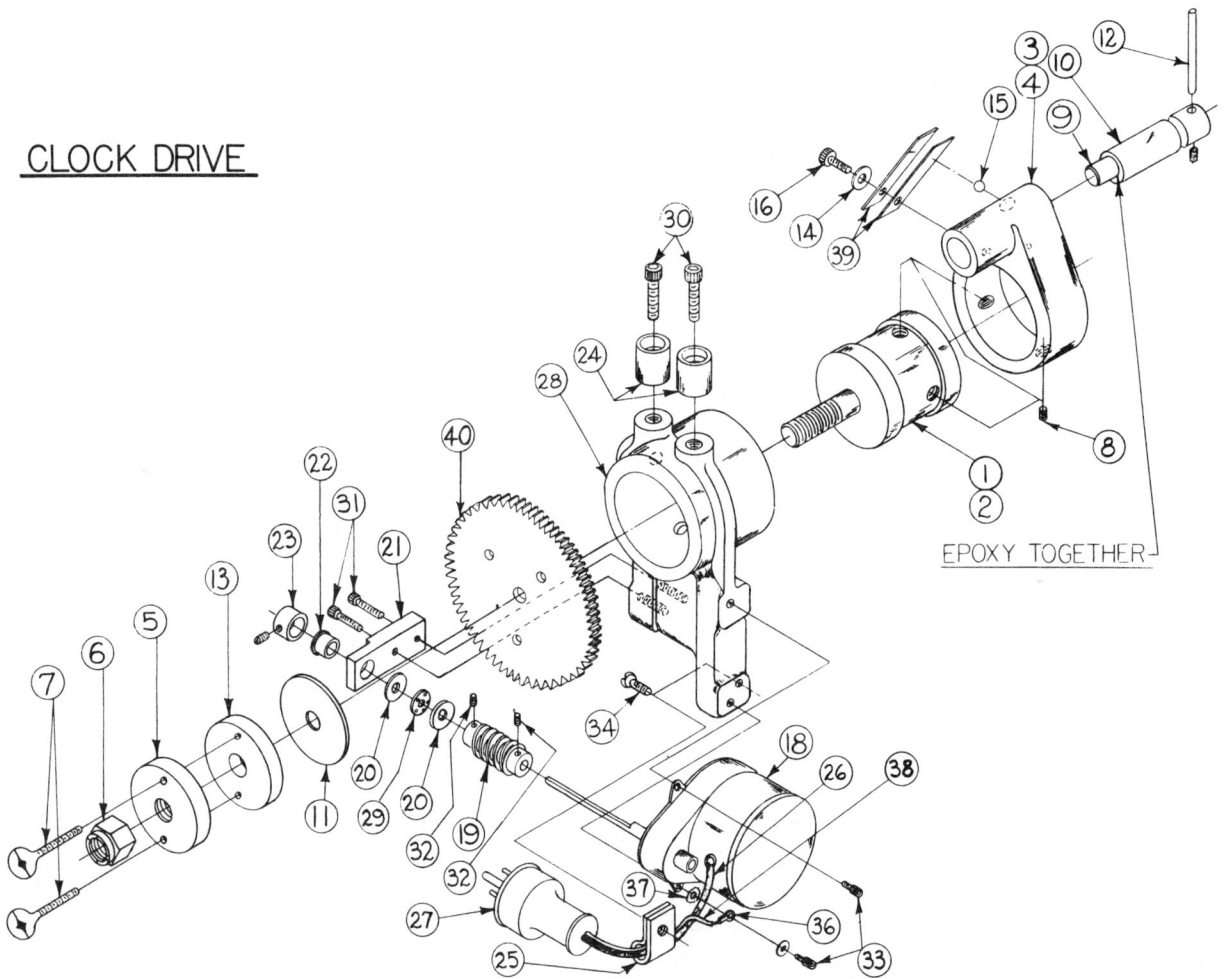

EPOXY TOGETHER

KEY NO.	DESCRIPTION	REQ.
1	Gear Shaft	1
2	Gear Shaft	1
3	Pin Support	1
4	Pin Support	1
5	Pressure Plate	1
6	3/8-24 Elastic Stop Nut	1
7	Thumb Screw #10-32 x 1" St'l. Cad. Pl.	2
8	1/4-20 x 1/4 Lg. Socket Hd. Set Screw-Flat Point	4
9	5/16" Diam. x 1-1/4" Dowel Pin St'l. Cad. Pl.	1
10	Eccentric Shaft	1
11	Washer, Vim Leather	1
12	Spring Pin-3/16" Diam. x 1-1/4"	1
13	Clutch Plate	1
14	#8 Flat Washer	1
15	Comm. Steel Ball -1/4" Diam.	1
16	#8-32 x 3/8 Lg. Socket Hd. Cap Screw	1
18	Clock Motor	1
19	Worm	1
20	Washer	2
21	Shaft Holder	1
22	Boston Bearing	1
23	Collor, Boston	1
24	Pin Clamp	2
25	#832 Smith Clamp	1
26	Spaghetti Tubing	1
27	Plug Ground	1
28	Clock Drive Body	1
29	Thrust Retainer	1
30	#10-32 x 3/4 Lg. Socket Hd. Cap Screw	2
31	#6-32 x 5/8 Lg. Socket Hd. Cap Screw	2
32	#4-48 x 1/8 Set Screw-Knurled Cup Point	2
33	#4-40 x 1/4 Lg. Socket Hd. Cap Screw	2
34	#6-32 x 1/4 Lg. Round Hd. Screw-Slotted	1
36	Ring Tongue	1
37	#4 Ext. Tooth Washer	1
38	Wire #18 GA.	1
39	Ball Retaining Spring	2
40	Worm Gear	1

MOTORIZED CLOCK DRIVE

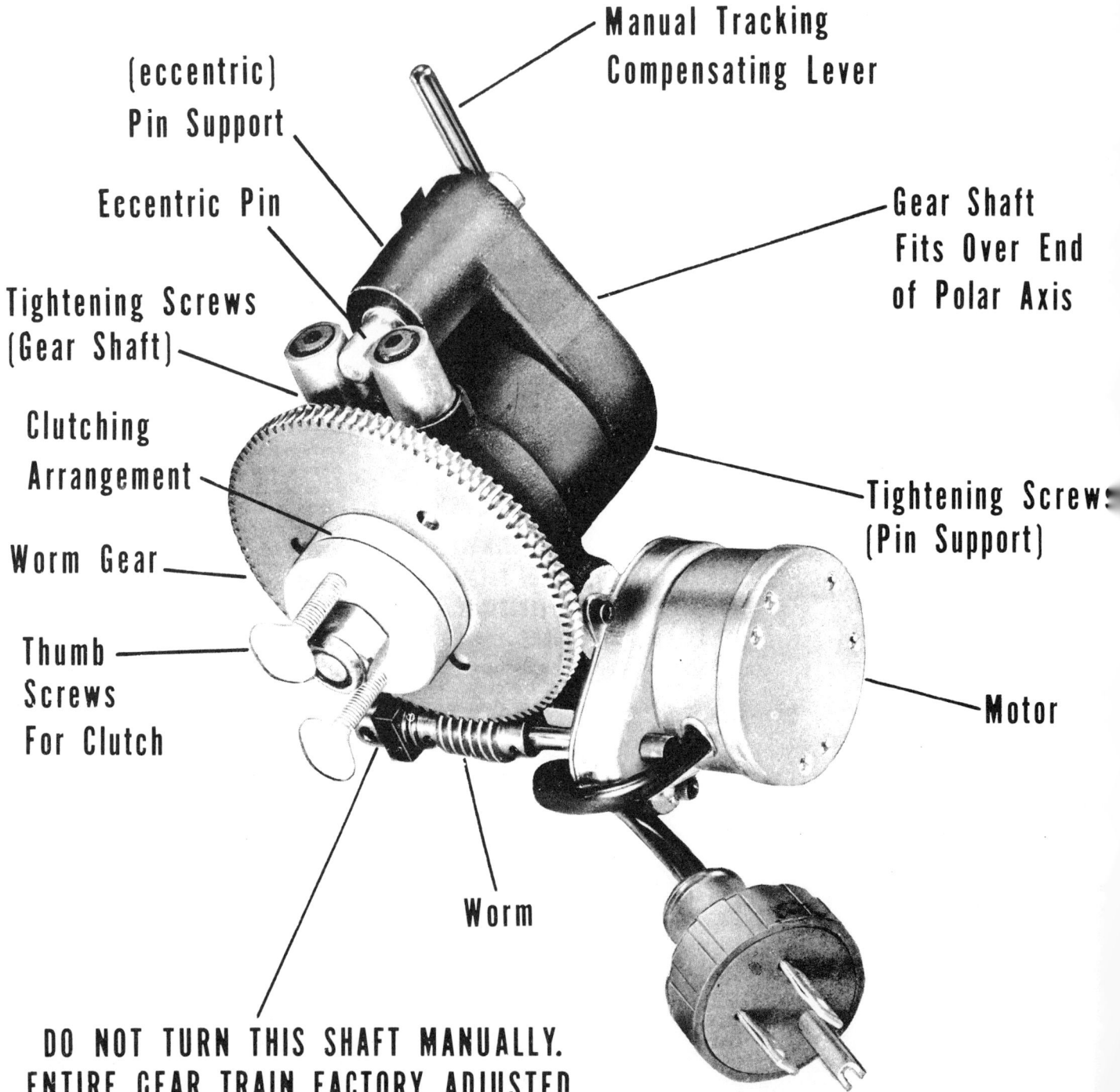

Manual Tracking
Compensating Lever

(eccentric)
Pin Support

Eecentric Pin

Gear Shaft
Fits Over End
of Polar Axis

Tightening Screws
(Gear Shaft)

Clutching
Arrangement

Tightening Screws
(Pin Support)

Worm Gear

Thumb
Screws
For Clutch

Motor

Worm

DO NOT TURN THIS SHAFT MANUALLY.
ENTIRE GEAR TRAIN FACTORY ADJUSTED.
−DO NOT TOUCH−

ASTRONOMICAL PHOTOS WITH
THE POLAROID® INSTRUMENT CAMERA

The Polaroid® Land Instrument Camera is a lensless camera specifically designed for photographing the images formed by optical instruments with eyepieces, such as microscopes and telescopes. All of the advantages of the Polaroid® photographic system are available for these specialized applications: the high speed films allow shorter exposures; you see the print moments after taking; corrections for optimum results can be made immediately; all without darkroom, chemicals, or other equipment.

Since the camera has no lens, the overall image quality is dependent on the instrument optics. These, and the skill of the operator, determine the quality of the finished pictures.

How It Works

The camera works on the principle of using the eyepiece as a projection lens. Figure 1 shows the instrument in focus for visual observation. Light from object A is focused by objective lens B to form an image at point C in the telescope. This image is magnified by the eyepiece D, emerging as parallel light rays, which, when operated on by the lens in the eye E, form an image on the retina F.

Figure 2 shows the instrument with camera focusing tube in place. The viewing lens G of the focusing tube automatically makes the eye look at point F inside the tube, which is the exact distance of the camera film plane from the eyepiece. As the eyepiece is moved closer to the objective, the rays converge. When adjusted for maximum sharpness, the image plane is at point F.

Figure 3 shows the focusing tube replaced by the camera. Note that the distance from the eyepiece D to the film plane is exactly the same as the distance from eyepiece D to the image plane F in Figure 2. The image will, therefore, be in sharp focus on the camera film.

Because the instrument eyepiece functions as a projector lens with the camera, the following changes in magnification or power occur:

When used with a Microscope:

$$\text{Magnification (Diameters)} = (.8)(\text{Power of Objective})(\text{Power of Eyepiece})$$

When used with a Telescope:

$$\text{Magnification (Diameters)} = \left(\frac{7.375}{\text{F.L. Eyepiece (inches)}}\right)\left(\frac{\text{Focal Length of Objective}}{\text{Focal Length of Eyepiece}}\right)$$

132

How To Use It

Since the other instructions supplied with the instrument camera fully describe its applications when used with a microscope, these instructions will be concerned only with its use with telescopes of the Newtonian reflector or the refractor type.

Since the problems are largely concerned with securing the camera, the use of camera support or something similar is almost a must. The post support should be secured to the tube with the hardware supplied.

For telescopes not drilled for the support, holes should be drilled as shown in Figure 4 for a reflecting telescope.

For a refractor type telescope, the same hole pattern should be drilled on the major diameter of the tube, as close to the eyepiece as possible. A typical installation is shown in Figure 5. Because of wide variations, only a typical installation can be shown.

The camera adapter is next installed over an appropriate eyepiece as shown in Figure 6. A similar arrangement is employed when using a refractor. Where eyepieces of smaller than 1-1/4" outside diameter are to be used, they must be

inserted in a centering washer held between the two threaded portions of the adapter. See the Polaroid[R] instructions for details.

After focusing through the camera focusing tube, the next step is the replacement of the tube with the camera. Since the focusing mount of the telescope is rarely vertical, the support problem is complicated by the fact that the camera must be positioned on the eyepiece adapter from the rear...ruling out any type of support which would restrict rearward movement.

We have found that the judicious applications of a 1/4-20 bolt and nut to the camera bracket and careful adjustment of the bracket on the post will provide support in the required two dimensions: one side of the camera body rests on the flat of the camera body; the adjacent 90° camera slide rests against the 1/4-20 screw and nut to prevent lateral slipping along the bracket. In cases where the mount is so positioned that gravity will not hold the camera, these supports can be augmented with a large rubber band around the camera and the camera bracket.

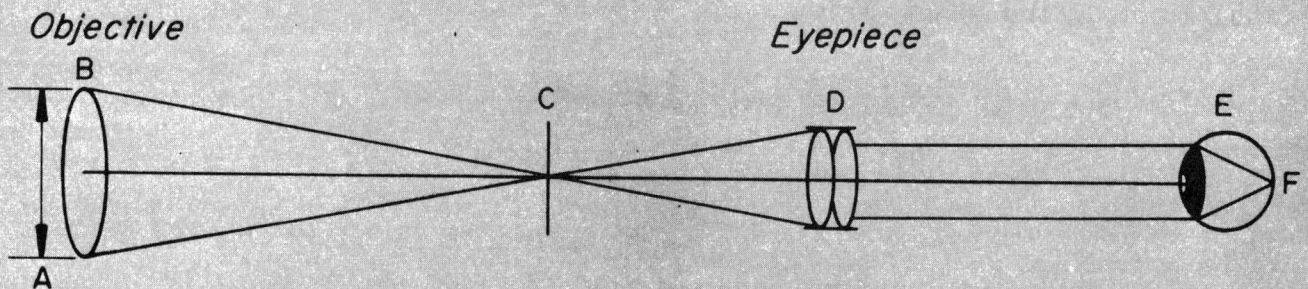

Figure 1. Telescope Optical System Focused For Visual Observation

Objective

Eyepiece Focusing Tube

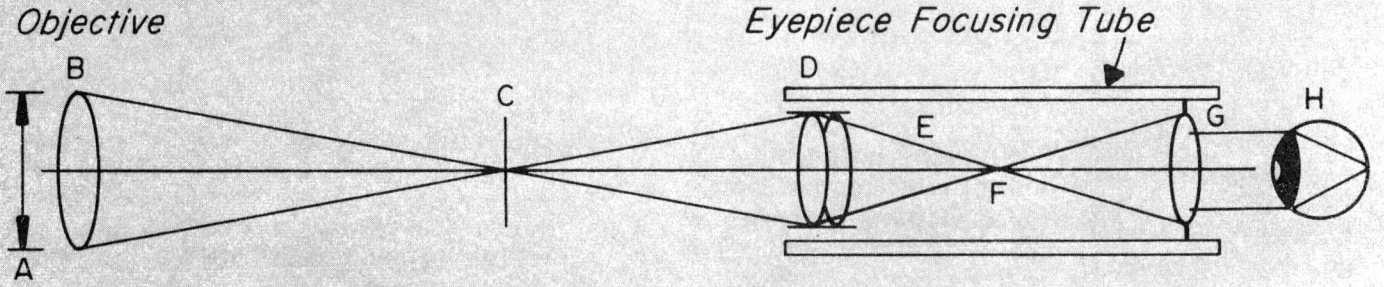

Figure 2. Telescope Optical System With Camera Focusing Tube In Place

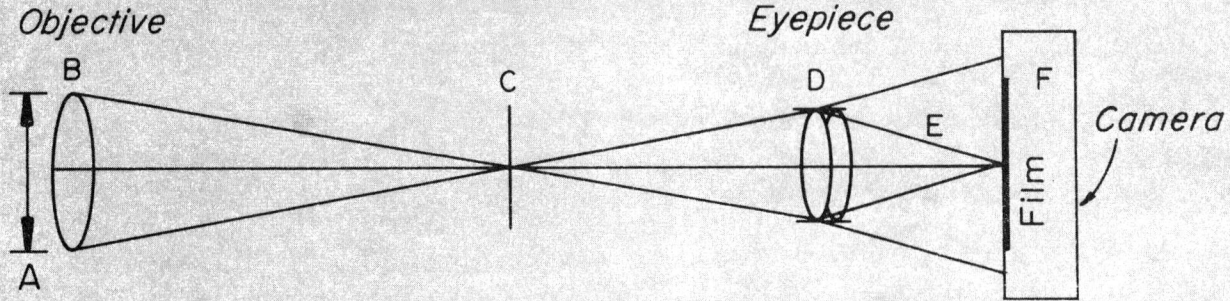

Objective

Eyepiece

Camera

Figure 3. Telescope Optical System With Camera In Place

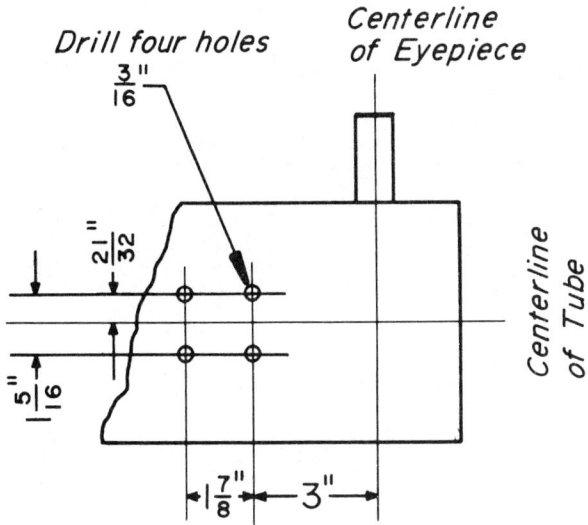

Drill four holes $\frac{3}{16}$"

Centerline of Eyepiece

Centerline of Tube

Figure 4. Mounting Holes For Post Support On Reflecting Telescope

Exposure

Using Land Pack Film No. 107 (ASA 3000), most exposures will be short. Suggested points of departures are listed below. These trial exposures were made with a F8 Newtonian reflecting telescope with a 25mm eyepeice.

Full moon approx. 1/4 sec.
Jupiter approx. 1 sec.
Sun (Herchel wedge diagonal and sun type eyepiece filter) approx. 2 sec.
Polaris approx. 1 sec.

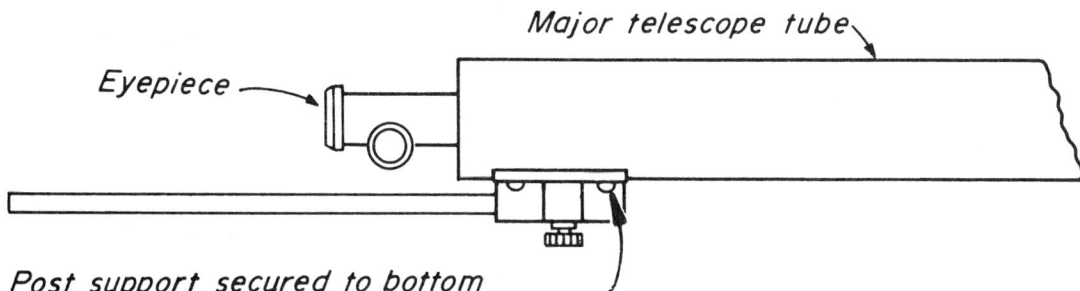

Major telescope tube

Eyepiece

Post support secured to bottom side of tube with four machine screws (Use drilling pattern of Fig. 4)

Figure 5. Camera Mounting Bracket Installation On Refracting Telescope

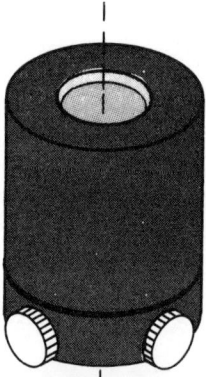

CAMERA ADAPTER
Slide over focusing tube
until adapter rests on top
of focusing rack; center
and secure with light pressure
on three plastic screws.

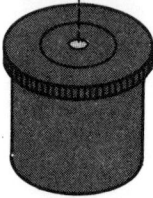

EYEPIECE
Insert in focusing tube

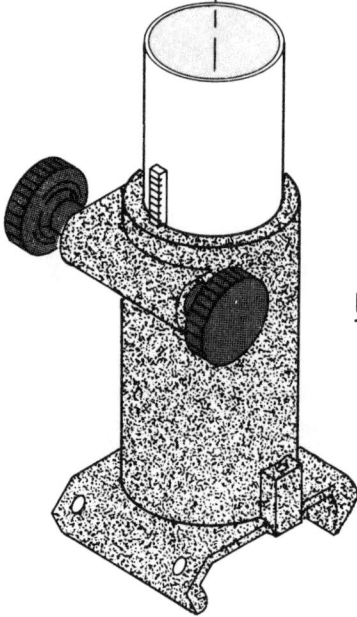

FOCUSING MOUNT

Fig. 6.   Adapter Eyepiece Focusing Mount
Arrangement

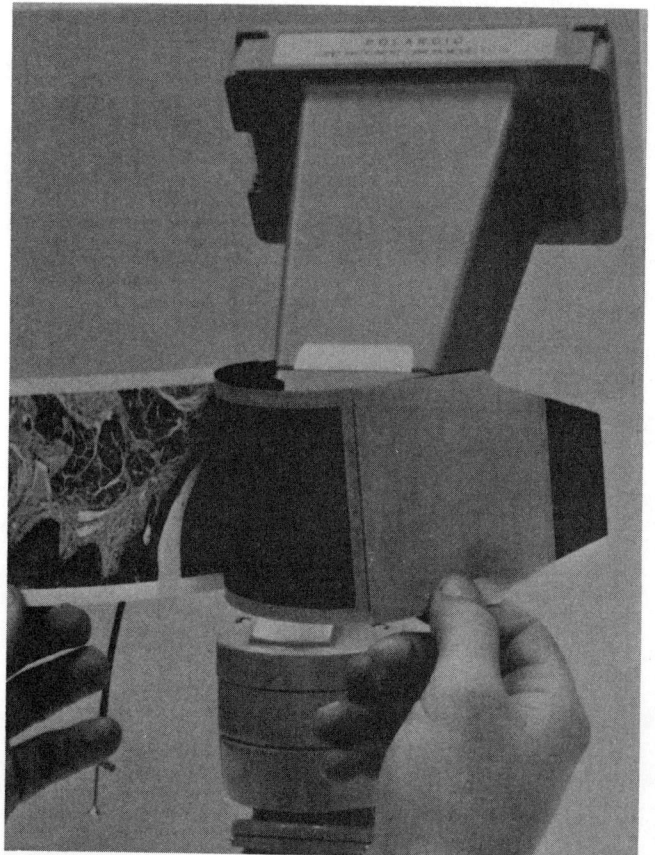

HEAVY DUTY MOUNT FOR LARGER TELESCOPES

Proper orientation of the telescope mount is essential to good observation of heavenly objects. The fundamental approach to this subject is simply stated: one must have the optical axis of the telescope properly aligned and the polar axis of the mount properly positioned. When these two requirements are met, the ease of observation becomes greatly enhanced.

The adjustment of the mount can be properly carried out following a number of methods, many of which can be found in the publication, AMATEUR ASTRONOMER'S HANDBOOK, by J. B. Sedgwick. One method commonly used by amateurs lends itself most easily for an initial setting of the mount.

Once the location and the desired pier or pedestal has been erected or placed, we may proceed with the installation. It is important to bear in mind that the pier should be constructed firmly and massively if possible (Fig. 1). With the completion of the pier, screw the cap on the threads. With a small compass, indicate the North Pole of the earth and screw the cap down until the short end of the polar axis housing points in this northerly direction. It is not necessary to use a wrench to tighten this cap at this stage, but merely to thread it as far as possible by hand, not exceeding the desired position of the polar axis pointing north. Any clear night the telescope is to be preliminarily aligned, remove the polar axis shaft and loosen any of the set screws in the cap holding the latitude shaft. Position the latitude arm in the center of the cap by adjusting either or both of the two set screws just enough to hold the arm firmly (Fig. 2).

Observe the North Star through the polar axis housing with the eye about a foot behind the south end of the housing. Alter the position of the mount until the North Star can be observed directly through and centered in the housing. With the Allen wrench, secure one of the set screws in the latitude arm locking the housing, keeping the North Star centered through the bearings. The cap may now be tightened on its threads. It is not necessary to have this mount cap overly tight on the threads, but it should be brought around until it is as snug as possible, yet still permit observation of the North Star through the polar axis bearings. When you feel that the mount has been preliminarily aligned, secure the set screw in the cap moderately tight against the threads, locking the cap and preventing it from rotating. Secure the two set screws in the latitude arm firmly—the other set screws which go against the latitude axis should not be secured, but made snug. Return the polar axis and the rest of the mount to its proper position. Place the telescope in the cradle and balance it by properly positioning the counterweights.

It is assumed at this point that the optical system in the tube is properly aligned. Proper collimation is a necessity. Reference for optical collimation is given in the instructions for the telescope. Alignment of the optical axis with the declination axis is fundamental. A relatively simple check (explained in the book by J. B. Sedgwick or AMATEUR TELESCOPE MAKING, Book One) should be carried out even though in manufacturing the mount caution was taken to properly machine the parts for good declination alignment.

With the telescope preliminarily set in this manner, you may use it for an indefinite period of time. However, when closer positioning is to be undertaken, the north celestial pole can be located with relation to the stars about it. From the diagram, it can be seen that the true pole lies about a degree from Polaris, and that a straight line drawn from a star in Cassiopeia to a star in the Big Dipper will pass through Polaris and very close to the pole. Whenever the stars are in a position where this straight imaginary line is either horizontal or vertical, adjustment of the telescope mount can easily be made. When this line is horizontal, the adjustment of the polar axis can be made through the latitude axis; and when the imaginary line is vertical, adjustment can be made by rotating the entire assembly about the threads. Both adjustments are necessary and can be easily complied with. If both adjustments are to be completed in the same night, there will be a six hour delay between the two. It is not necessary to have either one of the two adjustments first, but the position of the stars at the time of the adjustment will dictate which will be first.

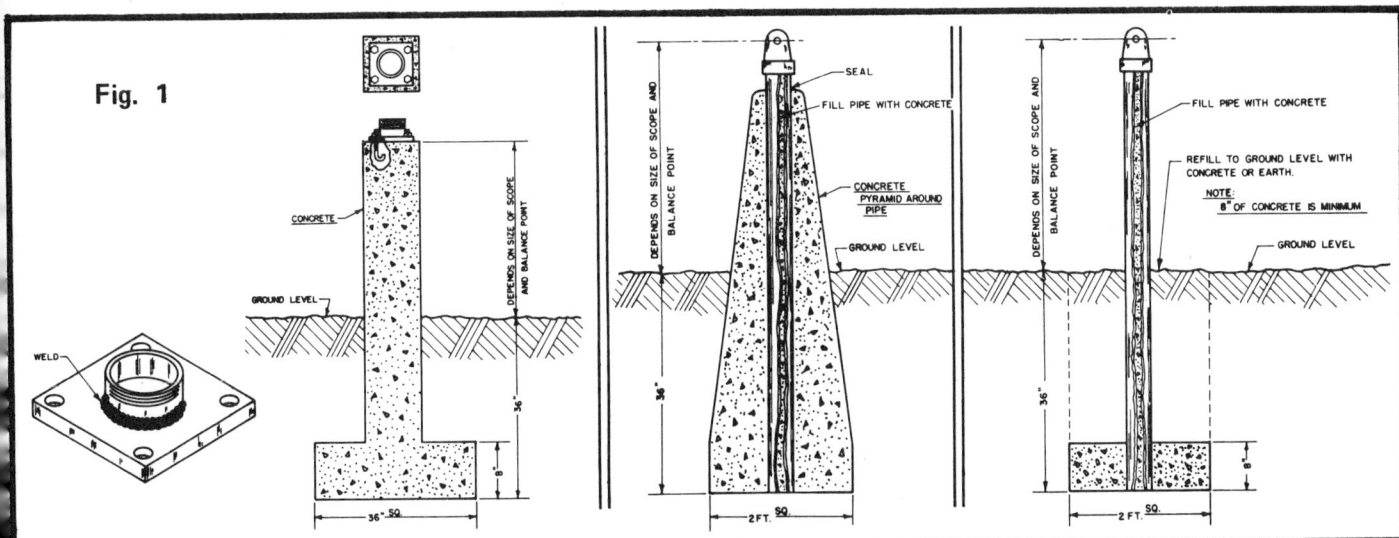

Fig. 1

Let us assume that Cassiopeia is just rising (or setting) and that the imaginary line is horizontal as in Fig. 3.

Arrange the telescope so that it is centered over the pier and mount, and point it in the general direction of the North Star. Carefully observe the mount and see that the telescope and mount are rotated and positioned in such a way that the assembly is on the meridian and in line, pointed toward the north.

Secure the polar axis shaft firmly by tightening the clamp. Do not permit this shaft to rotate. With a 1" eyepiece, observe the North Star through the telescope by only moving the declination axis. If the North Star can not be observed, alter the position of the latitude lever until the star can be observed in the eyepiece. Continue to move the lever and/or the telescope in the declination axis only until the star can be brought into the center of the low power eyepiece field. (Slight motion of the latitude axis arm produces a great deal of change in the sky.) Once the star has been centered in the low power eyepiece, insert an intermediate eyepiece and center the star in the same manner. Repeat this now with as high a power an eyepiece as you have, a four or six millimeter one if possible, positioning the star in the center of the field. When the star is centered to your satisfaction, very carefully tighten the two screws holding the latitude arm, while observing the star. Drive each of them into the arm locking it securely in place. Continue to observe the star and carefully secure the remaining four screws in the cap against the latitude axis. Do not attempt to tighten one at a time, but step up all four a turn at a time while observing the star as securely as you can, using only the Allen wrench. The latitude axis is now securely locked in place.

By waiting for six hours to elapse or until the sky has assumed the proper position another night, the second adjustment can be made by positioning the telescope as in Fig. 4. This is when the declination axis is horizontal. **Do not disturb the previous setting.** With the telescope in this position, secure very firmly the polar axis clamp, locking it. Loosen the single set screw in the cap, previously set snugly against the threads. The telescope and mount are now permitted to move in two directions only: for declination and rotation about the threads. By adjusting these two motions, observe the North Star in a 1" eyepiece. Once the North Star has been observed in this eyepiece by changing the declination and rotating the cap about the threads if necessary, replace the 1" eyepiece with a ½" eyepiece. Make the same observation, keeping the star in the center of the field, altering the position of the mount in either of these two directions if necessary. Repeat this same procedure with a short focal length eyepiece of four or six millimeters, keeping Polaris in the center of the field and altering only the two motions of declination or rotation. Once Polaris has been so centered, tighten the single set screws against the threads very securely. The mount is now favorably positioned quite close to the north celestial pole.

Care and Maintenance

A little lubricant occasionally put on the bearing faces is all that is required. This lubricant, however, should be sure suited to the temperature ranges of your locality. A protective cover over the assembly is desirable, even though precaution was taken to eliminate rust damage as much as possible.

To prevent scratching of your telescope tube in the cradle, if you use the rotating facility, it might be desirable to glue a small piece of felt on the four corners of the cradle which are in contact with your tube, as well as on the face of the handle which bears against the cradle.

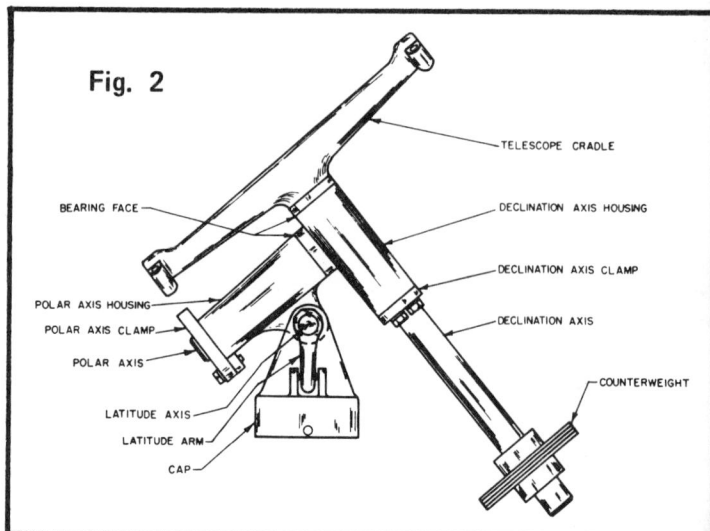

Fig. 2

TELESCOPE CRADLE
BEARING FACE
DECLINATION AXIS HOUSING
DECLINATION AXIS CLAMP
POLAR AXIS HOUSING
POLAR AXIS CLAMP
DECLINATION AXIS
POLAR AXIS
COUNTERWEIGHT
LATITUDE AXIS
LATITUDE ARM
CAP

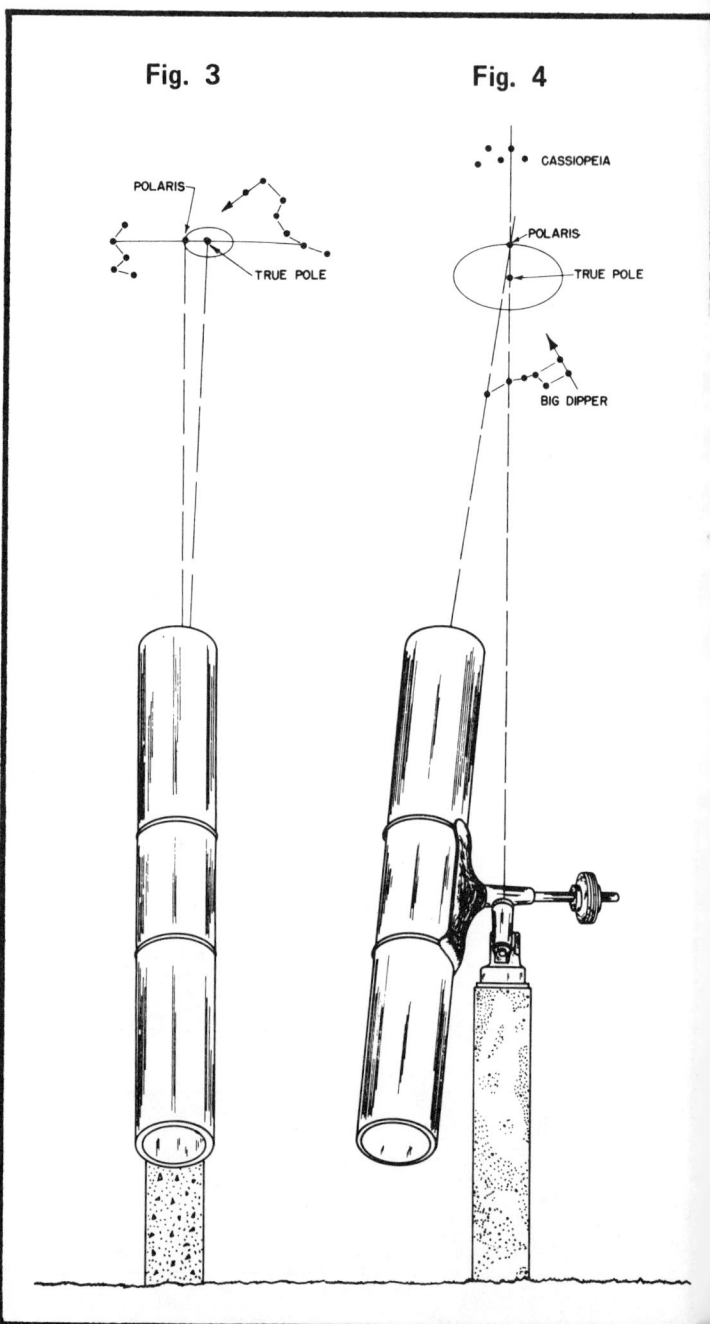

Fig. 3   Fig. 4

POLARIS
TRUE POLE
CASSIOPEIA
POLARIS
TRUE POLE
BIG DIPPER

8″ TELESCOPE

After removing the telescope from the box, centrally locate and secure it on its mount in a horizontal position.

Three screws hold the mirror cell and mirror in the telescope tube. (See Fig. 1.) Remove these three screws (being careful that spacer between cell and inner tube walls does not fall) and slip the cell out. Remove the shipping tapes and wrapping from the mirror and cell and return the unit to the tube in the same manner and position shown in Fig. 1. The cell and tube have index marks (put on with a china marker) to match up when returning the cell. Once matched up, your telescope will be collimated with only minor corrections to be made. The surface on this mirror is highly polished and should be handled with extreme care.

If minor collimation is necessary, have a second person adjust the thumb nuts one at a time. Observe through the eyepiece holder until you see your own eye looking back at you from the center of the mirror.

After checking the collimation of your telescope and making any necessary adjustments, check the alignment of your finder. This is easily accomplished by inserting the finder telescope through the two rings of the holder, and securing the six long thumb bolts.

The next step is to set up the telescope and focus it on a small object at least a quarter of a mile away. Adjust the scope until the object is in the center of the eyepiece, which should be, in this case, a one inch eyepiece. Loosen the finder and reposition it until the object is observed in the center of the field. Focus on the object by rotating the eyepiece, then focus the crosswires by loosening the thumb screws and sliding it back and forth. Observe through the eyepiece until the crosswires are in sharp focus. Lock the finder in place with the object being intercepted by the crosswires. For greater accuracy, now substitute the half-inch eyepiece for the one inch eyepiece, and see if any further adjustment is necessary to center the two telescopes.

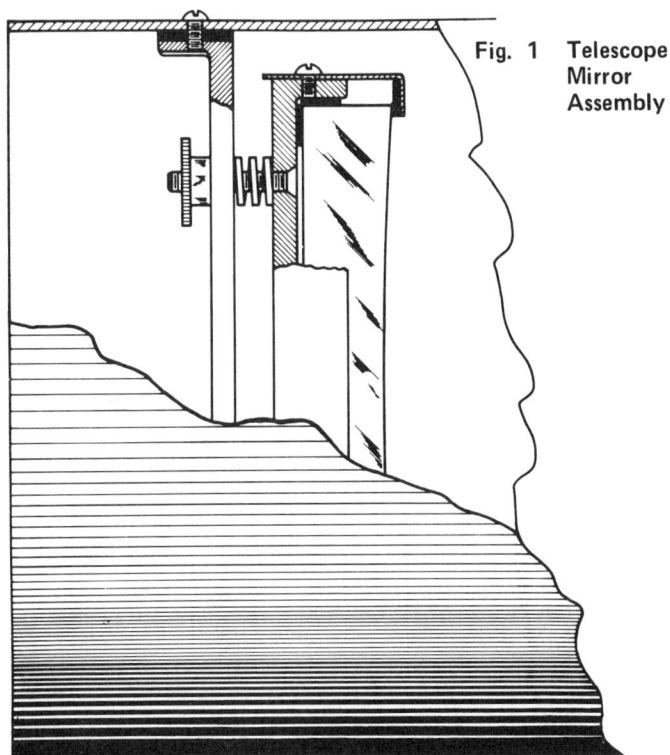

Fig. 1 Telescope Mirror Assembly

NORMALIZING YOUR TELESCOPE

When you take your telescope out of storage and set it up for outdoor use, you will have to wait for it to become normalized. This allows the air, mirror and other parts within the tube to reach the temperature of the air outside the telescope. Until normalization is achieved, there may be noticeable image distortion. If the temperature of the air changes suddenly while you are observing, the mirror may become fogged. If this happens do not try to wipe off the fog or you may severely damage the surface of the mirror. There is nothing to do but wait until normal air circulation has again normalized the telescope and the moisture has evaporated. If the dewing of your mirror does not cure itself naturally with the passing of time, give up, put the telescope away and try again another night. Severe dewing or fogging on the mirror must, like overcast skies, be looked upon as one of the unfortunate circumstances that make telescopic work temporarily impossible.

The telescope should be mounted in its cradle securely and positioned so that the center of gravity of the telescope passes

ADJUSTING AND USING THE FINDER

The field of your telescope is so limited, about half a degree with a one inch eyepiece, that locating a specific star or other sky object with it would be very difficult. Thus, it is desirable to have an auxiliary telescope with a field large enough to help aim the big telescope. A finder telescope is arranged so that whatever is centered in the field of the finder, will be visible through the main telescope (if both are properly aligned).

138

along the declination axis. This can easily be determined by mounting the telescope in a horizontal position and removing all the clamps. If it is out of balance, it will have a tendency to dip either one end or the other. In this case, readjustment is necessary until it is stabilized. Other necessary counter-balancing is accomplished by positioning the weights on the other end of the declination axis.

SPECIFICATIONS

The mirror is 8″ in diameter, f/8, 64″ focal length. It is made of Pyrex® sheet glass, parabolized, aluminized and over coated. The phenolic tube is 9-1/4″ O.D. and 63″ long. The spider diagonal supports an eliptical mirror 1-7/8 x 2-21/32″. The closest stars that can be divided are 0.57 seconds of arc. The faintest star that can be seen is 13.5 magnitude. The approximate size of the field that can be viewed with a 25mm

eyepiece, giving 64X, is 37 minutes of arc; for a 12mm eyepiece giving 128X, 19 minutes of arc; and for a 6mm eyepiece giving 256X, 9 minutes of arc. The maximum practical power to be used should be 400. The minimum practical power would be 32. The finder telescope has a field of view of 6 degrees.

STORING THE TELESCOPE

The telescope can be stored with the tube either horizontal or vertical. If space is not a problem, the horizontal position is probably better as there is very little strain on the clips holding the mirror and little tendency for dust to settle on the mirror surface. If the mirror is stored with the tube vertical, be sure that the mirror is at the bottom, otherwise, the unit will be top-heavy and easily knocked over. Protecting the telescope from dust is always a wise precaution.

SHORT FOCAL LENGTH EYEPIECES

Focus Travel

Short focal length eyepieces must come into focus closer to the objective than longer focal length eyepieces. If you have moved your eyepieces as far as you can go towards the objective and you cannot get a clear image of an infinite object such as a star or a planet, (see Figure 1) it will be necessary to either move your objective closer to the eyepiece, or change your focusing arrangement to allow the eyepiece to come closer to the objective. (See Figure 2.)

Atmospheric Conditions

On some nights turbulence in the air may cause blurred images of the stars, planets, etc., when using high powered eyepieces as defects in the air are magnified as well as the object in view. On these nights you will find that lower powers will give you better results.

Rigidity of Mount

When using high powered eyepieces a rigid mounting is a necessity, as any movement for the telescope is magnified as many times as the power you are using. Windy nights, passing trucks, etc., will cause the telescope to vibrate and poor images will result.

Quality of Objective, Diagonal

While each size objective has its power limit, the quality of the objective also limits the power that can be used with it. A poorly made objective may give good performance at low powers, but very poor performance when near its theoretical power limit for its diameter. Most astronomers figure about 50-power per inch of objective diameter as the practical limit.

Diagonal Mirror

The diagonal mirror of a reflector type telescope also has an effect on the performance of the telescope at high powers. A poor quality diagonal will also give poor images at high powers.

Alignment

It is also necessary to have perfect alignment of optics to get maximum performance from your telescope when using high powered optics.

FIGURE 1

Focusing tube at maximum travel towards objective. Focus of eyepiece cannot meet focus of objective. Image will not form.

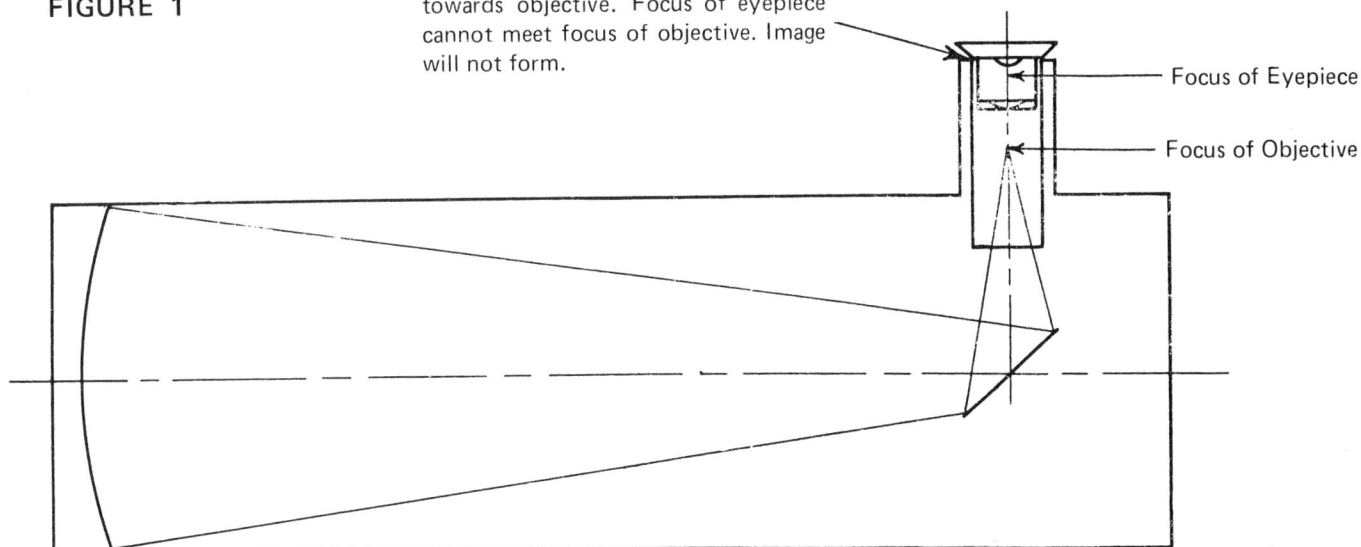

Focus of Eyepiece

Focus of Objective

NOTE: These drawings show how to use short focal length eyepieces on reflector type telescopes. On some refractor telescopes it is not possible to move the objective or change the focusing arrangement. If this is the case the main tube must be shortened.

Focus of objective and Eyepiece meet to form image.

Objective is moved in tube closer to Eyepiece.

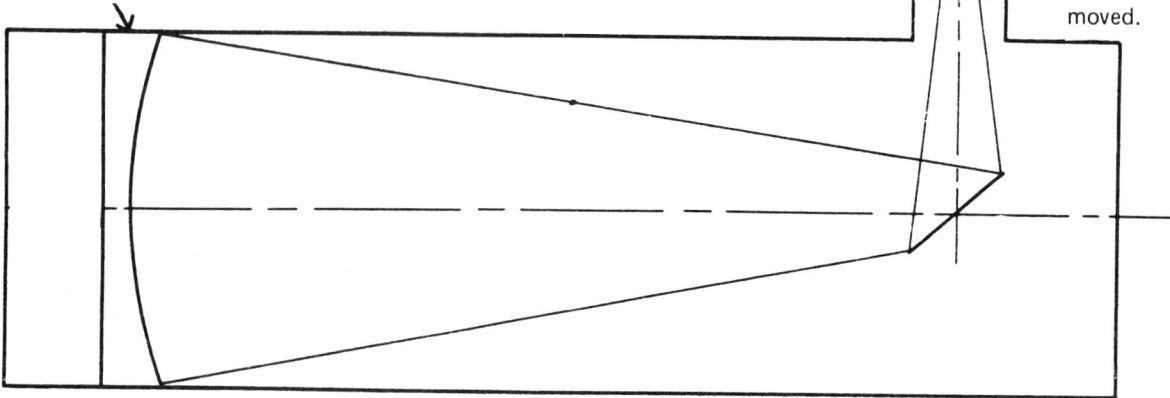

This tube can be cut shorter to allow eyepiece to come closer to objective in cases where objective cannot be moved.

FIGURE 2

Objective is moved toward Eyepiece to allow image to form.

CAUTION: When moving objective or changing focusing arrangements, test your longest and shortest focal length eyepieces to see that they both come into sharp focus before you make permanent alterations, as moving objective too close to eyepiece may make it impossible to focus long focus eyepieces.

Starfinder

The Starfinder is an excellent introduction to the fascinating science of astronomy. Without knowing the exact location of where you live or the exact time, you will be able to view in the sighting tube any of the named stars in the sky. You will be able to locate any of the constellations. The instrument may be used two ways—from the chart to the sky or from the sky to the chart. No calculation or prior knowledge of astronomy is needed to introduce you to the exciting and manifold wonders of the nighttime heavens.

Before attempting to use the instrument in the dark outdoors, it is strongly recommended that you become familiar with its various parts and motions by daylight or room light. Reference to the instructions and labeled drawings in good light will allow your subsequent use in the dark to be extremely simple.

For actual use we must choose a dark, clear night and an observing site which provides a maximum area of visible sky. It is important that a location be chosen which affords a clear view to the north, for in that region will be found the two reference stars we shall use in setting up the Starfinder. It may be interesting to note that while many stars put in only seasonal appearances our two reference stars will be visible every clear night of the year anywhere in the northern hemisphere from the North Pole down to about the latitude of southern Florida. A tree or building which obscures part of the eastern, southern or western horizon will cause no great harm since the stars move at about the same rate as the sun (15 degrees per hour) and an "eclipse" by an earthly obstruction is usually a temporary thing.

All of the stars on the charts are not visible on one given evening. Any particular star rises about 4 minutes earlier each night. This produces a westerly drift of the heavenly bodies and leads us to identify certain constellations and stars with particular seasons of the year. Glorious Orion, the finest constellation of them all, is essentially a winter group. Brilliant Vega and mellow Arcturus belong to the summer time. As you learn the sky, you will find there is more involved than mere position or pattern. Each of the more prominent stars vary somewhat in color and brightness and you will come to recognize them for their individual characteristics as much as for their relation to each other.

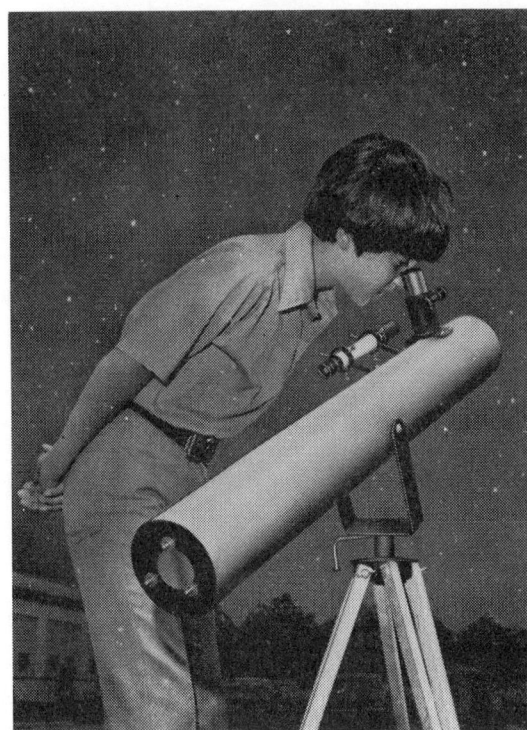

You will not exhaust the uses of your Starfinder in a few nights for during the length of a year new objects will be rising out of the east presenting themselves for your identification and adding to your lore of the sky.

When working outdoors at night, a light is needed to read the charts and the Starfinder dials. To preserve your "night sight" (which takes 10 to 15 minutes to acquire) it is strongly suggested that a small, not too bright flashlight be used and that the lens of this light be covered with fairly dark red cellophane.

INSTRUCTIONS FOR SET-UP

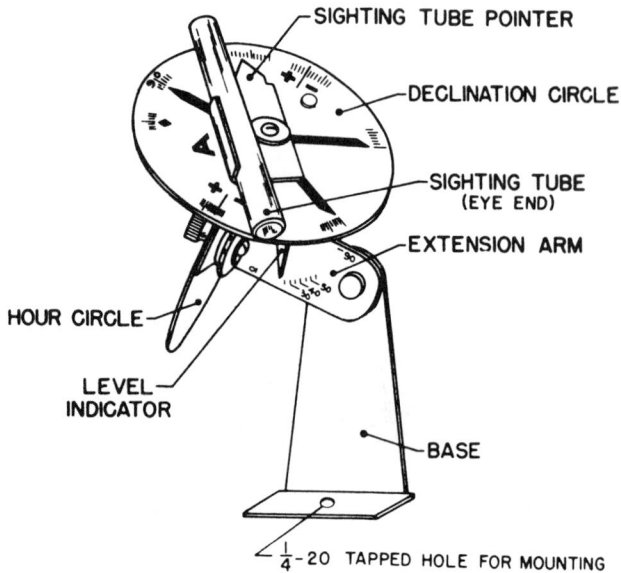

- SIGHTING TUBE POINTER
- DECLINATION CIRCLE
- SIGHTING TUBE (EYE END)
- EXTENSION ARM
- HOUR CIRCLE
- LEVEL INDICATOR
- BASE

$\frac{1}{4}$-20 TAPPED HOLE FOR MOUNTING

FIG. I

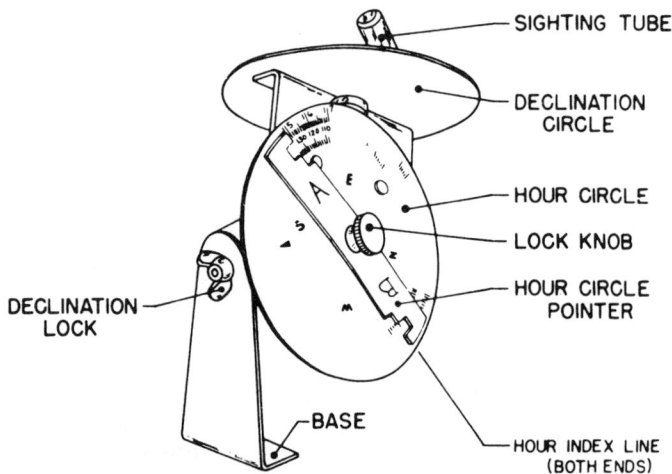

- SIGHTING TUBE
- DECLINATION CIRCLE
- HOUR CIRCLE
- LOCK KNOB
- HOUR CIRCLE POINTER
- DECLINATION LOCK
- BASE
- HOUR INDEX LINE (BOTH ENDS)

FIG. II

A If you cannot locate the North Star (Polaris) without aid, use these instructions to set up the Starfinder. If you can find Polaris, proceed directly to instruction B.

1 Obtain your LEVEL INDICATOR SETTING from chart C.

2 Place your Starfinder on a mount—camera tripod or similar. Determine North with the compass supplied. Face the numbered dial of the HOUR CIRCLE to the North. LEVEL INDICATOR must swing freely.Swing EXTENSION ARM up or down to place LEVEL INDICATOR to proper setting. Lock with DECLINATION LOCK wing nut.

3 Set the SIGHTING TUBE POINTER to 90. Sighting alongside the SIGHTING TUBE you will find you are aiming closely at a moderately bright star which stands quite alone in the sky. This is the North Star (Polaris). Proceed to Step 2, Instruction B.

B If you can find Polaris without aid, use these instructions.

1 Face the HOUR CIRCLE to North and place Starfinder on a mount—camera tripod or similar. Set SIGHTING TUBE POINTER to 90.

2 Swing BASE left or right and EXTENSION ARM up or down until POLARIS is centered in SIGHTING TUBE. Lock.

3 Check "Dipper Finder", instruction D, for relative position of star Dubhe to Polaris. Set SIGHTING TUBE POINTER to 62 A (diamond).

4 Swing HOUR CIRCLE until Dubhe automatically centers in SIGHTING TUBE. Loosen LOCK KNOB on HOUR CIRCLE POINTER. Place A end of HOUR CIRCLE POINTER on 11 RA (triangle). Lock.

The Starfinder is now oriented to the sky and is ready for use.

NOTES:

a Repeat the 11 RA setting on Dubhe at least once every ten minutes. This is the only setting in which HOUR CIRCLE POINTER LOCK KNOB is released. This keeps your Starfinder "in time" with the sky.

b If SIGHTING TUBE comes to an unusable eye position, transfer SIGHTING TUBE POINTER setting to other sector (A to B or B to A) and swing HOUR CIRCLE setting (not HOUR CIRCLE POINTER) to matching letter on POINTER. This feature prevents any blind spots in the sky.

c If you lack confidence in the star you have selected as Polaris, center it in the SIGHTING TUBE and do not disturb the instrument for about 15 minutes. If you can detect no movement after that time, you have Polaris. No other star will stand this test. If your selection was wrong, repeat the set up steps with more care.

LEVEL INDICATOR SETTING
C

Find the city nearest you (preferably to the East or West) and take its number for your LEVEL INDICATOR SETTING. For a number such as 35-40, set your POINTER between the two numbers. Please note that 30, 40, and 50 on the extension are referenced to the bent index lines.

Alamosa	35-40	Duluth	45-50	Ottawa	45
Albany	40-45	El Paso	30	Philadelphia	40
Albuquerque	35	Fargo	45-50	Pocatello	40-45
Amarillo	35	Fort Worth	30-35	Portland	45
Atlanta	30-35	Galveston	30	Prescott	35
Bangor	45	Halifax	45	Regina, Sask.	50
Birmingham, Ala.	30-35	Harrisburg	40	Reno	40
Bismarck	45-50	Helena	45-50	Richmond, Va.	35-40
Boise	40-45	Houston	30	San Antonio	30
Boston	40-45	Indianapolis	40	San Diego	30-35
Brownsville	25	Jacksonville	30	San Francisco	35-40
Buffalo	40-45	Kansas City	40	Salt Lake City	40
Calgary	50	Klamath Falls	40-45	Seattle	45-50
Casper	40-45	Little Rock	35	Sheridan, Wyo.	45
Cedar City, Utah	35-40	Los Angeles	35	Shreveport	30-35
Charleston, S.C.	30-35	Louisville	35-40	Sioux Falls	40-45
Charlestown, W. Va.	35-40	Macon	30-35	Spokane	45-50
Charlotte	35	Memphis	35	St. Albans	45
Chattanooga	35	Miami	25	St. Pauls	45
Chicago	40-45	Milwaukee	40-45	St. Louis	35-40
Cincinnati	40	Minneapolis	45	Syracuse	40-45
Columbus, Ohio	40	Missoula	45-50	Tacoma	45-50
Corpus Christi	25-30	Montreal	45	Tonopah	35-40
Couer d'Alene	45-50	New Bern	35	Tucson	30-35
Dallas	30-35	New Orleans	30	Traverse City	45
Denver	40	New York	40	Wichita	35-40
Des Moines	40-45	Oklahoma City	35	Winnepeg	50
Detroit	40-45	Omaha	40	Vancouver	50

DIPPER FINDER
D

On a loose sheet you will find printed a circle and rectangle which comprise the "Dipper Finder". It is suggested this be glued to a piece of light cardboard, the drawings cut out and the dial installed over the rectangle, a round head fastener passing through the center. While the Dipper Finder is not essential to the use of the Edmund Starfinder, it will be helpful when performing step 3, instruction B. Facing North, hold the unit vertically at eye level. Set the approximate date under your viewing hour. The dial will then show you the approximate area in the sky around Polaris where you will find the "Big Dipper" and its pointer star Dubhe. Step 4, instruction B does this automatically, but it is hoped that this unit will simplify the operation.

INTRODUCTION TO CHARTS

Following is a list of 77 named stars and the constellations to which they belong. These stars were selected for their brightness, distribution in the sky and the spread of their appearance through the seasons.

Planets do not appear on the chart since they do not have a fixed position in the sky. They are best found with the aid of information in the daily papers, the Almanacs or any of the popular monthly astronomy publications.

DECLINATION locates the stars North or South of the equator.

R.A. (right ascension) locates the stars in an East-West direction using hours and minutes. R.A. increases eastward.

SHA (Sidereal Hour Angle) also locates the stars in an East-West direction using degrees. SHA increases westward. For the purposes of the Edmund Starfinder, R.A. and SHA may be regarded as being the same thing. You may use either system but SHA is probably easier since you will use the single unit, the degree.

The stars apparently move to the West 1 degree every 4 minutes. The stars rise (and set) 4 minutes earlier each night, thereby drifting slowly to the West and by so doing, changing the seasonal aspect of the heavens.

All the stars on the chart are not visible every night of the year. To find those that are, subtract your LEVEL INDICATOR SETTING from 90; then, any star whose plus DECLINATION is larger than your answer will never set. Any star of minus declination greater than your answer is below your southern horizon and cannot be seen.

Alongside the DECLINATION column you will find symbols indicating the four seasons of the year. These show the periods when a given star will be highest in the sky at approximately 9 P.M. You look at stars of the "season past" by observing earlier in the evening, you preview the coming season by observing later in the evening. This information is given to prevent, for instance, a situation where the observer might attempt to find Sirius in July when it is in the direction of the sun and cannot be seen.

Use the DECLINATION column to set your SIGHTING TUBE POINTER. Use the R.A. or SHA column to set your HOUR CIRCLE (not the HOUR CIRCLE POINTER). Repeat the 11 RA setting on Dubhe frequently to keep your Starfinder in step with the "time in the sky".

ALPHABETICAL LIST OF THE BRIGHT STARS

	STAR		CONSTELLATION	R.A.		SHA	DEC.	
	Acamar	e	Eridanis	2h	55m	316	-40	W
	Almach	c	Andromeda	2		330	42	W
*	Albireo	b	Cygnus	19	30	68	27	Su
*	Aldebaran	a	Taurus	4	32	292	16	W
	Alderamin	a	Cepheus	21	18	40	62	F
	Algeiba	c	Leo	10	15	206	20	Sp
	Algol	b	Perseus	3	5	314	41	W
	Alhena	c	Gemini	6	35	261	17	W
*	Alioth	e	Ursa Major	12	48	168	56	Sp
	Al Na'ir	a	Grus	22	4	29	-47	F
*	Alnilam	e	Orion	5	34	276	- 1	W
*	Alnitak	z	Orion	5	38	274	- 2	W
	Alphard	a	Hydra	9	24	219	- 8	Sp
	Alphecca	a	Corona Borealis	15	32	127	27	Su
	Alpheratz	a	Andromeda		6	359	29	W
	Alshain	b	Aquila	19	52	62	6	Su
*	Altair	a	Aquila	19	48	63	9	Su
*	Antares	a	Scorpio	16	28	113	-26	Su
*	Arcturus	a	Bootes	14	12	147	19	Su
	Arneb	a	Lepus	5	30	277	-18	W
*	Bellatrix	g	Orion	5	24	279	6	W
*	Benetnasch	e	Ursa Major	13	44	154	50	Sp
*	Betelgeuse	a	Orion	5	52	272	7	W
*	Capella	a	Auriga	5	12	282	46	W
*	Caph	b	Cassiopia		8	358	59	W
*	Castor	a	Gemini	7	32	247	32	W
	Cor Corali	a	Canis Venatici	12	53	167	38	Sp
	Cursa	b	Eridania	5	5	284	- 5	W
*	Deneb	a	Cygnus	20	40	50	45	F
	Denebola	b	Leo	11	48	183	15	Sp
	Diphda	b	Cetus		40	350	-18	F

STAR		CONSTELLATION	R.A.		SHA	DEC.	
* Dubhe	a	Ursa Major	11	00	195	62	Sp
El Nath	b	Taurus	5	25	279	28	W
Enif	e	Pegasus	21	44	34	10	F
Eltanin	g	Draco	17	56	91	51	Su
* Fomalhaut	a	Piscis Australis	22	56	16	-30	F
Hamal	a	Aries	2	4	329	23	W
Izar	e	Bootis	14	43	139	27	Su
Kaus Australis	e	Sagittarius	18	22	84	-34	Su
Kochab	b	Ursa Minor	14	52	137	74	Su
Kornephoros	b	Hercules	16	28	113	22	Su
Markab	a	Pegasus	23	4	14	15	F
* Megrez	d	Ursa Major	12	12	177	57	Sp
Mekab	a	Cetus	3	00	315	4	W
Menkalinan	b	Auriga	5	55	271	45	W
Merak	b	Ursa Major	11	00	195	57	Sp
* Mintaka	d	Orion	5	30	277	0	W
Mira	o	Cetus	2	16	326	- 3	W
Mirach	b	Andromeda	1	10	343	35	W
Mirfak	a	Perseus	3	20	310	50	W
* Mizar	z	Ursa Major	13	20	160	55	Sp
Mirzam	b	Canis Major	6	20	265	-18	W
Nekkar	b	Bootes	15	00	135	41	Su
Nunki	s	Sagittarius	18	52	77	-26	Su
Phecda	c	Ursa Major	11	50	183	54	Sp
Polaris	a	Ursa Minor	1	48	333	89	
* Pollux	b	Gemini	7	44	244	28	W
* Procyon	a	Canis Minor	7	36	246	5	W
Rasalhague	a	Ophiuchus	17	32	97	13	Su
* Regulus	a	Leo	10	8	208	12	Sp
* Rigel	b	Orion	5	12	282	- 8	W
Rotanev	b	Delphinus	20	40	50	14	F
* Saiph	k	Orion	5	45	274	-10	W
Sabik	e	Ophiuchus	17	8	103	-16	Su
Scheat	b	Pegasus	23	2	15	28	F
Schedar	a	Cassiopia		40	350	56	W
Sheliak	b	Lyra	18	50	78	33	Su
Sheratan	b	Aries	1	52	332	21	F
Shaula	l	Scorpius	17	32	97	-37	Su
** Sirius	a	Canis Major	6	44	259	-17	W
* Spica	a	Virgo	13	24	159	-11	Sp
Tarazed	g	Aquila	19	44	64	10	Su
Unuk	a	Serpens	15	42	124	7	Su
* Vega	a	Lyra	18	36	81	39	Su
Zosma	d	Leo	11	12	192	21	Sp
Zuben el Genubi	a	Libra	14	50	138	-16	Sp
Zubenesch	b	Libra	15	15	132	- 9	Sp

*Bright Star - easy to identify

**Brightest Star in the sky

ADDITIONAL INFORMATION

MOUNTS:
While the use of a camera tripod (high enough to bring the Starfinder to eye level) is recommended, other mounts may be used or improvised. A simple mount would be a light board attached at proper level to a step ladder. Come up through the board with a ¼-20 screw to the Starfinder Base. A pipe or post sunk into the ground with a small plate at the top and the same screw arrangement as above will serve as a sturdy permanent mount ready for use at any time.

If you happen to be an amateur telescopist and have exhausted the more obvious sky objects, mount the Starfinder nearby and use it as an "area locator" to help you find double stars, nebulae, cluster, etc. These are listed in the publications noted at right.

NAVIGATION AND SURVEYING:
To illustrate the priciples of these two sciences, set the LEVEL INDICATOR to 90, orient the HOUR CIRCLE with the compass or Polaris to true North; the SIGHTING TUBE POINTER will read altitude, the HOUR CIRCLE will read azimuth. You are now using the Starfinder as an altazimuth mount. When sighting stars you are using it as a German Equatorial.

ADDITIONAL OBJECTS:
Your Starfinder will work with any chart or atlas which list objects by the standard Declination and R.A. (or SHA) method.

TO GO FROM SKY TO MAP:
Orient Starfinder. Aim at star you wish to identify (only the brighter ones are shown on the map supplied, this to prevent confusion), take off the Declination and Hour Circle readings being sure to read A and A or B and B. At the top of the map find the nearest corresponding R.A. (or SHA); drop down to the Declination line and identify the star or, if preferred, the constellation. If your declination reading is between +50 and +90, use the circular map. If between +50 and -50 use the rectangular map.

PUBLICATIONS:
The following publications will be found valuable for a continued or expanded interest in the sky.

"Norton's Star Atlas"
No. 9464. 8½ x 11" Hardbound. 116 pp.
Edmund Scientific Co.
Barrington, N. J. 08007

"Sky and Telescope"
Sky Publishing Corp.
Harvard College Obs.
Cambridge, Massachusetts 02138

"The Review of Popular Astronomy"
Sky Map Publications, Inc.
P.O. Box 231
St. Louis, Missouri

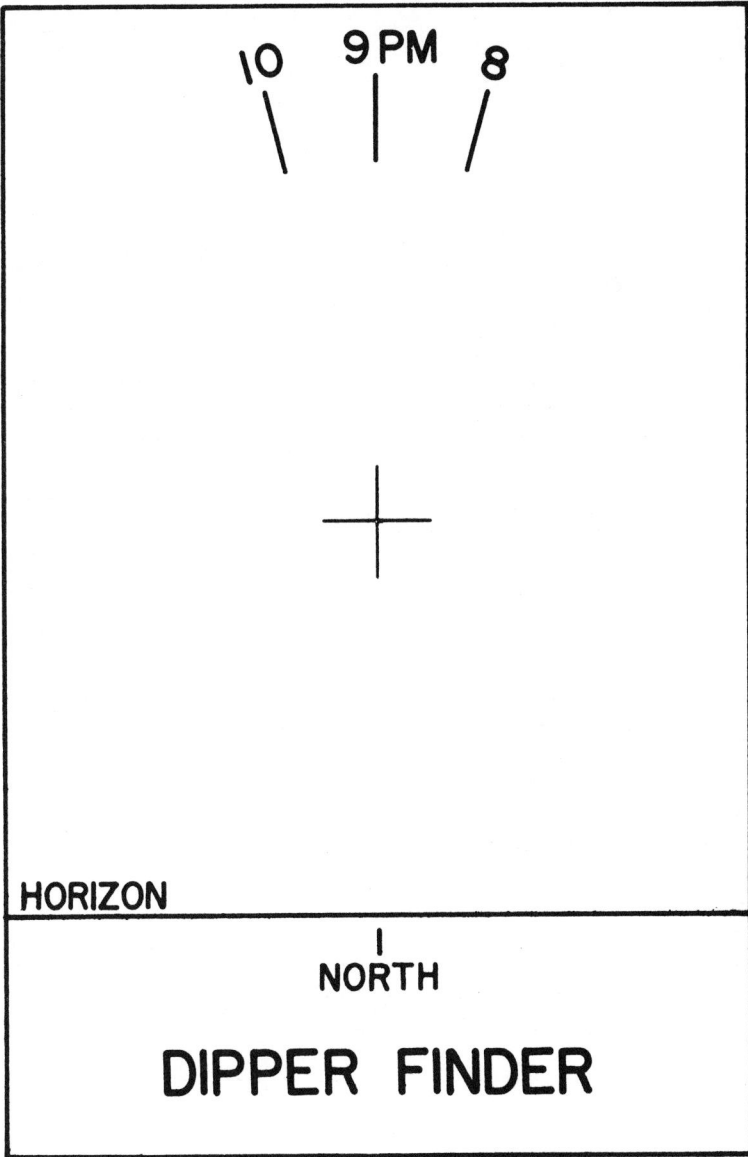

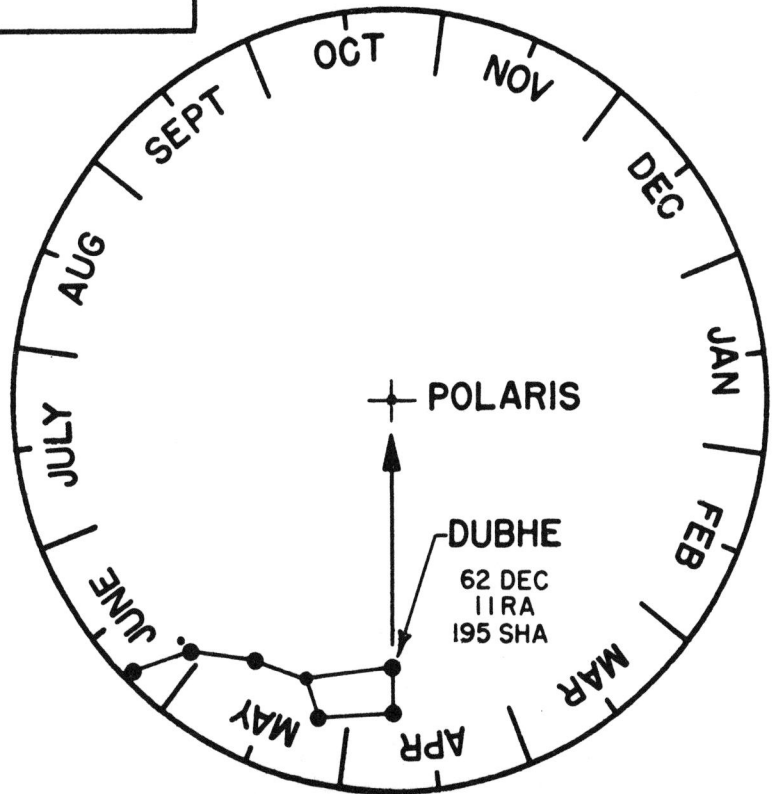

148

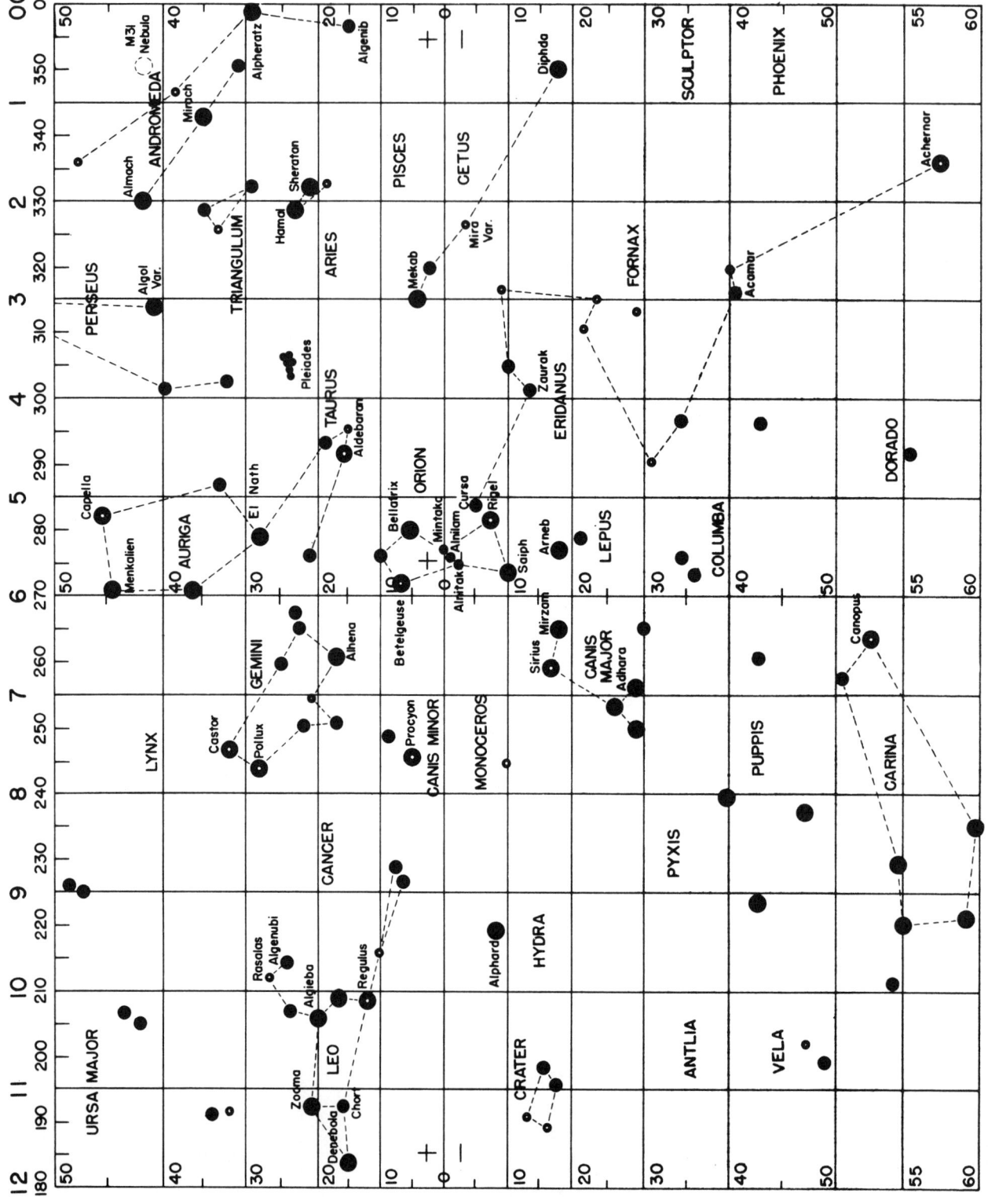

PART OF 70,501 "A"

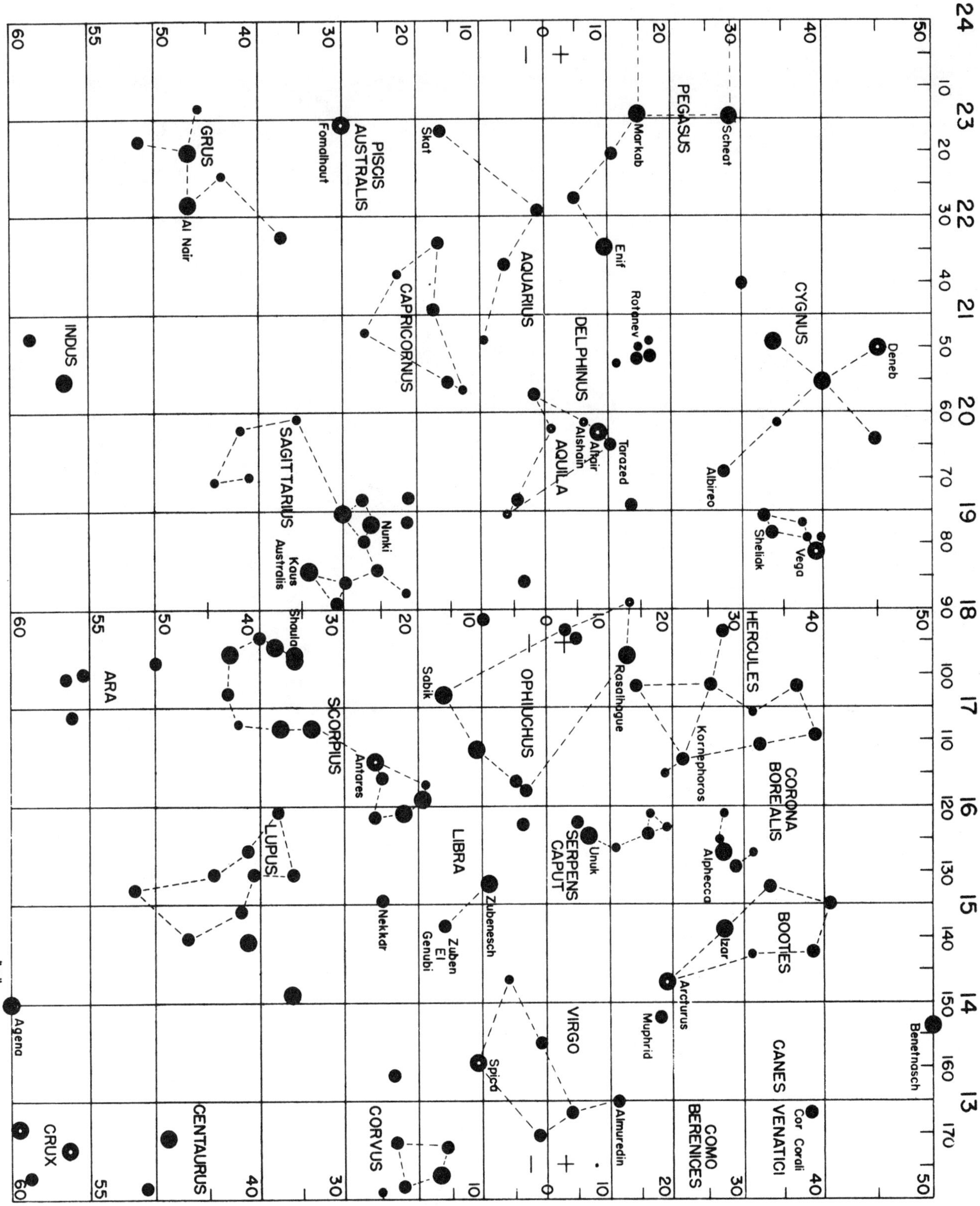

PEGASUS

Scheat

Markab

CYGNUS

Deneb

Albireo

PISCIS AUSTRALIS

Fomalhaut

GRUS

Al Nair

Skat

Enif

Rotanev

AQUARIUS

DELPHINUS

Tarazed

Altair

Alshain

AQUILA

Sheliak

Vega

INDUS

CAPRICORNUS

SAGITTARIUS

Nunki

Kaus Australis

Shaula

HERCULES

Rasalhague

Kornephoros

CORONA BOREALIS

Alphecca

Sabik

OPHIUCHUS

SCORPIUS

Antares

Unuk

SERPENS CAPUT

BOOTES

Izar

Arcturus

ARA

LUPUS

LIBRA

Nekkar

Zubenesch

Zuben El Genubi

Muphrid

CANES VENATICI

Cor Caroli

COMO BERENICES

Almuredin

Benetnasch

Agena

VIRGO

Spica

CENTAURUS

CRUX

CORVUS

PART OF 70,501 "B"

TRIM TO THIS LINE AND ATTACH AT 12 R.A. ON OTHER MAP

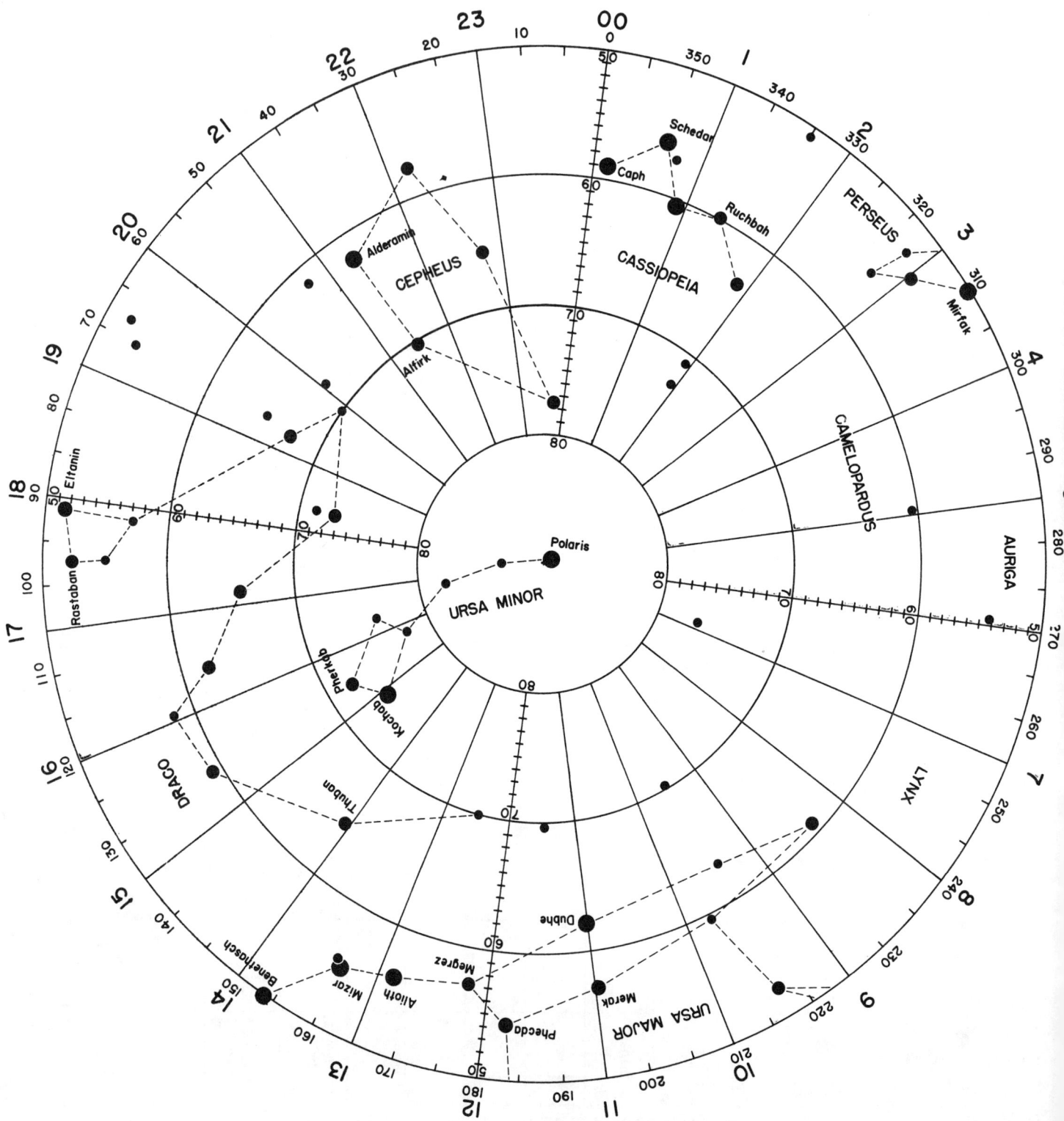

EYEPIECE FILTERS FOR ASTRONOMY

Astronomical filters are made from solid optical glass. This is the most satisfactory material for this use, far superior to laminated glass-gelatin types. Your filters, with reasonable care, will last a lifetime; they are immune to humidity changes, can be cleaned without damage and they will not fade or change color even when exposed to solar radiation.

The filters are 21mm diameter for mounting in a standard metal filter cell. They may also be mounted directly in standard microscope eyepieces.

The mounting cell is precision machined from aluminum and carefully anodized. It is externally threaded (28.5mm x .6mm pitch) for mounting in our 1-1/4 inch diameter orthoscopic and kellner eyepieces. A threaded retaining ring secures the filter within the cell. Use one cell and change filters or, for maximum convenience, mount each of your filters in a separate cell.

ASTRONOMICAL FILTER SUMMARY

COLOR	LONGEST WAVELENGTH (50% transmission)
Med. Red Filter	600nm
Dark Red Filter	680nm
Med. Green Filter	533nm
Med. Yellow Filter	480nm
Light Orange Filter	580nm

GENERAL

Color filters are a necessity to any serious planetary observer. Judicious selection of filters can improve image quality by minimizing scattering in the planets atmosphere; they reduce prismatic dispersion in our own atmosphere and they may be used to increase contrast between areas of differing colors. In addition, selective viewing of different levels of a planets atmosphere is possible. For very bright images, the use of a darkening filter will reduce irradiation effects.

In order to understand the operation of astronomical filters, let us consider each of these factors separately.

Scattering of the light rays has the effect of interposing a luminous veil between the image and the observer. The phenomenon of scattering is the result of light being refracted around and reflected by molecular and sub-microscopic particles. Lord Rayleigh has shown that scattering is inversely proportional to the 4th power of the wavelength of the light. Therefore violet light (4000Å) is scattered 16 times more than deep red (8000Å). This is why the daytime sky is blue and why better image quality is obtained using the longer wavelengths of light.

Mars and Jupiter exhibit a form of light scattering which appears to change with depth of atmosphere. By eliminating or minimizing the scattered blue light we are better able to observe the planetary features using the red and yellow portions of the visable spectrum.

Prismatic Dispersion by our own atmosphere is most pronounced when observing a celestial object close to the earth's horizon. The light is refracted by the earth's atmosphere with the shorter wave lengths being refracted the most. The result of this refraction makes objects near the horizon appear to be redder than those at greater elevation.

Irradiation is a distortion of size as a result of viewing objects of different brightness. A bright area will encroach upon a darker area and will appear larger. This is a purely physiological condition that originates in the working of the eye itself. Examples of its effect on astronomical observations are the apparent enlargement of the polar cap of Mars and apparent reduction in the size of canals and dark spots.

Wherever dark spots or areas are displayed against a light background, irradiation causes these features to shrink in size and sometimes to disappear compleately. Examples are the lunar rills and the narrow Martian Canals.

Atmospheric penetration can be made somewhat selective by using the effects of molecular scattering of light. Since the shorter wave lengths are scattered more, it follows that ultra violet light barely penetrates the atmosphere, blue penetrates to a greater extent and blue-green may penetrate to the surface. By the proper selection of filters, various levels of atmospheric penetration can be observed and studied.

Color Contrast is affected by the differences in color and brightness. Where color differences exist, contrast control is possible by employing appropriate filters. Light orange and yellow filters will enhance the contrast of the cloud belts on Jupiter and Saturn. A yellow filter will make the polar cap of Mars stand out from the surrounding ochre desert. A green filter will increase the contrast of the atmospheric clouds above this same desert.

General-Light; White light can be broken down into three primary colors; blue, green and red. When mixed together, these three colors produce white. When white light is reflected from a colored surface, certain wavelengths are reflected and others are absorbed. A surface which appears red, for instance, when illuminated with white light, reflects red light and absorbs green and blue.

When white light is transmitted through a colored filter, the effect is similar. When a red filter is placed ahead of white light,

the red is transmitted and the blues and greens are absorbed.

Similar actions will result when other colored reflective surfaces and other colored filters are employed. A rule of thumb is that filters transmit similar colors and eliminate their complements. Filters are often used by planetary observers in the following ways: In observing Jupiter and Saturn, yellow and orange filters are useful for cloud blanks and zones. A blue filter is helpful in determining the positions of cloud blanks. Green is most useful in the low contrast red and blue of the Jovian atmosphere. It cuts out red and blue, enhancing contrast of surface detail.

Venus may be observed during daylight hours if a red filter is used to darken the blue sky. It will enhance surface detail at all times. Most viewing of Mars is done with that planet quite low in the sky. This is the worst condition for prismatic dispersion. This dispersion can be minimized by the use of the red filter which will produce maximum contrast. The scattered blue light of Mars can be filtered out with an orange or yellow filter also for increased contrast.

FILTER SELECTION: The tabulation below may be used as a guide for filter selection. It should be emphasized that this is only a guide to start you on your way. Experience and a general knowledge of filter application will provide many cases of image enhancement which may not be covered in the tabulation.

Color	Sun	Mercury	Venus	Moon	Mars	Jupiter	Saturn	Uranus	Neptune	Pluto	Stars	Nebulae	Comets
Green	A	C	C	A	A	B	B	B	C	B	B	C
Yellow	A	A	A	A	A	A	A	A	A	A	A	A	A
Orange	A	C	B	A	A	B	-	B	B	B	B	B	B
Red	A	A	A	A	A	B	A	A	A	A	A	A	A

A-used a great deal
B-used occasionally
C-used rarely

Unfortunately, most youngsters don't spend sufficient time preparing their projects and themselves. It's not always the contestant's fault. The school may not announce the Science Fair until late, and then give the youngsters minimal time to make preparations. This, of course, shows up in the work when the judging takes place.

You've got to look at your project from the judge's point of view, too. Many young people have parents who are actively interested in their work, and enjoy participating with their children. Unfortunately, sometimes this participation shows up during the judging, too. You see massive projects that are almost professionally prepared by misinformed fathers who will spare no cost in furnishing the very best. One father at a recent science fair in an elementary school really went all-out. In his position as an executive at a leading chemical and pharmaceutical firm, he gathered together materials and aids that included audio-visuals, enough glass apparatus to set up a research laboratory, and had a demonstration of advanced chemistry that no youngster without these resources could possibly hope to duplicate. The child had memorized a "canned" speech explaining everything, but when one of the judges asked a question, it became apparent that the youngster had little knowledge of the subject, and even less to do with assembling the project.

Other youngsters seem to think that the experiment they're demonstrating is the be-all and end-all. It's not. How you present it is of extreme importance, too. If your clothing is unkempt, if your speech is slurred or unclear, you're going to hurt your chances, even if your experiment is a cure for the common cold. Be neatly dressed, have a clean experiment to show, and know what you're doing. Be prepared to answer questions put to you by the judges, and if the judge's questions are not as sophisticated as you'd expect them to be, avoid the chance to be a smart aleck. Be polite at all times, for this judge can cast a vote for or against you.

Don't just learn all there is to know about your own subject either. When this writer was a judge at Chicago's Science Fair, he saw a demonstration of tunnel diodes. The youngster running the demonstration knew more about tunnel diodes than Dr. Esaki did... but he had no knowledge of Ohm's Law, basic and fundamental to any electronics research.

Be dramatic, too. Don't be afraid to dress things up with informative posters, colorful bunting, or spotlights that can call the judge's attention to you and your project.

Do the job right, make a nice presentation, and you won't rule yourself out by defaulting.

Picking the right project is important, too. Don't overreach your own abilities by any means. If your project depends for its success on having a working cyclotron, forget it. You're out of the running at once, for where are you going to get a cyclotron?

Don't over-simplify, either. We remember one young man who demonstrated "gravity" simply by dropping a ball on the floor. The ball went down, hit the floor, bounced up again and was caught by the "experimenter" who proceeded to explain, quite seriously, that "gravity made the ball drop." The judges looked at him, looked at each other, and moved quietly to the next exhibit.

You're supposed to prepare your experiment at home, then bring the result and the proofs to the Science Fair at your school where you will exhibit and demonstrate your findings. Believe it or not, the judges are going to want to see evidence of the "scientific method" so keep extensive notes in proper form, with the name of the experiment, the experiment number, the date, the problem, experiment and solution. This sort of thing is very impressive.

Judges of course, are only human. When they've spent the entire morning looking over the various entries, they will then go to lunch and discuss what they've seen. An exuberant judge can easily sway one who is less forceful, or one who hasn't as yet made up his mind. This is where the impression that you make on a judge will really tell. This is where the winners are decided.

Is it "fair?" Not really. The judge that doesn't know much about electronics, for example, might have been terribly impressed with your laser demonstration, but another judge might pooh-pooh it by saying "Yeah, but he built it from a kit!" The message? If you *did* build something from a kit, dress it down by substituting a front panel cut from Masonite and painted. It won't look as nice, but it sure will look original, and that will work better for you.

The real secret of winning is originality. Show the judge something that *you* did by *yourself*, and you've got a much better chance than the student who puts forth the shiniest, fanciest equipment.

Originality! Show something really new -- however humble it might be, and you'll make a far better impression than the guy who repeats an old-hat experiment, no matter how important it might have been in its time. The opportunity is there, and if you are so bent, you must seize it.

What it all comes down to, is that your first step is to select a project that has great potential for winning. Not at your local school level alone, but one that could walk off with top honors at the Nationals. That business of picking the right project -- the one that's right for *you* is what it's all about.

You're going to read books like this one, you're going to eye the catalogs and you're going to come out with your own winner. Not by copying word-for-word what you see, but by creating something out of nothing. By combining the best of several individual projects perhaps, and by applying your own inventiveness and creative genius to what you're doing. That's what separates the winners from the losers. If all you do is copy, chances are that you'll impress some of the judges, but all you need is one judge that's seen it all before, and you're done for.

Time pressure is another big bug-a-boo for the student. You've got a deadline by which time you must complete your work. They won't hold up the Fair because your project isn't quite ready, and you don't want to go in with an incomplete job, either. If you do get close to finished, by all means make an effort to get it done -- *right* -- and in time. If you can't make it, just relax and keep working anyway, there's going to be another Science Fair next year anyway, right? The next most important thing to *selecting* the project right for you, is the *preparation* of that project so it will be most appealing to the judges. Spend some time and effort on this. Obtain the backgrounds and charts that you may need, and the ones you have to make up yourself certainly deserve more than a crayon and some freehand artwork. A visit to your local art-supply shop will yield some professional-looking letters which can easily be pressed on your display material. A few colors of Magic Marker can add some brilliance to your display. And if you have a friend that's into art, by all means employ the services of that friend!

Want an idea of a winning project? One of the winners that this writer still remembers, consisted of a small black box on wheels. Under the box was a small photo-electric cell and a light bulb. Sensors in the unit operated a small motor that steered the thing. The experimenter drew a white line on the dark floor, placed the "bug" on the line, and it ran around actually following the line, stopping only when it ran out. The underneath light would reflect off the line up to the sensing photocell, controlling the little vehicle.

This project was unique, unusual and different, but it also showed a practical application. Built in a larger scale, this unit could perform routine delivery functions in industry.

As you can see, it's the unusual and unique that will stick in the judge's mind.

If all of this is true, what is the purpose of this book? The object, of course, is to stimulate your creative processes in the right direction. Don't make exact duplicates of the experiments shown here. Chances are that at least one of the judges will also have seen this book, and the closer you get to the top, the better the chances are that a judge will have already seen the project. Instead, apply a little ingenuity by combining projects, by changing them, by building further upon them to make them unique. Let's take, as an example, telescopic photography.

You're going to photograph the night sky through a telescope. Set up your reflector, the camera holder and camera. Shoot lots and lots of photos, then enlarge the best to use as a background. For the exhibit, set the telescope and camera in front, and you've just about got it made. One young man created a telescope using clear plastic tubing, to show how the telescope worked, too. He used black thread to show image inversion through his model telescope, and as you must know, while what he showed was not new, it was an attractive and interesting set-up that took the judge's eye.

Be careful about your demonstration, too.

We remember a youngster who had built a huge box with a clear plastic cover. There was a single hole in the cover. Inside the box were literally hundreds of small mouse traps, each with a ping-pong ball on the spring. To demonstrate this experiment, he would drop another ping-pong ball through the hole in the cover. Instantly, traps would be sprung, and inside the cover, balls would fly all over the place with a tremendous clatter. The system demonstrated the principle of chain reaction.

Well, during the Fair, one of the judges approached the demonstration, and asked, "What have we got here?" The young man obliged by dropping the ping-pong ball through the hole. All heck broke loose. The balls bounced, the traps sprung, and eventually, the demonstration came to rest. The judge beamed, "Hey, that's great." He went to get the other judges to see the demonstration, but it had to be set up first. This meant re-setting all the mousetraps, placing a ball on each, and it would take forever to accomplish this, even with help. When the judges went to lunch to discuss possible winners, the kid was still setting mousetraps. At lunch, the one judge who had seen the demonstration was verbal enough, but just didn't swing enough weight to sway the others. As far as I know, the poor guy is *still* there, setting mousetraps and feeling terribly unhappy.

Okay. It's getting late, and I'm tired. I'm sure the neighbors are having kittens over the sound of this typewriter, so I'm going to turn off and go to bed. I'm sure you've enjoyed this book, and I hope you were able to get a winning project idea out of it. By all means, give the next science fair at your school a good shot. You have nothing to lose and everything to gain.

Got any questions? Write to me, care of the publisher, and I'll be sure to answer any questions you might have. Goodbye, and good luck. I'm rooting for you.

Byron G. Wels

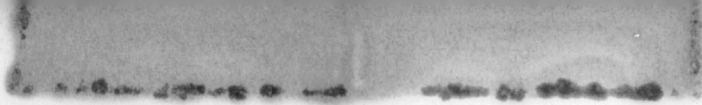